WOMEN AND THE ENVIRONMENT

PREPARED BY ANNABEL RODDA

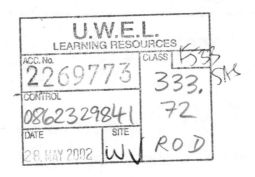

Zed Books Ltd · London & New Jersey

Women and the Environment was first published by Zed Books Ltd,
57 Caledonian Road, London N1 9BU, United Kingdom and 165 First Avenue,
Atlantic Highlands, New Jersey 07716, United States of America, in 1991.

Copyright © United Nations Non-Governmental Liaison Service, First Reprint, 1993

Cover and book design by Lee Robinson
Cover photo: Jean Mohr
Typeset by Goodfellow & Egan, Cambridge
Printed and bound by Forum Enterprise, Kuala Lumpur
Third Impression, 1997

British Library Cataloguing in Publication Data

A calalogue record for this book is available from the British Library

ISBN 0-86232-984-1 hb
ISBN 0-86232-985-X pb

Library of Congress Cataloging-in-Publication Data

A catalogue record for this book is available from the US Library of Congress

CONTENTS

ACKNOWLEDGEMENTS

This book has been prepared by Annabel Rodda on behalf of the Joint UN-NGO Group on Women and Development, and made possible through financial contributions from:

- Swedish International Development Authority (SIDA)
- United Nations Environmental Programme (UNEP)
- World Food Programme (WFP)
- United Nations Children's Fund (UNICEF)
- United Nations Educational, Scientific and Cultural Organization (UNESCO)
- International Labour Office (ILO)
- United Nations High Commissioner for Refugees (UNHCR)

LOGISTICAL SUPPORT AND TECHNICAL ASSISTANCE

- United Nations Conference on Trade and Development (UNCTAD)

The content of this book has been approved by the Joint UN/NGO Group on Women and Development. The following organizations have made a special contribution through their participation in the editorial panel formed for this publication:

- Associated Country Women of the World
- International Council of Women
- International Fund for Agricultural Development (IFAD)
- International Labour Office (ILO)
- World Conservation Union (IUCN)
- Medical Women's International Association
- United Nations Conference on Trade and Development (UNCTAD)
- United Nations Economic Commission for Europe (ECE)
- United Nations Environment Programme (UNEP)
- United Nations High Commissioner for Refugees (UNHCR)
- Women's International League for Peace and Freedom
- World Health Organization (WHO)
- World Wide Fund for Nature (WWF)

Special thanks to Irene Dankelman for her help and advice in the initial stages of preparation. Overall co-ordination and management of the Joint UN-NGO Group on Women and Development is provided by the United Nations Non-Governmental Liaison Service (NGLS), an inter-agency unit which fosters dialogue and co-operation between the UN system and the NGO community on development policy issues and North-South relations.

PREFACE

THIS BOOK FOCUSES on the importance of women in relation to environment and development. In the developing countries, many women's relationship with the environment is vital to their daily lives, for example, in the provision of water, fuel, food and other basic needs. These women not only bear the brunt of environmental degradation, but also play a crucial part in environmental management. Their importance as key agents in achieving sustainable development cannot be overstated. In addition, women everywhere are influencing the environmental debate in many ways—as consumers, as campaigners and as educators and communicators.

The issue of women, environment and development is now recognized in some areas, but does not yet feature as the prime focus of many programmes of the UN system or other organizations. It is an issue which is highly relevant to the agenda of the 1992 United Nations Conference on Environment and Development.

The information in this book brings together material from a wide range of sources; it provides numerous examples and includes original contributions from experts. It is hoped that as well as providing a valuable resource, *Women and the Environment* will enlighten and inform the reader and serve to stimulate action.

ANNABEL RODDA

1 INTRODUCTION

The state of the world's environment is of growing concern. Its present deterioration has come about mainly as a result of human activities, especially those concerned with industrialization. Over the past 200 years industrial processes have been responsible for the pollution and degradation of the air, water and land. In addition the environment is being degraded as a result of unsustainable exploitation of natural resources and environmentally unsound agricultural practices. The spread of urbanization and the development of transport systems also have an environmental impact, as does armed conflict. Furthermore, in many parts of the world, there is the problem of the increased pressure of a rapidly expanding population.

I am concerned about the wounds and bleeding sores on the naked body of the earth.

Have we not seen the long-term effects of these bleeding sores? The famine? The poverty? The chemical and nuclear accidents?

The small wars and deaths in so many parts of the world? When we have seen all these calamities, have we done no more than ask: Who is responsible?

For me, personally, I know that I may be responsible for some of it.

I am sure that everybody else is responsible for some of it.

We are responsible directly or indirectly. We are all of us strangling the earth.

Wangari Maathai
Founder, Kenya Green Belt Movement
as featured in *UNICEF Staff News*,
January–March 1991

THE IMPORTANCE OF PROTECTING the environment is now recognized by national governments and intergovernmental agencies. Non-governmental organizations (NGOs) are playing a substantial role in the environmental movement, from small groups acting locally (some of which can gain national recognition and influence governments), to large international environmental organizations. The scientific community is providing the knowledge and expertise and presents the evidence that is used not only by these organizations but also by the media, which communicate to the public at large. The environment has only recently become a prime interest of the media, with the major news stories of the disasters in Ethiopia, then Bhopal and Chernobyl. Now the media are concerned with wider environmental issues such as global warming and deforestation. The images of the burning of the Amazon rainforest inspire a genuine worldwide concern that something must be done to help Brazil save the greatest rainforest on earth.[1]

Growing awareness of environmental problems led to the United Nations Conference on the Human Environment in Stockholm (1972), which adopted the Action Plan for the Human Environment and initiated the United Nations Environment Programme (UNEP). This conference was significant for founding the concept of sustainable development and for the part played by NGOs in presenting the views of the people. It set a new pattern for the relationship between the UN and NGOs in dealing with global issues. For the first time, facilities were provided for NGOs in consultative status with the Economic and Social Council of the United Nations (ECOSOC) and other interested organizations to meet parallel to the UN conference and to be able to present their views to the official body. Since then, NGOs have been associated with all world gatherings held under the auspices of the United Nations.[2]

Following the 1972 conference, the International Union for the Conservation of Nature (IUCN), World Wildlife Fund (WWF) and United Nations Environment Programme (UNEP) launched the World Conservation Strategy in 1980,[3] as a framework and guidance for conservation, to help achieve sustainable development. A second, more far-reaching version will soon be published.

In 1987 the World Commission on Environment and Development (WCED), under the chairmanship of Gro Harlem Brundtland, published its report, *Our Common Future*.[4] This focuses on the concept of sustainable development, which is defined as: 'development that meets the needs of the present without compromising the ability of future generations to meet their own needs'. The problem of the world's poverty was addressed, but without denouncing economic growth: 'We see instead the possibility for a new era of economic growth, one that must be based on policies that sustain and expand the environmental resource base. And we believe such growth to be absolutely essential to relieve the great poverty that is deepening in much of the developing world.' The report's policy directions focus on population, food security, loss of species and genetic resources, energy, industry and human settlements. The report also considers the international scene, and institutional and legal reform and, in a call for action, states 'the time has come to break out of past patterns and that action must be taken to reduce risks to survival and to put future development on paths that are sustainable'.

Twenty years after the Stockholm Conference another UN Conference on Environment and Development is to be held in Brazil in 1992. The overall agenda is basically the same, but whereas, in 1972, the main purpose was to create awareness and to set out principles, in 1992 the focus of the conference will be action, and it will set the agenda into the twenty-first century.

Recognition of the importance of the environment is reflected in the development of environmentalism, a movement which began in the nineteenth century as a response to the effects of industrialization. A concern for wildlife led to the establishment of national parks and wildlife protection organizations; this interest in conservation continued into the twentieth century, with environmentalism essentially synonymous with wildlife conservation, and of limited extent. But since the late 1960s environmentalism has increased its popular support and broadened its scope to a concern to include all aspects of the natural environment: land, water, minerals, all living organisms and life processes, the atmosphere and climate, the polar icecaps, remote ocean depths and even outer space. Attention turned from looking at the environment *per se* towards its interrelationships with human activities, with an emphasis on the relationship between human and natural environments, and between poverty and environmental degradation.[5]

As well as the development of environmentalism, the twentieth century has seen the rise of another influential movement, the women's movement. Like environmentalism, this first appeared much earlier, but it was not until the present century, and in particular until the 1960s, that the women's movement became established as a worldwide influence.

In the Western world, the status of women was founded in the civilizations of Greece and Rome, where the men had public responsibilities and status, while women's role was to bear children and manage the household. Western women's rights were limited until the nineteenth century, when women's movements concerned with efforts to obtain greater educational opportunities, rights to income and property, employment and the right to vote

Bangladesh: Women remove soil from silted-up canals to prevent flooding.

developed. In many other parts of the world women did have rights, but these were often lost during the colonization process. Women farmers, for example, lost their right to land, and when Western education became available it was open only to boys.

In the early years of the twentieth century, around the time of the suffragette movement and World War I, many influential international women's organizations were founded. The 1960s brought the Women's Liberation Movement, as women examined their status as second-class citizens and became increasingly frustrated by their inequality *vis-à-vis* men, especially with regard to their careers. At the same time there was the expansion of women's organizations in the newly independent countries of the Third World. There has since been a great mobilization of women around the world and a wider application of the feminine perspective, both within existing systems and through the formation of new groups and organizations.

Within the women's movement there is a range of different groups and ideologies. The Third World group, DAWN (Development Alternatives with Women for a New Era), for example, sees feminism as an essentially political movement with, at its core, a commitment to breaking down the structures of gender subordination, and a vision of women as full and equal participants with men at all levels of societal life.[6]

A particular type of feminism, ecofeminism, owes its origins to the relationship between women and nature, and perhaps, also, to the fact that the environmental and women's movements both became prominent about the same time. Ecofeminism has been described as 'a philosophy made flesh by our passion to create ourselves in deep communion with our planet'.[7] Different forms of feminism and different aspects of ecology have been brought together by ecofeminist writers and thinkers; and,

fundamentally, many women perceive ecofeminism as expressing how, in some sense, they are intimately connected to, and part of, the earth.[8]

Different types of women's organizations have played an important part in the women's movement, enabling women to make their voices heard and press for changes that have led to their advancement. These various organizations include the longstanding traditional service-oriented organizations particularly involved in the areas of education and health, those affiliated to political parties and workers' organizations, and those related to development projects or to research activities.[9]

The importance of the role of women was recognized by the UN and 1975 was declared International Women's Year, to be followed by the UN Decade for Women (UNDW), 1976–85. The end of the Decade for Women was marked by two conferences in Nairobi, a UN conference and an NGO conference. The primary task of the former was to draw conclusions about the experiences and obstacles encountered in the attainment of the goals of the UNDW, and to prepare forward-looking strategies for the advancement of women up to the year 2000. The System-wide Medium Term Plan 1990–95 provides guidance for individual organizations in the framing of their own plans and programmes.

The Non-governmental World Conference of Women – Forum 85 was held in parallel with the UN conference. One of the characteristics of the forum was that women were actively involved and there was a constant exchange of views, experiences and opinion, and a sharing of research and knowledge.[10] During the course of these discussions, the importance of women as daily managers of natural resources and carers of the environment became apparent.

However, although the subject of women and development was a focus of the 1985 conferences and the following World

Survey, the link between women and the environment was not a major theme, and even the Brundtland report makes only brief reference to women. The role of women was highlighted in the UNEP State of the Environment Report 1988,[11] and the publication of the books *Women and Environment in the Third World*, by Irene Dankelman and Joan Davidson (1988),[12]

and *Staying Alive – Women, Ecology and Development*, by Vandana Shiva (1989)[13] brought the issue to a wider audience. The topic has been the focus of discussions in various conferences, seminars and workshops, especially those in connection with the 1992 UN Conference on Environment and Development.

Women's contribution to making the

WOMEN AND ECOLOGY MOVEMENTS

To say that women and nature are intimately associated is not to say anything revolutionary. After all, it was precisely just such an assumption that allowed the domination of both women and nature. The new insight provided by rural women in the Third World is that women and nature are associated not in passivity but in creativity and in the maintenance of life.

This analysis differs from most conventional analyses of environmentalists and feminists. Most work on women and the environment in the Third World has focused on women as special victims of environmental degradation. Yet the women who participate in and lead ecology movements in countries like India are not speaking merely as victims. Their voices are the voices of liberation and transformation which provide new categories of thought and new exploratory directions. The women and environment issue can be approached either from the categories of challenge that have been thrown up by women in the struggle for life, or it can be approached through an extension of conventional categories of patriarchy and reductionism. In the perspective of women engaged in survival struggles

which are simultaneously struggles for the protection of nature, women and nature are intimately related, and their domination and liberation similarly linked. The women's and ecology movements are therefore one, and are primarily counter trends to a patriarchal maldevelopment.

A science that does not respect nature's needs and a development that does not respect people's needs inevitably threatens survival. In their fight to survive the onslaughts of both, women have begun a struggle that challenges the most fundamental categories of Western patriarchy – its concepts of nature and women, and of science and development. Their ecological struggles are aimed simultaneously at liberating nature from ceaseless exploitation and themselves from limitless marginalisation. They are creating a feminist ideology that transcends gender, and a political practice that is humanly inclusive; they are challenging patriarchy's ideological claim to universalism not with another universalising tendency, but with diversity; and they are challenging the dominant concept of power as violence with the alternative of non-violence as power.

Vandana Shiva

Extract from 'Let Us Survive – Women, Ecology and Development', *Sangarsh 2*, Sangarsh Editorial Collective, Bangalore

WOMEN AND ENVIRONMENT

It is common knowledge that as far as the Environment is concerned, there is no better person to be informed or used than the Woman.

In Kenya it is an accepted fact that the children are taught to speak their 'mother tongue'. It is therefore imperative that the first words uttered by a child are those he or she has learned from the mother. It can therefore be taken that the role of women in Environmental matters is so important and crucial that no one can afford to take it lightly. As in Education, if the woman is enlightened on the environmental issues, as goes with Health and Nutrition, then the whole Nation will be enlightened and consequently the whole world. In Africa, and to be more specific in Kenya, the role of women in fetching water, firewood, and cleaning and clear-ing the homesteads and fields is obvious. Thus it becomes even more crucial that when we talk of environment and devel-opment, the woman should be the key figure since her life is closely woven with the very issues at stake.

It is therefore important that the Environmentalists should address them-selves and make use of the very key people that are directly concerned with the environment and that is the women. Someone said, if you want a message to go out to the whole world there are three ways of telling it, that is TELEVISION, TELEPHONE AND TELEWOMAN! Nothing could be more true. It is there-fore important that WOMEN be used and be placed in the correct place if the message concerning our environment and sustaining the same is to be best developed and kept.

Kenya Water for Health Organization

environment a central issue has been sig-nificant. In 1962, the publication of Rachel Carson's '*Silent Spring*' focused attention on the dangers of pesticides. Since the 1970s, women's groups and organizations have been very active in promoting environ-mental awareness, education and protec-tion. Women make up a large part of Western Europe's Green parties, both as members and party leaders. All over the developing world, women play a crucial role in environmental management; as farmers, stockbreeders, suppliers of fuel and water, they interact most closely with the environment. They are the managers, and often the preservers of natural resources.[14] The crucial role of women in environmental issues has long been recog-nized in the developing countries. The empowerment of women is vital if they are to participate fully.

As Joan Davidson emphasizes:

Women as producers and carers are wholly dependent upon the renewability of natural systems to provide food, fuel, water and shelter.

As cultural guardians and the first educators, women value the environment in many ways. Over much of the Third World, they are the main environmental managers.

But the close and symbiotic relationship that these women have with the natural world – built up over generations – is breaking down. Recognizing and restoring that good relationship is not only crucial for any lasting improvement in women's own development position, it will be fundamental in the move

towards sustainable development.

What matters now is how the link between women and the environment is perceived and acted upon. Above all, governments, aid agencies and local communities must see women as central figures in environmental management: they should be shaping policies and projects and benefiting directly from them. It is not enough to reduce the damaging effects of conventional development; women need positive action to enhance their role as resource managers.[15]

This book is concerned with women and the environment and development. The contents reflect its main purpose as a resource tool to provide information and to raise awareness. Essential background information on the environment is provided in Chapter 2, which sets out salient environmental issues, showing the complexity of the interaction between human activities and the physical environment.

Chapter 3 focuses on the importance of women in the environment in their different roles, as users, producers and managers. It details their work as collectors of forest products and of water, and as farmers and income earners, as well as their contribution as discerning consumers and practising environmental managers. The effect of the environment on women's lives, and the fact that they are so often the innocent victims of its degradation are detailed in Chapter 4, which also includes social considerations and environmental health.

Chapter 5 highlights the positive action taken by women, despite the limiting constraints. Attention is given to their key role in education and communication and the practical ways in which they are improving and conserving the environment. These activities are illustrated by specific case studies in Chapter 6, which not only provide detailed information, but can also serve as models. The final section of this chapter is concerned with women's participation and includes strategies for planning and suggestions for research.

More detailed reference information, together with guidance for study and action is contained in the annexes.

1 Lamb, Robert (1990) *TVE News*, London, Television Trust for the Environment.
2 Ballantyne, Edith, Women's International League for Peace and Freedom, personal communication.
3 IUCN, UNEP, WWF (1980) *World Conservation Strategy*, International Conservation Union, Gland, Switzerland.
4 World Commission on Environment and Development (WCED) (1987) *Our Common Future*, Oxford, New York, Oxford University Press.
5 UNEP (1988) *The State of the Environment*, *The Public and the Environment*, Nairobi, UNEP.
6 Development Alternatives with Women for a New Era (DAWN) (1985) *Development, Crisis, and Alternative Visions; Third World Women's Perspectives*, New Delhi, DAWN.
7 Hynes, Patricia (1989) 'Ecofeminism: A Way Back to Ourselves', *IDOC Internazionale* 3/1989, Rome, excerpted from 'The Feminism of Ecology', a paper presented at the conference 'Women and Life on Earth'.
8 Davies, Katherine (1989) 'What is Ecofeminism', *IDOC Internazionale* 3/1989, Rome.
9 DAWN, op. cit.
10 Pietila, Hilkka and Vickers, Jeanne (1990) *Making Women Matter: The Role of the United Nations*, London, Zed Books Ltd.
11 UNEP, op. cit.
12 Dankelman, Irene and Joan Davidson (1988) *Women and Environment in the Third World, Alliance for the Future*, London, Earthscan Publications Ltd.
13 Shiva, Vandana (1989) *Staying Alive: Women, Ecology and Development*, London, Zed Books Ltd; Delhi, Kali for Women.
14 United Nations (1990) Department of Public Information (factsheet).
15 Davidson, Joan (1989) 'Restoring Women's Link with Nature', *Earthwatch* 37, London, International Planned Parenthood Federation (IPPF).

2 LOOKING AT THE ENVIRONMENT: THE MAIN PROCESSES AND ISSUES

This chapter provides basic information on the environment and is intended primarily for those who do not have a detailed knowledge of the subject. The main environmental issues are presented as a broad overview; further information on specific issues can be obtained by following up the references at the end of the chapter. This chapter looks at environmental issues in the global context without particular reference to women; the links between women and the environment and their role in sustainable development are dealt with in subsequent chapters.

THE NATURAL ENVIRONMENT □ This means all the various facets that comprise our planet and its surroundings.

THE ATMOSPHERE The atmosphere is the layer of gases that surrounds the earth. An average example of pure, dry air consists of nitrogen (78%), oxygen (21%) and argon (0.9%). Other gases such as carbon dioxide, hydrogen, helium and ozone are present in small quantities. Besides these gases, the atmosphere contains variable quantities of water vapour in the lower layers.

The troposphere, or lower atmosphere, is in contact with the earth's surface. It is about eight kilometres high at the poles and about 18 kilometres high at the equator, and it is in this layer that most phenomena take place. The next layer is the stratosphere, which extends up to 50 kilometres above the earth and contains a layer of ozone which absorbs harmful ultraviolet radiation from the sun. Above the stratosphere are the two outer layers of the atmosphere: the mesosphere and the upper atmosphere.

THE HYDROSPHERE This is made up of the oceans, lakes, rivers and other bodies of water on the earth. Water covers nearly 71 per cent of the earth's surface, is essential for life and is an important natural resource (see section on Water).

THE GEOSPHERE The earth consists of a central core surrounded by a mantle and the outer layer of the earth's crust. The crust and upper mantle are made up of rigid plates which float over denser material. Internal heat provides energy for the movement of these plates, causing great earth movements such as folds, faults, earthquakes and volcanic activity. These processes result in a variety of physical landscapes which are further modified by weathering and erosion. Of great significance is the soil cover; this is indispensable for the growth of plants, which provide food for people and animals.

THE BIOSPHERE The biosphere is the narrow zone where different types of organisms live on the earth – a little above and below the surface of the land and in water and air. It is inhabited by an immense variety of living species as well as more than 5,000 million human beings. The types of organisms and their spatial distribution vary depending on the climate and land conditions.

ECOSYSTEMS The biosphere can be

divided into smaller units, or ecosystems, which are based on the similarities in the characteristics of the landscape and the life forms it supports. All the plant and animal life that inhabit a particular area make up a community, which interacts to obtain food and shelter (see Diagram 2.1).

GLOBAL CYCLES These are the energy, the hydrological and the biochemical cycles, which are briefly explained below.

The energy cycle is fundamental as it involves the flow of energey which links the various components of the planetary system. Solar energy heats the atmosphere and the oceans, particularly in the equatorial regions. It is this flow of energy and the associated latitudinal imbalances that produce the global circulation of the atmosphere and the oceans (see Diagram 2.2).

The hydrological cycle is perhaps the most basic of the global cycles, as it influences circulation in the atmosphere and the oceans, and acts as the route for the biochemical cycles. The hydrological cycle involves the movement of water from the oceans to the atmosphere, to the land and its return to the oceans through the processes of evaporation, precipitation and runoff (see Diagram 2.3).

Biochemical cycles, that is the cyclic movements of chemicals such as carbon, nitrates and sulphur are also important in the global environmental system. Of these the carbon cycle is the most significant. Carbon dioxide is used by plants, through the process of photosynthesis, to make carbohydrates, and carbon is moved along the food chain to the animals. Carbon dioxide is returned to the atmosphere by the processes of respiration and decay, and by the burning of plant material and fossil fuels – coal, gas and oil (see Diagram 2.4).

NATURAL RESOURCES A natural resource is a part or product of the environment which is of use and value to the earth's inhabitants. These resources are often classified according to whether they are renewable or non-renewable. For example, forests can be replanted and are renewable, but coal and oil supplies become exhausted and are non-renewable.

SOCIO-CULTURAL ENVIRONMENT □ Like the natural environment, the human or socio-cultural environment is also regarded as a set of interlocking systems. It refers to all the physical infrastructures built by humankind and the social and institutional systems which have been developed. It also includes historical, cultural, economic, political, moral and aesthetic aspects of human life. The socio-cultural environment has developed as a result of the interaction of human beings with one another and with the natural environment.

ENVIRONMENTAL ETHICS An environmental ethics is basically a human ethics based on social justice for all without discrimination of race, sex, religion, ideology, caste, region or nation. Most current environmental problems are essentially a result of people's activities and their attitude towards the socio-cultural and natural environments. Historically, individual and societal values have not always been in the best interests of preserving a high-quality environment. The present-day environmental crisis demands a change in attitude, in order that initiatives can be taken to rescue the environment from destruction.[1]

THE MAIN ENVIRONMENTAL ISSUES □ The present problems of the environment and the threat they pose to the future give rise to a number of pressing issues.

GLOBAL WARMING, ITS CAUSES AND EFFECTS It is now generally accepted that the continuing build-up of greenhouse gases in the atmosphere will lead to substantial global warming. Using computer models

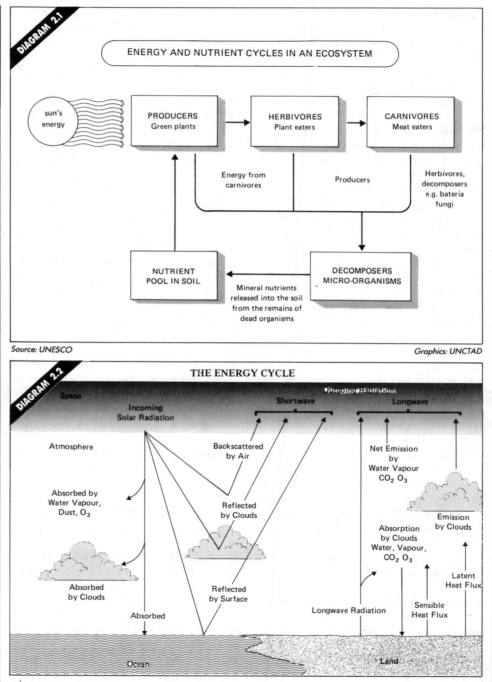

DIAGRAM 2.1

ENERGY AND NUTRIENT CYCLES IN AN ECOSYSTEM

sun's energy

PRODUCERS
Green plants

HERBIVORES
Plant eaters

CARNIVORES
Meat eaters

Energy from carnivores

Producers

Herbivores, decomposers e.g. bateria fungi

NUTRIENT
POOL IN SOIL

Mineral nutrients released into the soil from the remains of dead organisms

DECOMPOSERS
MICRO-ORGANISMS

Source: UNESCO

Graphics: UNCTAD

DIAGRAM 2.2

THE ENERGY CYCLE

Space

Outgoing Radiation

Incoming
Solar Radiation

Shortwave

Longwave

Atmosphere

Backscattered
by Air

Net Emission
by
Water Vapour
CO_2 O_3

Absorbed by
Water Vapour,
Dust, O_3

Reflected
by Clouds

Emission
by Clouds

Absorption
by Clouds
Water, Vapour,
CO_2 O_3

Absorbed
by Clouds

Reflected
by Surface

Latent
Heat Flux

Absorbed

Longwave Radiation

Sensible
Heat Flux

Ocean

Land

Source: Our Future World, Natural Environment Research Council (UK)

Graphics: UNCTAD

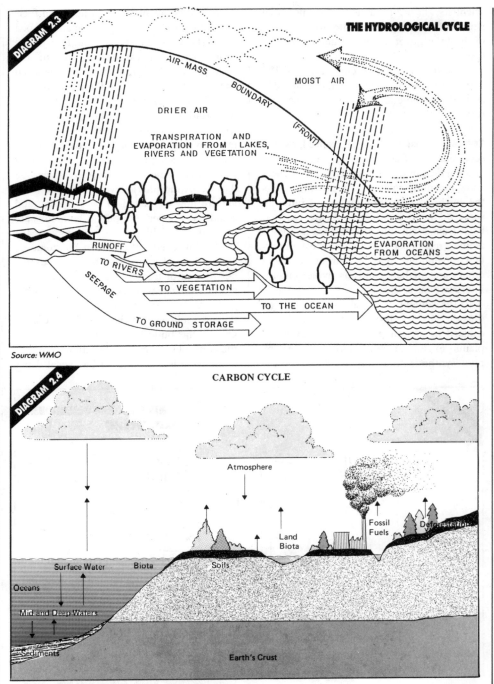

DIAGRAM 2.3

THE HYDROLOGICAL CYCLE

AIR-MASS

BOUNDARY

MOIST AIR

DRIER AIR

(FRONT)

TRANSPIRATION AND EVAPORATION FROM LAKES, RIVERS AND VEGETATION

RUNOFF

TO RIVERS

SEEPAGE

TO VEGETATION

TO THE OCEAN

TO GROUND STORAGE

EVAPORATION FROM OCEANS

Source: WMO

DIAGRAM 2.4

CARBON CYCLE

Atmosphere

Fossil Fuels

Deforestation

Surface Water

Biota

Soils

Land Biota

Oceans

Mid and Deep Waters

Sediments

Earth's Crust

Source: Our Future World, Natural Environment Research Council (UK)

Graphics: UNCTAD

scientists have predicted the potential degree of warming. According to the report of the Inter-governmental Panel on Climate Change (IPCC), there is likely to be an increase in global mean temperature of 1°C above the present value by the year 2025 and 3°C by the end of the twenty-first century.[2]

Causes Global warming is caused by the accumulation of certain gases, called greenhouse gases, in the atmosphere. These gases allow incoming solar radiation, which heats the earth, to pass through easily, but trap some of the heat which is being radiated back from earth into space. This is known as the greenhouse effect. The most important greenhouse gas is carbon dioxide; others are methane, nitrous oxide, chlorofluorocarbons and ozone.

In the context of global warming carbon dioxide (CO_2) plays a vital role. It is exhaled in breathing and utilized by green plants to manufacture carbohydrates by photosynthesis. It is also produced by the process of decay and by burning fossil fuels (coal, oil and gas). By analysing air trapped in ice-sheets, scientists are able to estimate earlier levels of carbon dioxide in the atmosphere. They are thought to have been about 270 parts per million by volume (ppmv) in the early nineteenth century, and this steadily increased as large-scale industrialization took place, necessitating burning growing quantities of coal and oil, through which process carbon is oxidized and released into the atmosphere as carbon dioxide. Atmospheric levels of carbon dioxide are now estimated to be 350ppmv and could rise to over 500ppmv if emissions are not reduced. This is due not only to the increase in energy production for domestic and industrial purposes, but also to the destruction of tropical forests; much of the wood is cleared by burning and, as healthy, growing trees absorb carbon dioxide from the air it follows that the fewer the trees the greater the build-up of carbon dioxide in the atmosphere (see Deforestation).

Methane is a product of biological decay

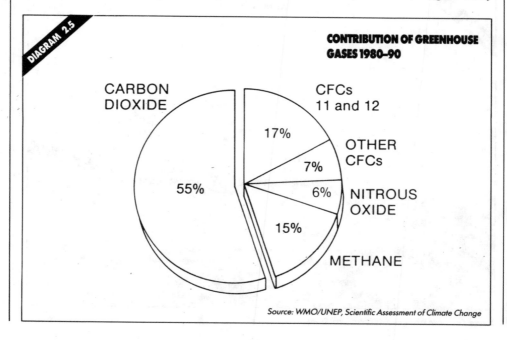

DIAGRAM 2.5

CONTRIBUTION OF GREENHOUSE GASES 1980–90

CARBON DIOXIDE

CFCs 11 and 12

17%

OTHER CFCs

7%

55%

6%

NITROUS OXIDE

15%

METHANE

Source: WMO/UNEP, Scientific Assessment of Climate Change

and is produced in water-logged areas such as rice fields; it is also released during the digestive processes of cattle. Other sources are the burning of fossil fuels and industrial waste, and the extraction of coal and natural gas. Methane concentrations in the atmosphere have been rising steadily, keeping pace with the increase in world population and related agricultural development.

Nitrous oxide is produced as a result of biological activity, its release being primarily associated with the use of fertilizers and the burning of biomass material (plant and animal matter) and fossil fuels. It is estimated that by the year 2030, nitrous oxide levels will show an increase of 34 per cent over pre-industrial levels.

Chlorofluorocarbons (CFCs) do not occur naturally, they are a product of the chemical industry. They are used in aerosols, refrigeration systems, air conditioning, solvents and foam insulation. Because of their commercially attractive properties (cheap to produce, non-inflammable, non-poisonous end product), production of CFCs has increased rapidly over the past 50 years. In addition to acting as a greenhouse gas, CFCs are largely responsible for the destruction of the ozone layer.

Ozone is a natural constituent of the atmosphere found in the lower (troposphere) and upper levels (stratosphere), where it forms a layer. It is in the troposphere that ozone could play a role as a greenhouse gas, and there has been a noticeable increase of ozone concentrations at this lower level due mainly to the combustion of fossil fuels. (Ozone is considered in more detail in the next section.)

Effects The predicted increase in global temperatures would have a considerable impact on the environment and on society. One of the principal effects would be the overall rise in sea level due to the melting of the ice caps and expansion of the oceans. Thus, low-lying coastal land – agriculturally productive, densely populated, and containing major urban settlements – would be threatened. Areas at risk would be fertile deltas such as those of the Ganges and Nile, low-lying islands such as The Maldives and Tonga, and major cities such as London, New York and Tokyo. The rise in sea level would also threaten the natural environment by the loss of coastal conservation areas, and of species such as ice algae.[3]

The increase in temperature would result in a change in the present world pattern of winds and rainfall, and this would affect the global distribution of forests and farming systems. For example, the North American grain-producing lands could become desert and no longer able to provide a larger proportion of the world's food; on the other hand, Siberia could become productive farmland.

It is possible that as a result of global warming there will be a greater frequency of weather-related extremes such as storms, floods and droughts. This would exacerbate the environmental problems of soil erosion and desertification, and would also have a considerable impact on water supply.

In order to reduce the impact of global warming there needs to be worldwide limitation on the emission of greenhouse gases, especially carbon dioxide. All countries will be affected by global warming in some way, both directly by the environmental impact, and indirectly by the change in lifestyle demanded by future internationally agreed prescriptions to reduce greenhouse gas emissions. Some industrialized countries are already committed to reducing CO_2 emissions, and the UN is preparing a framework convention on climate change to be ready for signing at the UN Conference on Environment and Development in Brazil in 1992.[4]

OZONE DEPLETION AND ITS EFFECTS
The ozone layer is found at an altitude of 20–25 kilometres in the stratosphere, and

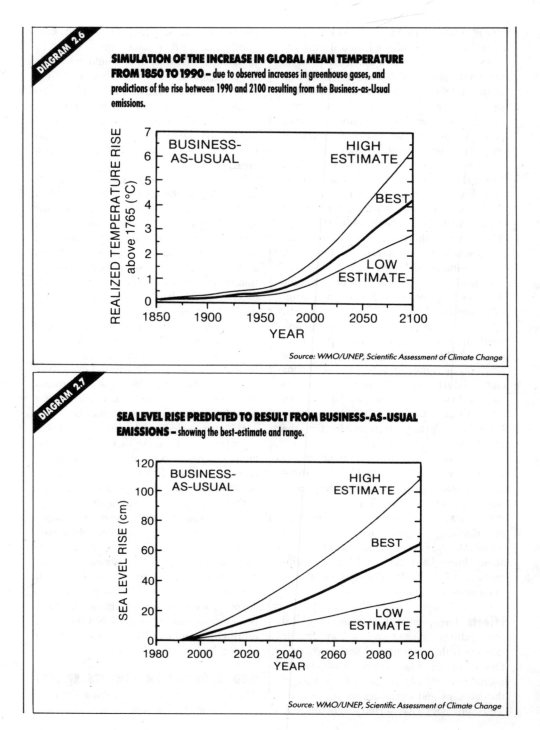

DIAGRAM 2.6

SIMULATION OF THE INCREASE IN GLOBAL MEAN TEMPERATURE FROM 1850 TO 1990 – due to observed increases in greenhouse gases, and predictions of the rise between 1990 and 2100 resulting from the Business-as-Usual emissions.

BUSINESS-AS-USUAL

HIGH ESTIMATE

BEST

LOW ESTIMATE

REALIZED TEMPERATURE RISE above 1765 (°C)

YEAR

Source: WMO/UNEP, Scientific Assessment of Climate Change

DIAGRAM 2.7

SEA LEVEL RISE PREDICTED TO RESULT FROM BUSINESS-AS-USUAL EMISSIONS – showing the best-estimate and range.

BUSINESS-AS-USUAL

HIGH ESTIMATE

BEST

LOW ESTIMATE

SEA LEVEL RISE (cm)

YEAR

Source: WMO/UNEP, Scientific Assessment of Climate Change

provides a protective screen which keeps out most of the sun's harmful ultraviolet radiation. The discovery of the ozone hole above the Antarctic by Dr Joe Farman and his team from the British Antarctic Survey in 1985 confirmed that the depletion of ozone was much greater than had been predicted. There has also been a noticeable decline in ozone over the Artic.

The main threat to the ozone layer is the presence of CFCs (see Global warming) in the atmosphere; halons which are used in fire extinguishers are also damaging. These gases cause the destruction of ozone through chemical reactions which take place in the upper atmosphere. Of particular concern is the long lifetime of CFCs and halons in the atmosphere, which gives them time to drift up into the stratosphere and destroy the ozone.

Effects Continued depletion of the ozone layer would result in an increase in ultraviolet radiation which would lead to a rise in the occurrence of skin cancers and cataracts. Agriculture would also be affected. Many crops, for example peas and beans, are sensitive to increased ultraviolet radiation; photosynthesis would be inhibited and therefore overall growth and yields would be reduced. Ultraviolet radiation can penetrate deeply into clear water and this would damage the primitive life-forms which are at one end of the aquatic food chain, eventually affecting fish supplies. An increase in ultraviolet radiation can also cause deterioration of synthetic materials such as paints and other products used in the building industry.

Combating ozone depletion This is perhaps one of the less complicated environmental issues to tackle, as far as international agreements are concerned, in that there is one known principal cause – the emission of CFCs into the atmosphere, and that these products can be replaced

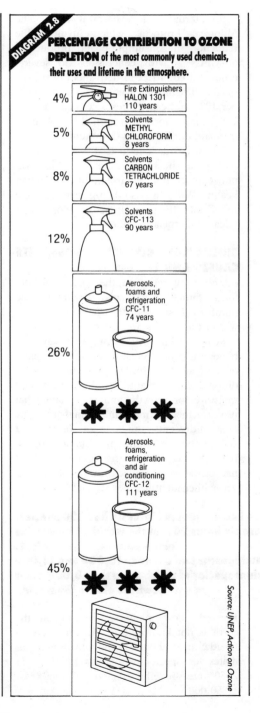

DIAGRAM 2.8

PERCENTAGE CONTRIBUTION TO OZONE DEPLETION of the most commonly used chemicals, their uses and lifetime in the atmosphere.

4% Fire Extinguishers HALON 1301 110 years

5% Solvents METHYL CHLOROFORM 8 years

8% Solvents CARBON TETRACHLORIDE 67 years

12% Solvents CFC-113 90 years

26% Aerosols, foams and refrigeration CFC-11 74 years

45% Aerosols, foams, refrigeration and air conditioning CFC-12 111 years

Source: UNEP, Action on Ozone

with alternative less harmful ones. The Montreal Protocol, which involves the reduction in consumption and production of CFCs – with concessions to several groups of countries to help them over particular difficulties – was agreed in September 1987 and came into force on 1 January 1989; the protocol was ratified by 29 countries and the European Community.

There is much industrial activity in the search for substitute chemicals which will not damage the environment or human health. Work is also being done on the re-use of CFCs in order to avoid their release into the atmosphere.[5]

BIOLOGICAL DIVERSITY LOSS, ITS CAUSES AND EFFECTS

The term biological diversity refers to the variety of life-forms found on this planet, that is: the number of species, the genetic diversity within the species and in the different eco-systems which they form. The range of biological diversity varies in different parts of the planet according to the climatic conditions. Most plants need warmth and moisture for growth, and it is plants that produce food to maintain animal life. The greatest diversity is to be found, on the land and in the sea, within the humid tropical regions. Tropical forests contain at least half of the world's species, most of them as yet neither identified nor studied.

A one hectare plot in Malaysia had 220 species. Amazonia holds 20% of the world's bird species and Indonesia a further 16%. Madagascar had between 10,000 and 12,000 plant species of which more than 8,000 occur nowhere else in the world.[6]

Precisely how many species inhabit the earth is not known, but scientists have so far identified about 1.4 million; rough estimates for species extinctions by the year 2050 are in the region of 660,000–1,860,000.[7]

Causes The loss of biological diversity is mainly caused by the destruction of habitats, as land is cleared for farming, industrial development, urban settlements and so on. Pollution is a further significant cause. Aquatic life, both in the oceans and in waters of highly populated and industrial regions, is particularly at risk; the effects of acid rain on trees has been apparent for over 20 years and acidification of lakes and rivers is also a serious problem (see Pollution). Of major concern is the disppearance of the world's tropical forests, which cover less than one-tenth of the earth's land surface, but are home to 40 per cent of the planet's terrestrial species. The world's natural wetlands are also disappearing as they are increasingly being drained for agricultural purposes. The overall degradation of the environment is affecting the habitat of species worldwide, from the tropics to the polar regions.

Exploitation of species can lead to their reduction and even extinction. Throughout history humankind has exploited species of wild plants and animals through such activities as hunting, fishing, whaling and lumbering. The most sought after species are those which are rare and, therefore, more commercially valuable and desirable.

Modern farming is also responsible for species reduction. As farming has become more commercialized there has been a concentration on a smaller number of varieties of crops and animals, and greater emphasis on large-scale monoculture.

Effects An obvious effect of the loss of species is the loss of basic natural resources. Not only the loss of food from fishing grounds, and timber from forests, but other valuable products such as waxes, resins, fibres and chemicals used for a variety of purposes. Many drugs now produced synthetically originated from plants, for example, aspirin, and a wide variety of natural products is used in industry.

PHOTO: NORMAN MYERS/WWF

Loss of the genetic base is also a cause of grave concern as all cultivated plants and domesticated animals originated from wild species. It is therefore vital to protect and maintain wild species in order to continue breeding new, improved varieties and for the resuscitation of exhausted domesticated species. Large reserves of genetic material will also be needed for the future developments in biotechnology and genetic engineering (see Biotechnology).

The loss of biological diversity also has significance in the context of ethical and cultural values.

The appreciation of biological diversity as beautiful, inspiring and vital defines our humanity and enriches our spiritual life. Humankind has an ethical responsibility not to tamper with the evolution of life on earth.[*]

Combating biological diversity loss

Biological diversity can be maintained by the *in situ* establishment of protected areas and effective management of plants and animals by controlling their utilization and exploitation. *Ex situ* conservation in human-altered ecosystems, such as zoos and through gene banks is also important and can complement *in situ* conservation.

Many countries have completed or are preparing their conservation programme in accordance with the World Conservation Strategy. There have also been other international conservation efforts such as the Convention on International Trade in Endangered Species (CITES).

Although ecosystems and species are being threatened worldwide, the greatest concern today is centred on the tropical forests most of which are in the developing countries. The response of developing

countries to the threat of biological impov-
erishment is particularly constrained by
pressing social and economic issues and by
the burden of international debt. Many
actions that can be taken to stem the loss of
biodiversity do provide short-term economic benefits, for example, maintaining
natural forests so that wild species can be
harvested for food, medicines and industrial
products, or establishing protected areas to
encourage tourism or downstream water
developments that do not become clogged
with silt. But the long-term conservation
needed will not take place in the developing
world unless developed countries provide
their fair share of the funding, technology
and knowledge needed for its implementation. It is in all countries' interest to
share responsibility for conserving biodiversity.[9][10]

BIOTECHNOLOGY AND ITS EFFECTS Biotechnology (as defined in Annex 1) is a
generic term for those technologies that use
living organisms (or parts of) to modify
existing life-forms in order to generate new
life-forms. It also involves the application of
biological organisms, systems or processes
in industry.

Selective breeding of crops and farm animals has been practised for some time, but
scientists are now applying sophisticated
techniques such as cell transfer and tissue
culture. Also included in biotechnology is
the technology of genetic engineering,
which involves the transfer of genes
between unrelated species.

Biotechnology can bring great benefits to
humankind; already much progress has
been made in the field of medicine with the
development of new vaccines and drugs.
Plants can be produced that contain their
own pesticide, generate their own fertilizers, and resist common plant diseases
and lethal doses of week-killers. Biotechnology can also increase the milk production
of dairy cattle by one-third.[11]

The application of biotechnology could
provide opportunities to promote sustainable development. Farming could benefit
from the use of biotechnological agents to
control insect pests and diseases affecting
crops, and from the breeding of crop varieties such as those which give greater yields
or are adapted to local conditions. The use
of tissue culture could assist propagation of
certain tropical tree species and this would
be an advantage in reforestation. Fish production could also be increased by the
application of *in vitro* fertilization and
improved fish nutrition.

There is, however, a growing concern
about the control of biotechnology and
about the potential risks to health and the
environment, as well as the ethical implications. It is important to develop international procedures to assess these risks and
to identify environmentally sound types of
biotechnology. One problem is that
biotechnological research and development
are mostly in private hands, in industrialized countries and oriented to short-term
commercial profit. Furthermore, potentially
dangerous biotechnological products, for
which testing is forbidden or restricted in
industrialized countries, may be tested in
developing countries where, so far, regulations governing such tests are either lax or
non-existent.[12]

Effects Biotechnology is concerned with
the life-forms that make up one of the
components of the environment, the biosphere. The change in balance within the
ecosystem is a potential danger and is
almost certainly irreversible. The danger of
deliberately introducing species is known
from past experience, for example, the
introduction of rabbits into Australia. A
more recent example is that of a water weed
which clogged the Kariba Dam. Another
potentially adverse effect on the environment is that the development of pesticide-
resistant plants could encourage increased

use of pesticides, and thus exacerbate the damage this already inflicts on the environment.

There is also the importance of the link between biodiversity and biotechnology. The genetic material used in biotechnology is found in abundance in the areas of great biological diversity, the tropical forests. As noted in the previous section, the threat of the loss of this biological diversity is an important issue. The exploitation of the rich genetic diversity of developing countries by transnational corporations and institutions and industrialized countries is of pressing concern to some developing countries.

We must formulate mechanisms for effective cooperation with reciprocal benefits between biotechnology-rich developed countries and gene-rich developing countries and to ensure preferential treatments for owners of genetic resources with regard to biotechnological manipulated resources.[13]

DEFORESTATION, ITS CAUSES AND EFFECTS

The clearing of forests is not a recent activity. Timber has played a vital part in the development of humankind, providing a basic resource for fuel, building material, tools and equipment and, more recently, paper. Most of the world's temperate deciduous forests have been replaced by agricultural land. The vast coniferous forests of North America and Europe are largely commercially managed, with a reasonable balance in favour of reafforestation being maintained, although this is now being counteracted by the damage caused by acid rain.

But, as we have noted, it is the destruction of the world's tropical forests which is of increasing environmental concern. It is estimated that every year 6.3 million hectares of tropical forests are cleared for agri-culture and 4.4 million hectares are degraded for logging, much of it unsustainable; 3.8 million hectares of tropical woodland are cleared or degraded for agriculture or fuelwood.[14] These figures far exceed the rate of reforestation.

Causes The main reason for deforestation is to clear land for agriculture, whether it is by landless farmers practising shifting cultivation, or for cattle ranching or commercial plantations. In the case of shifting cultivation, the forest is cleared, burnt, planted, harvested and then left fallow to return to forest and regain its fertility, but only if the fallow period is long enough. With greater population pressure, however, fallow periods became too short to allow the forest to regenerate. Farmers are also forced on to more marginal land which is unable to support this practice.[15] Some governments promote colonization of tropical forests through large-scale resettlement schemes which do not take into account the environmental implications; this has happened in the Amazon (Brazil and Ecuador) and in Indonesia. The demands of the international beef industry have led to the clearing of vast areas of rainforest for cattle ranching, particularly in Central and South America. Tropical forests are also cleared for the cultivation of plantation cash crops. This system was largely initiated and developed by European colonial governments, but many developing countries' governments encourage plantations as their products provide valuable exports.

Trees are also an important source of fuel for people living in and near the forests. Although this does not normally involve the felling of whole trees, as supplies diminish the trees will be threatened. Commercial logging is one of the major causes of the destruction of tropical forests. This involves big corporations and multinationals buying forestry concessions in order to fell and export timber to Europe and Japan. One-tenth

Nine square meters of rainforest for every hamburger

Source: IOCU

of all the timber for this market comes from the tropical forests, including half from South-East Asia (especially Indonesia, Malaysia, and the Philippines).[16] Cutting logging roads and opening up previously inaccessible areas result in further degradation. Large-scale construction projects, such as the building of highways, and dams for hydro-power and irrigation, are also responsible for destroying the forests.

Effects Forest soils are naturally fertile only as long as the forest cover remains to maintain the supply of humus. Once the trees are removed, soil erosion soon follows: the heavy, tropical rainfall rapidly leachs the nutrients out of the soil and, especially on slopes the unprotected soil is then washed away.

In mountainous areas, tropical forest cover protects the watersheds of large rivers. Forest clearing promotes rapid run-off which not only causes soil erosion but

also landslides. The resultant increased deposits silt up the lower course of rivers and this can precipitate more frequent flooding. For example, deforestation in the Himalayas is a contributory factor to the frequent and devastating floods in Bangladesh. The increase in run-off can also cause silting-up of reservoirs and other water installations, and this affects the overall control of water resources.

Tropical forests play a crucial role in regulating the world's climate: by absorbing the sun's heat; by absorbing carbon dioxide in the process of photosynthesis; and by returning water to the atmosphere through the process of transpiration. Large-scale deforestation is therefore a contributory factor to global warming.

Unless management of tropical forest and woodland ecosystems is significantly improved, by the year 2000 more than half the population of

the developing world will be short of fuelwood or lack it altogether; many indigenous peoples will have been displaced, their cultures lost; some 10–20 per cent of the world's plant and animal species will have become extinct; many more watersheds will be severely degraded and the potential for continuing to harvest valuable timber will have disappeared.[17]

Combating deforestation It is unlikely that deforestation could be halted altogether, but it is possible to reduce the rate of destruction. The introduction and implementation of sustainable forestry management would mean that logging must be limited to the quantity that would allow for regeneration. Another way of using the forest sustainably is to encourage the collection of non-timber products. Reforestation may seem an obvious solution in areas where the forest has been destroyed; however, for the forest to return to its original state would take centuries. Reforestation can provide the valuable functions of a forest cover in protecting the soil and watersheds, and in regulating the climate. But it is important that appropriate tree species are chosen in any reforestation project. The planting of vast areas with commercially valuable eucalyptus, for example, has been criticized as inappropriate for local needs, and this species' demand for water can result in lowering the water table.

Despite recent initiatives aimed at combating the decline of tropical forests (the SILVA Conference (1986); Tropenbos (1986): the Tropical Forest Action Plan (1985); and the International Tropical Timber Organisation (1986)), the situation remains alarming. All these initiatives propose basic strategies and investment plans necessary for corrective action; practical implementation, however, remains slow.[18 19] The initiatives have been broadly welcomed, although they have been criticized

as inappropriate by some experts and observers.

DESERTIFICATION, ITS CAUSES AND EFFECTS
Desertification is the process whereby lands bordering true deserts are reduced to desert-like conditions. The areas prone to desertification are the savannas, desert scrublands and dry forests surrounding the true deserts. The climate of these areas consists of a short rainy season, allowing for rapid plant growth and a long dry season. Plants in these areas have adapted to withstand the dry conditions and are able to take advantage of any available water. Some have very long roots to reach permanent underground sources of moisture, others store water in stems or leaves; some plants are ephemeral, appearing during times of rainfall and producing seeds which remain dormant until favourable conditions for growth return. There is a delicate balance in the ecosystems of these drylands and once these plants are unable to revive, the process of desertification sets in. When the sparse vegetal cover is reduced, the dry, light soil is open to erosion by wind, and by rainfall which, although infrequent, is intense and washes away the fragile soils rapidly.

Causes The underlying cause of desertification is the detrimental effect on the vegetal cover mainly as a result of inappropriate farming practices. In some cases cultivation methods lead to overcropping on the arid soils which soon become exhausted. Intensification of the traditional grazing practices leads to overgrazing, and the resultant destruction of the ground cover. Pressure on the land becomes greater as more land is cultivated and pastoralists are forced to use more marginal land. The use of trees for fuelwood and the spread of bush fires also contribute to the destruction of the protective vegetal cover. The damaging results of

PHOTO: PHILIPPE ROCH/WWF

these practices become most obvious at times of below average rainfall, especially when, as is often the case, this occurs in successive years. According to Professor F. Kenneth Hare, 'properly defined, climatic drought is the failure of expected rainfall; it is hence a shock to any economy that is already overstressing its food system and natural resources'.

Traditional human societies, due to their indigenous knowledge and understanding of their environment, were adept at conquering drought. But the rise in population and various forms of land regulation have made this adaptation more difficult. Nomadic pastoralism, for example, has declined, as has shifting cultivation. Drought has, in some areas, driven the pastoralists into the zone of cultivation, with resulting conflict.[20]

Effects Land affected by desertification is no longer able to support the basic farming economies of its indigenous people. This often leads to famine and enforced migration and the related social implications. The effects of desertification often spread to the more productive neighbouring areas receiving the migrants, as greater pressure is then put on those lands. The full impact of the human tragedy resulting from desertification is seen in Africa; in the Sahel in West Africa and in Ethiopia and Sudan.

Combating desertification Desertification can be curtailed only by careful long-term planning. Measures can be taken to arrest the spread of desertification and to rehabilitate the degraded land as shown in Diagram 2.9.[21]

WATER Water by its presence in the hydrosphere and through its role in the hydrological cycle is central to many environmental issues. The quantity and distribution of water determines types and diversity of the

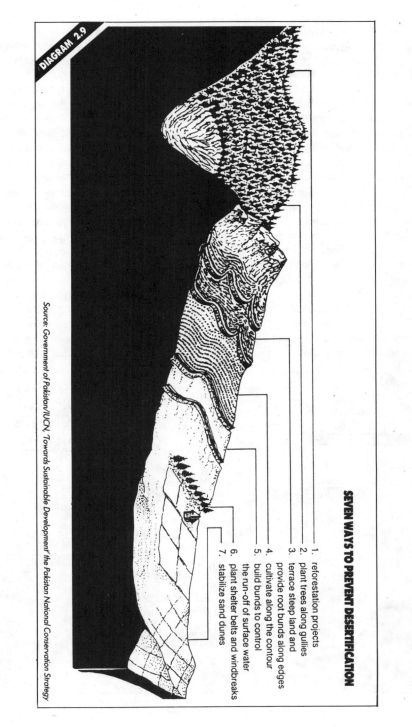

DIAGRAM 2.9

SEVEN WAYS TO PREVENT DESERTIFICATION

1. reforestation projects
2. plant trees along gullies
3. terrace steep land and provide root bunds along edges
4. cultivate along the contour
5. build bunds to control the run-off of surface water
6. plant shelter belts and windbreaks
7. stabilize sand dunes

Source: Government of Pakistan/IUCN, 'Towards Sustainable Development' the Pakistan National Conservation Strategy

fauna and flora as well as the nature of people's activities.

It is estimated that the total volume of water on the earth is 1,454 million cubic kilometres. Of that, 94 per cent is salt water in the oceans. The remaining 6 per cent forms the freshwater resources essential to life; some of this freshwater is underground (and mostly unexploitable), some is in the form of ice in glaciers, and some in lakes, and 0.0001 per cent is present in the rivers. Yet it is this 0.0001 per cent of the earth's water which forms the main source of potable water for human use.[22]

Water is essential to life itself; for example the human body is 70 per cent water. The rate of water consumption has increased as society has developed. In farming, it has increased with the use of modern techniques and irrigation, which now account for 73 per cent of global water use. Industry consumes 21 per cent of global water, which is an essential ingredient in the manufacturing processes of many products, for example, chemicals, paper and textiles. Water is used in energy production, as a source of energy in hydropower, and as a cooling agent for thermal and nuclear power stations. In some countries, rivers and canals are an important means of transport, expecially for bulky, heavy products. Water is also a valued amenity as a visual asset and for leisure activities.

Water is used for a variety of domestic purposes, including personal hygiene and sanitation, cooking, washing clothes and for domestic cleaning. In the developed countries there is an increasingly high consumption of domestic water (see Box). The consumption of water for domestic purposes is also increasing in developing countries as more households in urban areas are connected to a water supply, and in rural areas more wells and pumps are installed in the villages. This is happening even though many people in developing countries still

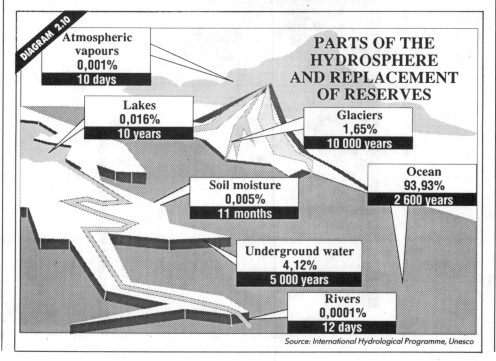

DIAGRAM 2.10

Atmospheric vapours
0,001%
10 days

PARTS OF THE HYDROSPHERE AND REPLACEMENT OF RESERVES

Lakes
0,016%
10 years

Glaciers
1,65%
10 000 years

Soil moisture
0,005%
11 months

Ocean
93,93%
2 600 years

Underground water
4,12%
5 000 years

Rivers
0,0001%
12 days

Source: International Hydrological Programme, Unesco

The average US citizen uses 160 (American) gallons of water per day.

Example	Water used
Each flush of a toilet	3 to 5 gallons
Showering	5 gallons per minute
Cooking (three meals)	8 gallons
Dishwashing (three meals)	10 gallons
Washing clothes	20 to 30 gallons
Taking bath	30 to 40 gallons

This personal use accounts for 8 per cent of the nation's total water consumption, compared with 33 per cent used by agriculture and 59 per cent by industry. It takes 2,500 gallons of water to produce one pound of beef and 100,000 gallons to produce one new car.

R. NORTH, 'THE REAL COST', *NEW INTERNATIONALIST*, 1986

do not have a supply of potable drinking water.

Water is a finite resource, and in some regions of the world the limit of its avail-ability has already been reached and in some others it is rapidly approaching. There is a need for a world water strategy to balance the demand for water with the available resource in a regional and river basin context. It is also important to consider the uneven global distribution of water with regard to the areas of greatest population increase (see Population). These concerns are to be addressed at the UN Conference on Water and the Environment in Dublin in January 1992.

Water and the environment Water is responsible for the creation and degradation of the land surface. Moving water in the rivers and sea and in its solid form as ice, erodes the rocks and, in transporting the fragments, grinds them into fine particles, which are later deposited to form new, mostly fertile land. This is the land of the river deltas and lowland plains where most of the world's inhabitants live. Intense rainfall

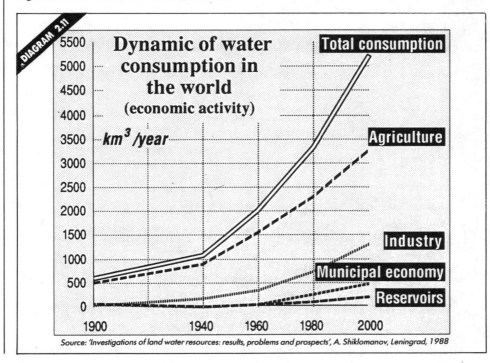

DIAGRAM 2.11

Dynamic of water consumption in the world
(economic activity)
km^3/year

Total consumption

Agriculture

Industry

Municipal economy

Reservoirs

1900 — 1940 — 1960 — 1980 — 2000

5500 5000 4500 4000 3500 3000 2500 2000 1500 1000 500 0

Source: 'Investigations of land water resources: results, problems and prospects', A. Shiklomanov, Leningrad, 1988

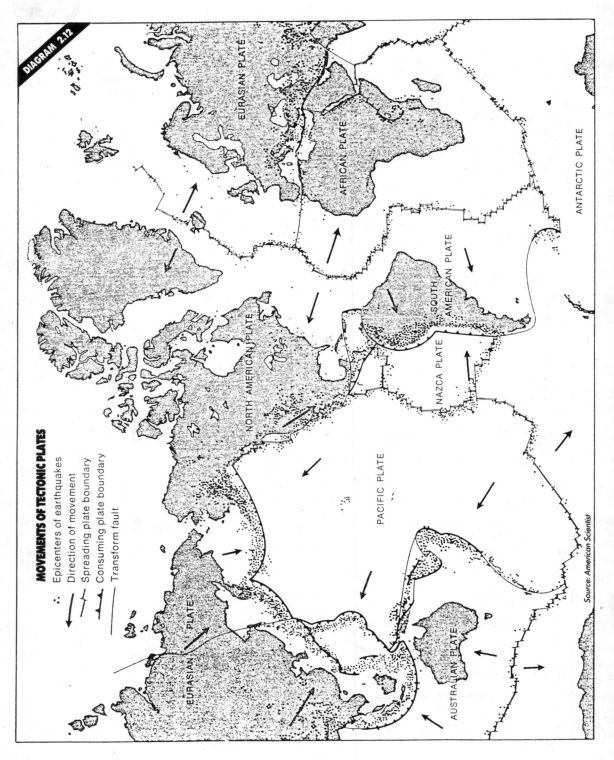

MOVEMENTS OF TECTONIC PLATES

∴ Epicenters of earthquakes

→ Direction of movement

Spreading plate boundary

Consuming plate boundary

Transform fault

EURASIAN PLATE

AFRICAN PLATE

ANTARCTIC PLATE

NORTH AMERICAN PLATE

SOUTH AMERICAN PLATE

NAZCA PLATE

PACIFIC PLATE

EURASIAN PLATE

AUSTRALIAN PLATE

DIAGRAM 2.12

Source: American Scientist

in some areas leads to widespread soil erosion and landslides, lubricated by water, not only displace large quantities of soil and vegetal cover or crops, but also cause considerable structural damage and loss of life.

Waterfalls, rivers and lakes are also of aesthetic value, as is recognized in the design of man-made environments, where ornamental water – pools and fountains – is a popular feature.

Many of today's pressing environmental issues involve water; it is the main receiving agent for liquid waste, from domestic sewage to toxic industrial waste, and water is the agent that transports harmful pollutants (see Pollution). Large schemes intended to manage water for human consumption can also damage the environment. By using water for irrigation, previously unusable land is made productive, but the high evaporation rates in hot dry regions lead to the salinization and consequent infertility of soils. Dams built to provide water for urban dwellers often entail flooding and submerging large areas of farmland, home to indigenous peoples, under these man-made lakes. In some areas large water schemes have resulted in lowering the water table, causing wells to dry up thus, for those dependent on this source, exacerbating the already difficult task of collecting water.

That a supply of safe drinking water and efficient sanitation is one of humanity's basic needs was recognized by the UN International Drinking Water Supply and Sanitation Decade (1981–90), which set as its goal the provision of clean water and sanitation for all the world's people.[23]

ENVIRONMENTAL DISASTERS AND THEIR EFFECTS An environmental hazard is accounted a disaster when the proportions are such that it causes mass destruction and loss of life. Environmental disasters may be natural or as a result of human activities. The extent of these disas-

ters is usually expressed in terms of loss of life and amount of destruction.

Natural disasters occur when there is a sudden change in the systems and processes within the physical environment and are classified according to their origin in the geosphere, atmosphere, hydrosphere and biosphere.

Earthquakes and volcanoes originate in the earth's crust and are caused mainly by disturbances at the unstable regions of the plate boundaries. They are therefore concentrated in specific regions of the earth, such as those bordering the Pacific Ocean, Southern Europe, a line across the southern USSR and northern Iran. The eruption of a volcano or movement within the earth's crust is violent but short lived, and in the case of earthquakes comes with little obvious warning. These events often inflict considerable damage (for example, the 1976 Tangshan earthquake in China) in a short time, and may precipitate others, such as tidal waves, mudflows and landslides.

Disasters associated with the atmosphere can occur anywhere. They include tropical cyclones/hurricanes, extra-tropical storms, tornadoes and thunderstorms. These violent activities of the weather often cause destruction of property and loss of life. Winds are particularly destructive, and unusual spells of extreme heat or cold can cause many deaths. But these climatic occurrences can be forecast and their progress tracked.

Disasters of the hydrosphere may be flooding or drought. Floods are one of the most widespread and severe of all natural disasters, frequently occurring in low-lying, fertile areas favourable for settlement and usually densely populated. Their impact is considerable. They may be the result of freak storms, prolonged periods of rain or, in coastal regions, exceptionally high tides and storm surges. Some are very brief, as in flash floods, some may persist for several weeks. At the other extreme, low rainfall over a long period of time leads to drought. Drought *per se* is not a direct cause of death, but it has an overall effect on people's health and livelihood, and the often resultant famine can be responsible for a death-toll of immense proportions.

Disasters of the biosphere include bush and forest fires and plagues of pests such as locusts. In addition to natural disasters, there are those caused by human activities. Man-made disasters, apart from those related to armed conflict, are usually associated with the accidental release of harmful substances, such as chemicals, oil and radioactivity. Disasters also result from human intervention, for example, cracks in dams and unstable waste tips. Recent examples of man-made disasters include the nuclear accident at Chernobyl and the escape of poisonous gases at Bhopal.

Effects One result of disasters can be degradation of productive land due to landslides or floodwaters, being buried under volcanic lava and ash, or contaminated by radiation or chemical pollution. More widespread is the destruction of buildings and infrastructure, including homes, schools, hospitals, factories, fractured water supply and sanitation pipelines, disruption of power supplies and the damaging of communication links. Apart from the immediate effects of injury, death and loss of homes, there is the subsequent effect on health due to the lack of clean drinking water and of food, the spread of disease and exposure to the elements. In the case of disasters from industrial pollution, there is the problem of the immediate and long-term health effects.

The impact of disasters in terms of loss of life depends not only on the intensity and nature of the disaster but also on the density of the population and the economic status of the country concerned.

Disasters are taking a greater toll because there are more people living in the areas affected. Many developing countries are in parts of the earth particularly prone to natural disasters, located at plate boundaries, or in the path of tropical storms. Many countries have less than rigid industrial regulations, which is seen as an advantage to companies setting up factories in developing countries, but means there is a greater risk of industrial accidents. Disaster preparedness is of prime importance, but not all countries have either the financial or technological resources available.

January 1990 saw the launching of the International Decade for Natural Disaster Reduction (IDNDR). The proclamation of the decade reflects two main developments, namely: the increasing impact of natural disasters in terms of loss of life, physical damage and effects on the economic development of vulnerable countries; and the progress achieved in scientific and technological knowledge which has been such as to allow its application to disaster mitigation through transfer of technology. Over the next ten years, nations throughout the world are asked to give special attention to programmes and projects designed to reduce loss of life, property damage and economic and social disruption due to natural disasters.[24][25]

ENERGY, ITS PRODUCTION, CONSUMPTION AND EFFECTS
Energy sources are classified as either non-renewable or renewable. Most of the world's energy is produced from the non-renewable sources of coal, oil and natural gas. These are fossil fuels, formed millions of years ago from decaying plants and animals, and found in certain sedimentary rocks that make up the earth's crust. The present rate of consumption of these fuels, predominantly in the developed world, is a crucial issue, as not only is the supply rapidly becoming exhausted, but their use is proving to be harmful to the environment. Nuclear energy is also a non-renewable source.

Of the renewable sources of energy, biomass (fuelwood and agricultural and animal waste) is a major source in many developing countries. But fuelwood, although technically a renewable source, is becoming severely depleted. The other most widely used source of renewable energy is water, once used to drive mill-wheels, but now used to produce electricity (hydropower). Other renewable sources are wind, tidal energy, solar power and geothermal energy.

Energy is a basic requirement for everyday life – for cooking, heating and lighting. In the developed, industrialized countries large quantities of energy are consumed by industry, transport and agriculture as well as for domestic purposes.

Effects The extraction and transporting of energy sources have a visual and structural impact. Mining can cause land subsidence, leaves unsightly waste tips, and in its opencast form destroys large areas of land. Also the dust from the coal is a health hazard. The construction of oil drilling installations and pipelines can also be detrimental, especially in areas where wildlife may be threatened. Accidents involving release of oil during drilling or transporting have disastrous effects on wildlife, for example the accident of the tanker Exxon Valdez off the coast of Alaska in 1989.

The continued unsustainable use of biomass in tropical regions is of increasing environmental concern. Unlimited collection of fuelwood is one of the causes of desertification, and the continued burning of plant and animal waste in some areas is affecting the fertility of the soil, because its use as a fuel prevents it from being added to the soil as fertilizer. Also, burning biomass in inefficient stoves can be an environmental health problem.

Electricity generating stations of all types have some effect on the environment. The burning of fossil fuels for electricity generation and heating systems, and by the internal combustion engine, pollutes the atmosphere, causing environmental health problems, acid rain and, through the emission of greenhouse gases, global warming. (More detail on these topics can be found in the appropriate sections of this chapter.) The production of nuclear power poses a threat to the environment due to potential contamination resulting from accidents, and the problem of disposal of nuclear waste. Nuclear power stations also have a relatively short life. Hydropower stations also affect the environment: their construction in remote areas disrupts ecosystems; large schemes involving dams and storage systems displace settlements and drown agricultural land. Other, less used, power systems also present problems. Geothermal plants, for example, emit unpleasantly smelling sulphur dioxide. Systems used in the transmission of energy, for example, electric power lines not only present a visual intrusion, but also affect agriculture, and human health.

The conservation of energy is of prime importance; on the one hand there is the need to conserve the limited reserves of fossil fuels, and on the other there is the need to reduce the emission of greenhouse gases. In this respect there is a need to consider more seriously alternative, less polluting sources of energy. Although some work has been done on the related technology, most governments are not, as yet, giving this full priority. Alternative sources already in limited use include wind power, tidal power, solar power and the utilization of biogas from animal and human wastes. The production of commercial electricity by means of nuclear fusion which, unlike nuclear fission, would avoid the problem of nuclear waste, is still not yet a viable alternative.[26]

POLLUTION CAUSES AND EFFECTS

Pollution takes place when potentially harmful substances are released into the environment. This mostly concerns the disposal of waste in some form, but some substances, such as fertilizers, are themselves useful, but become pollutants when there is an excess. Pollution is caused principally by the activities of humankind, but it can also be a natural process. It is usually classed according to the receiving agents – air (emissions), water (effluents) and land (dumps and disposals). Pollution can cross these divisions, as in the case of the acidification of lakes resulting from air pollution. Other forms of pollution are noise and aesthetic pollution of the environment by odours and unsightly constructions.

Pollution of some kind has always taken place, but it became a problem as a result of the Industrial Revolution, a problem which has accelerated during the twentieth century. Whereas before World War II, when the main concern was soot and sewage and now, in addition, there are the new, often highly toxic chemicals and radioactive substances.

Causes Some pollutants occur naturally, for example, radon gas, methane and minerals in the rocks, which enter rivers and water supplies. Volcanic activity can be responsible for the release of harmful gases and dust into the atmosphere.

Most pollution arises from people's economic and domestic activities. Modern agricultural practices involve the application of chemicals in fertilizers, herbicides and pesticides. These can pollute the atmosphere, enter water systems through seepage and run-off from the soil, be harmful to those handling them, and can contaminate the food which is being produced from the land. Even the cattle pollute the atmosphere by releasing methane during digestion, and cause an increase in nitrates in the soil from their dung. Intensive farming methods produce polluting waste, for example, methane from ricefields and slurry from intensive livestock farming.

Industrial activity is responsible for a wide range of pollution. Thermal power stations burning fossil fuels emit the harmful pollutants sulphur dioxide, nitrous oxide and carbon dioxide, the main causes of acid rain and global warming; smelting and refining ores and minerals are another source of pollution. But it is the chemical industry which is of particular concern. Over the past 50 years it has produced synthetic organic compounds used in products which have become part of everyday life, yet can be environmentally harmful. The disposal of the industry's hazardous wastes is a particular problem, as their deposition has not been confined to the countries of origin. Threatening toxic cargoes are sailing the oceans seeking an acceptable refuge. The potential danger of pollution from the nuclear industry is an even more ominous threat. Despite rigid controls and assurances from the industry, accidents have occurred, notably at Chernobyl in 1986.

Associated with social and economic development has been the development of transport systems which not only pollute the atmosphere by burning fuel, but are also responsible for noise and visual pollution. The noxious emissions from motor vehicles are especially a cause for concern.

Domestic waste includes sewage, garbage of all kinds, worn-out household equipment, as well as the emissions from domestic heating. The quantity of domestic waste is increasing, as are the environmentally harmful products such as non-biodegradable plastics, chemicals from detergents, mercury in batteries, and old refrigerators (releasing CFCs).

Effects Pollution is harmful to the environment and to the health and well-being of all living things. Pollutants released into the water and soil can find their way into the human body as a result of breathing, eating and drinking. (see Health). Pollution also

KILLER CAR

- Cars POLLUTE, even without lead! Cars produce:
  67% of carbon monoxide. Large amounts can kill
  17% of carbon dioxide, the main greenhouse gas
  50% of nitrogen and acid rain.

- Car MANUFACTURE releases paint thinners, degreasers and solvents into the atmosphere.

- Car MOULDINGS use 50% of all (ozone eating) CFCs.

- TYRES from synthetic rubber (250m/year) are difficult to recycle.

- The world's 386 million are the fastest growing users of FOSSIL FUELS.

- Discarded BATTERIES (100m/year) release lead-laden acids into soil.

- Burning scrapped PLASTICS releases toxic gases.

- One third of all LAND in cities is taken by cars; 10% of USA's arable land is paved.

One World Week, UK

causes the deterioration of buildings, dirt and decay, and impairs local amenities.

Agricultural land and production can be threatened by pollution: soil can be contaminated by chemicals or by radiation, crops can be harmed by incorrect use of agricultural chemicals, and forests are being destroyed by acid rain, which is formed when sulphur dioxide and nitrogen oxide are released into the atmosphere. The damage caused by acidification was first recorded in West Germany in the 1960s and now large areas of Europe and North America are affected.

Pollution of fresh water presents a serious hazard to human health through contaminated drinking water supplies (see Health) and it can also be harmful to crops and livestock. Polluted water damages aquatic life; it also limits the leisure and ornamental uses of water. Marine pollution is decimating the world's fisheries and marine life, as well as polluting beaches.

The impact of pollution on climate is on a truly global level as the circulation of the atmosphere has no boundaries. The link between pollution of the atmosphere and global warming and ozone depletion has already been explained in earlier sections.

The effects of environmental pollutants, particularly those caused by vehicle emissions, and by chemicals, are of continuing concern in all countries. The United Nations Environment Programme states that:

Additional data and better methods are needed to manage the risk of pollution comprehensively and to adapt available technology to the needs of developing countries. Information on the type and severity of pollution and its effects on the health of populations is scarce in most countries. There is therefore a need for improved monitoring, assessment and epidemiological surveillance. [27] [28]

URBANIZATION AND ITS ENVIRONMENTAL EFFECTS The city has its own particular environment, consisting of buildings, streets and planned open spaces. The hard impermeable nature of the surfaces, the heat island effect on temperatures, the alignment of buildings with regard to light, sun, wind and rainfall, the adaptation of wildlife to city habitats are all aspects of the human-made urban environment. The city is a focus of social and economic activities, and the cultural dimension is present in its architecture, museums and entertainments. Living conditions vary from luxury apartments, and spacious suburban houses to poor tenements and makeshift shacks of the squatter settlements characteristic of many large cities in developing countries. As UNESCO observed:

During this century, urbanization has become a major ecological driving force involving vast transformations in the use of land, air, water and energy resources and an unprecedented redistribution of human population. In 1920 only 14% of the world's population lived in an urban environment; by 1980 the proportion had risen to about 40%; by the year 2000, it is expected to be more than 50%."

There is an important relationship between the city and its surrounding area. The city provides the urban services, and the surrounding area is a source of food, resources and labour. On the other hand, any harmful pollution will extend well beyond the city limits. The city itself can be seen as an open system, depending on energy and nutrients for its existence, producing waste products which have to be removed (see Diagram 2.13).

People move to the cities to seek a better way of life. During the Industrial Revolution people in Europe moved from rural to

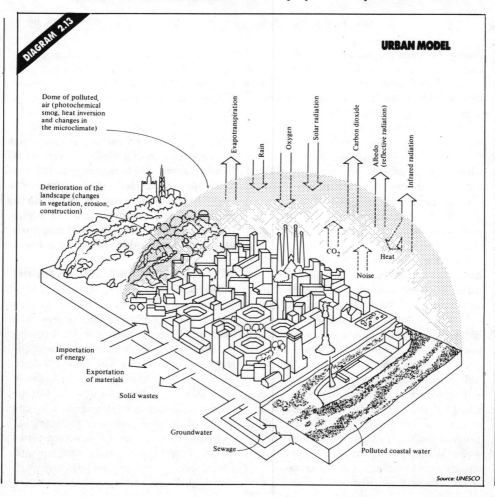

DIAGRAM 2.13

URBAN MODEL

Dome of polluted air (photochemical smog, heat inversion and changes in the microclimate)

Deterioration of the landscape (changes in vegetation, erosion, construction)

Evapotranspiration

Rain

Oxygen

Solar radiation

Carbon dioxide

Albedo (reflective radiation)

Infrared radiation

CO_2

Heat

Noise

Importation of energy

Exportation of materials

Solid wastes

Groundwater

Sewage

Polluted coastal water

Source: UNESCO

urban areas to work in the factories. Today rural poverty in developing countries is driving people to the cities for the opportunities not available to them in the countryside; but very few can expect to find employment. In the cities of developing countries migration is now a contributory factor to increased population which is currently showing an annual growth rate of 3.5 per cent a year.[30]

The nightmare of every urban planner is Mexico City. It was built in the wrong place, on a very marshy substratum in a valley and has expanded at an amazing speed. The population is likely to reach 30 million by the end of the century.

The city's growth took place in a spontaneous and unstructured fashion. Factories were sometimes located in the middle of residential areas, and millions of cars, all producing exhaust fumes, have to clear their way through the too narrow streets. If an earthquake occurs the results are catastrophic.

The more wealthy build their houses on the slope around the city, due to the unhealthy air which permanently hangs like a blanket over the lower part of Mexico City; the poor live closely packed together, sometimes around and on the rubbish tips.[31]

Effects UNESCO's Man and the Biosphere Programme sets out the following environmental effects of increased urbanization:

- land is lost through the paving over of natural and agricultural ecosystems by urban infrastructure (roads, houses, and so on);
- per capita demand for water and energy increases when people move from rural to urban areas;
- changes occur in regional and global atmospheric systems as a result of the concentration of air pollution and heat energy;

- cities produce huge amounts of solid and liquid waste, which can lead to environmental and human health damage when they become greater than the absorptive capacity of the surrounding terrestrial and aquatic ecosystems;
- urban systems are vulnerable to shortages of energy, water and food, to epidemics and the spread of disease, and to the risks attached to some industrial activities.

As far as the overall global pattern of urbanization is concerned, a significant change is taking place in the distribution of the world's largest cities. According to UN World Population report 1986, in 1970, of the 20 largest cities, nine were in the less-developed regions, and by the year 2000 16 of the 20 largest cities will be in the less-developed regions. Many of the developing countries will have to plan for cities of sizes never dreamed of in currently developed countries.[32]

ENVIRONMENT AND HEALTH Environment and human health are inevitably inter-linked, and a healthy environment is essential to the health and well-being of the planet, and its inhabitants, who depend on it for the air they breathe, the water they drink and the food they eat. Also, an unhealthy population produces less, and may be forced into practices damaging to the environment.[33]

The atmosphere provides the air we breathe. An average adult breathes 11 cubic metres of air each day. This air is becoming increasingly polluted from industry, transport systems, and agricultural and domestic chemicals. Air quality in many cities, especially the mushrooming capitals of developing countries, has already deteriorated to the point of causing respiratory problems for the less robust. WHO estimates that more than 600 people are exposed to a sulphur dioxide concentration well above what is calculated to be medically safe; more than one billion people are exposed to the hazards of microscopic airborne dust particles in excess of WHO's recommended limits. Recent studies point also to health hazards attributable to indoor air pollution. Wood, dung, peat, coal or other fossil-fuel fires for cooking and heating in poorly ventilated dwellings, largely in rural areas of developing countries, expose women and infants to continual high air pollution.

According to WHO, an individual needs 40–50 litres of water per day for drinking and personal and domestic hygiene. Yet this essential requisite is still unavailable to many people. In 1988 one billion people in developing countries (China excluded) lacked ready access (that is, within a 15-minute walk) to potable water, and about twice that number were without proper sanitation.[34]

The UN International Drinking Water Supply and Sanitation Decade was launched with the aim of providing water and sanitation for all by 1990. This ambitious target was not reached, but about 1,348 million more people in developing countries were provided with safe drinking water during the 1980s, and 748 million more people were provided with suitable sanitation services.[35] This improvement, however, barely kept pace with the increase in population.

Not only the simple provision of water, but its quality is very important. Untreated water leads to the spread of diarrhoea and other diseases. Water is also the habitat for vector-borne diseases such as malaria, which is still one of the most serious public health problems in the developing countries, and schistosomiasis, which is carried by a species of water snail and threatens children who wash and bathe in infected water. Even a naturally clean water supply may contain products such as fluoride which can be harmful, and water supply can be contaminated from lead pipes.

The land itself has an influence on health. There are examples of harmful products from the rocks such as radon gas, but it is land as the source of food which has the main impact. Millions of people today get insufficient food, or food lacking essential nourishment; the former leads to undernourishment the latter to malnourishment, both of which conditions are seriously debilitating and make the body more prone to infection. Degradation of the land by soil erosion, desertification and so on limits food production significantly. Also, land may be contaminated by chemicals or radioactivity, and this contamination can be passed on to people through the food supply.

The plants and animals of the natural ecosystems can also be a health hazard. Rats, for example, not only spread disease but along with other rodents consume or spoil vast quantities of cereal crops annually; insects such as mosquitoes and tsetse fly are carriers of disease. Pollen and other plant emissions, such as spores, can cause painful allergies.

People's health is greatly affected by the immediate environment in which they live and work, and by their social habits and lifestyle. Smoking, alcoholism and drug abuse have serious health consequences; accidents in the home and at work continue to give cause for concern, and stress-related health problems are increasingly associated with modern lifestyles.

By the year 2000, it is estimated that almost half of the world's population will live in cities. In many developing countries the overcrowded and squalid living conditions, often without piped water or sanitation, and the increasingly high pollution are major health hazards, particularly with regard to communicable diseases. In developed countries the problems of unhealthy industrial cities of the nineteenth century have largely been overcome, and the major infectious diseases are no longer a

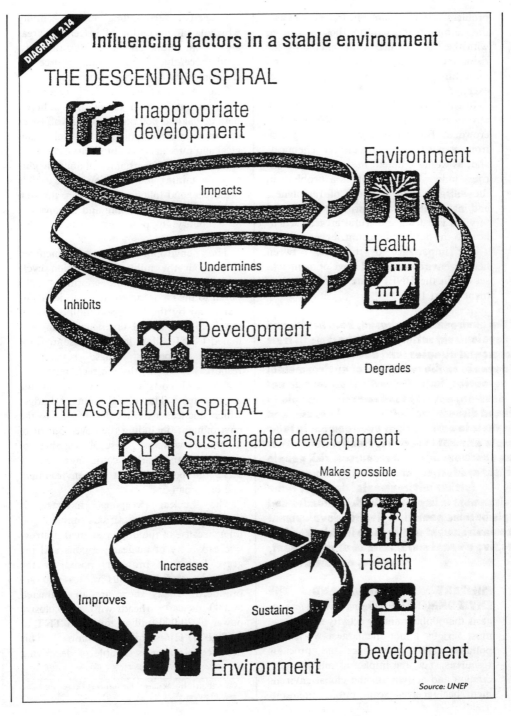

DIAGRAM 2.14

Influencing factors in a stable environment

THE DESCENDING SPIRAL

Inappropriate development

Impacts

Environment

Undermines

Health

Inhibits

Development

Degrades

THE ASCENDING SPIRAL

Sustainable development

Makes possible

Increases

Health

Improves

Sustains

Environment

Development

Source: UNEP

problem. Apart from respiratory disease, the main problems now are those associated with the stress of urban life, including the rising incidence of crime and violence, and unhealthy lifestyles, including lack of exercise.

In rural areas, the environment is generally more healthy, less polluted and less crowded. But there is an increasing risk from exposure to agricultural chemicals and, as we have noted, in developing countries, indoor air pollution is a problem in the villages. The problem of remoteness and inaccessibility from primary health care services is a feature of rural areas, particularly in the developing countries.

The importance of the link between health, environment and development was set out in the UNEP State of the Environment report 1986.[36]

If the environment is abused, both health and development suffer; people become ill from environmental diseases, and development, which depends on the [wise] use of environmental resources, fails. Similarly, if nations do not develop, poverty condemns their people to continued disease, debility and early death, and drives them to destroy their environment in their desperate attempt to survive. Finally, ill health is itself an enormous drain on resources, sick people are less productive, and are often driven to do further environmental damage. If the environment is improved, both economies and people become healthier. Health, development and the environment will become interlocked in a positive upward spiral instead of the present, negative, downward one.

MILITARY ACTIVITY AND THE ENVIRONMENT* Emerging evidence suggests that global military activity may be the most serious if not the largest worldwide polluter and consumer of precious resources. Yet, the impact of military production and activity on the global environment has received scant public attention.

The secrecy surrounding military activity which is often conducted in remote areas away from public and media scrutiny has, until recently, hidden this source of environmental destruction from view.

The impact of military activity on the environment is both direct and indirect, both actual and potential. It covers all types of weaponry (conventional, chemical, biological and nuclear) as well military activity in war and peace. Environmental abuse begins with the mining and diversion of the earth's resources, and follows step by step through the manufacturing, testing and deployment of weaponry, to peace-time military exercises and war.

The environmental costs incurred throughout the military production cycle are compounded by the enormous risks posed to the environment from accidents or wars, and by the lost opportunities resulting from the annual diversion of an estimated US $1 trillion in global resources for military purposes.[37] These squandered resources represent the indirect, but nonetheless real costs of the military to the environment. The global military budget which finances activities detrimental to the environment, including the development of a global weapons' arsenal capable of destroying the earth, could alternatively serve the betterment of the environment and of humankind.

The nuclear weapons' industry is undoubtedly the most serious military polluter because of the unprecedented destructive capability of nuclear weapons and the grave long-term problems posed by the explosives and hazardous wastes that are produced. Today there are an estimated 50,000 nuclear warheads with the explosive power of 20,000 million tonnes of TNT or 1,600,000 Hiroshima-size bombs.[38] This destructive power is capable of destroying

---

* Contributed by **Women's International League for Peace and Freedom**.

all of the earth's inhabitants and its ecosystems. Many scientists believe that a nuclear war would result in a phenomenon known as nuclear winter, with dense clouds of radioactive fall-out, and soot and smoke from the explosions and fires, blocking out the sun possibly for months.[39] Perhaps a greater threat than deliberate war is accidental war, or an accident resulting from human error or technological failure. Statistics indicate that errors and accidents are routine within the command, control and communications systems[40] that maintain nuclear weapons; accidents at sea involving nuclear vessels occur frequently.[41]

Radioactive materials release energy or atomic particles (radiation) into the environment. Some radioactive substances, such as uranium-234, occur naturally; other substances, such as plutonium, are produced artificially in nuclear reactors. The time span during which a substance emits radiation is known as its half-life. Many of the by-products of nuclear weapons production have long half-lives, and some will remain dangerously radioactive for fifty times longer than recorded history.

To date no effective solutions have been found for the long-term storage of radioactive waste or for clean-up following a nuclear disaster. Radiation can contaminate air, soil, groundwater and vegetation, with dire consequences for nearby populations and wildlife. It can cause cancers, genital defects, immune deficiencies from reduced monocyte levels in white blood cells, and consequently increased incidence of disease.[42] The danger can continue for thousands of years and can pose a threat to the environment and populations well beyond the initial area of contamination. Radioactive particles can be carried for long distances by clouds, winds and waterways; they can also be exported to other regions by entering the food chain.

During the early 1960s, strontium 90 was found in babies' teeth and was traced to the clouds of radioactive fall-out circling the earth as a result of atmospheric nuclear weapons' tests. Although this discovery led to a treaty banning atmospheric nuclear tests, testing has continued underground, with an estimated 20 per cent of tests resulting in the release of some radioactive gases to the atmosphere.[43]

The mining of uranium lays waste large tracts of land and produces vast amounts of radioactive waste. The reactors used for the production of weapons-grade uranium or plutonium also produce large quantities of lethal waste, and are subject to routine emissions, leakages and accidents. Wastes that remain radioactive for thousands of years can outlive any storage container produced today. The full extent of the health and environmental consequences of these operations is not yet known, but recent evidence from a variety of localities suggests that it is extensive. Such operations include the dumping of highly toxic radioactive wastes into rivers and seas, the contamination of soils and groundwater, in some instances affecting drinking water and soil well beyond the production site.

Other forms of military activity are also significant in their threat to the environment. Conventional weaponry has been employed in more than 135 wars that have occurred worldwide since 1945. War is ecologically destructive in a number of ways. It often results in widespread temporary and permanent destruction of both the human and physical environment, including dramatically increased consumption and destruction of natural resources.

Since World War II, the sophistication of high technology weaponry has dramatically increased the destructive nature of warfare and, at the same time, has increased its ecologically disruptive capability. The Vietnam War, 1961-75 with its widespread use of chemical defoliants, massive rural bombing and forest destruction alerted the public to the tremendous price that warfare inflicts on the physical and human environment, a price that will continue to be paid well into the future. The Gulf War of 1991 inflicted considerable environmental damage, the full impact of which has yet to be assessed.

But even in the absence of war, on-going military exercises, such as large manoeuvres using tanks and other heavy vehicles, and low-level flight tests, gouge the earth's terrain, disrupt animal and bird life, and damage societies.

The research and development of chemical and biological agents for military purposes is an additional concern. The accidental or intentional release of unknown biological and chemical agents, produced secretly in military laboratories, poses an undefined but alarming risk both to populations and the environment. Disposing of these agents once produced is yet another hazard. Under a Chemical Weapons Convention currently under negotiation, all national stockpiles of chemical weapons are to be destroyed. Plans to dispose of these weapons by burning them on one of the atolls in the Pacific has raised serious environmental concerns.

The industrialized countries, and especially the NATO and Warsaw Pact military alliances, have been responsible for the bulk of military activity and expenditure since 1945. Since the 1970s, however, there has been a significant increase in such activity amongst developing countries, with some nations spending as much as 50 per cent of their GNP on the military.[44]

While US$1,900,000 is spent each *minute* on the global military, most of the world's population lives in poverty.[45] The Brundtland Report on Environment and Development demonstrated that protecting the environment requires, amongst other things, dealing with underdevelopment. Stopping military production would not only free resources for development purposes, but it would also eliminate a major source of environmental destruction and waste.

POPULATION AND THE ENVIRONMENT

Population is at the centre of the issues affecting both the physical and social environments. As the world's population increases there is inevitably greater pressure on natural resources, and the greater the pressure, the more likely it is to lead to degradation of the environment. The world's population now exceeds five billion; the total for 1990 was 5.3 billion.[46] Growth will not stop altogether for perhaps another century, when world population may exceed ten billion, twice its present level. Most of these births will be in developing countries.

It was at the time when the world population reached its first billion, in the nineteenth century, that Thomas Malthus put forward his ideas on population: that whereas population increases geometrically, food production increases arithmetically, thus raising the whole question of balance between population and natural resources. Then the problem of the increasing population of industrial Europe could be solved by the expanding economy, and by migration to the New World. Since that time, not only has the world's population increased, but there has been a change in the regional distribution of that increase. The so-called demographic transition of the developed countries has meant that the fall in death rates, due to improved medical care, was followed by a reduction in birth rates as people started to limit their families. In the industrial countries, the over-60s make up 17 per cent of the population. At the same time, there has been a 'population explosion' in the developing countries where, with the improvement in health care, infant mortality rates have decreased and people are living longer. The population growth in developing countries reached its peak in the period 1965–70; the total numbers will reach their maximum in the last years of this century.

The rate of population growth has

increased the pressure on the world's natural resources, particularly concerning the availability of the basic needs of food and water. According to the UNFPA World Population Report 1990:

So far, in global terms, the struggle to keep food production level with population growth has been won, but the continuing advance of population growth has made it a struggle, and the fight continues.

In many of the local battles, especially in developing countries where population growth is higher, food production is losing ground to population. Between 1979–81 and 1986–87, cereal production per person actually declined in 51 developing countries and rose in only 43, out of the 94 countries for which FAO data are available.[47]

Another concern is the loss of productive land due to degradation processes such as desertification and soil erosion. On the other hand, yields have been increasing and, with genetic engineering, could continue to do so.

One of the major issues of the future is how the world's demand for water will be met. The hydrological cycle does not distribute water in an equitable manner. Most of Africa, much of the Middle East and North Asia, the western United States and north-western Mexico, parts of Chile and Argentina, and of Australia are areas of severe water deficits.[48]

The link between population and energy is another key issue. The high energy-consuming industrial countries exert pressure on the resources and cause more pollution by their use, whereas in the lower energy-consuming countries the large population exerts pressure on the environment and its natural resource base.[49]

Effects There are some clear links between population and degradation of the environment. Population growth is a major cause of deforestation, as land is cleared for farming and settlements. According to the United Nations Population Fund (UNFPA) 'when both agricultural and non-agricultural needs are taken into account, growing populations may be responsible for as much as 80 per cent of the loss of forest cover.' The impact of population on the environment can be explained in terms of an equation.

The equation has three components. First, lifestyles, incomes and social organization determine levels of consumption. Second, the technologies in use determine the extent to which human activities damage, or sustain, the environment, and the amount of waste associated with any level of consumption. These two factors determine impact per person. The third factor, population, determines how many persons there are: it is the multiplier that fixes the total impact.[50]

At any given level of technology or poverty, population growth is a prime cause of land degradation in most of the developing world, and slowing population growth will help to limit further degradation.[51] According to the Population and Natural Resources Programme of IUCN:

In coming decades, critical population/ resources interactions are projected to be:

- Increasingly large direct population pressures on natural resources.
- Massive population movements and significant changes in resource use by populations who depend primarily on the availability of specific natural resources for their livelihood and who find themselves in increasing competition with other human populations as well as with other species.
- Increasingly precarious equilibrium between people and resources among those populations who live at the mere

edge of survival (for example, in the Sahel), with the possible consequence of large-scale environmental destruction caused by practices adopted for short-term survival, rather than long-term sustainability.

- Significantly increased per capita demand for natural resources in the newly industrialised countries where average family size decreases rapidly, while resource consumption increases simultaneously.
- Continued high demand by the ageing and wealthy populations in the industrial countries for natural resources which are in short supply or absent in their own countries.[52]

ECONOMIC AND POLITICAL CONSIDERATIONS It is important to look at these two factors both in terms of their links and impact on the environment.

Environmental economics The concept of sustainable development as set out in the Brundtland Report is concerned with the future of the global economy, and thus it is important to investigate the link between the environment and the economy. Fundamental to an understanding of sustainable development is the fact that the economy is not separate from the environment in which we live. There is an interdependence, both because the way we manage the economy impacts on the environment, and because environmental quality impacts on the performance of the economy.[53]

Environmental economics is concerned with three broad categories: first, the environment is a source of raw materials and energy, which are the physical inputs to recurrent production; second, the environment absorbs the waste products of our civilization, through its air, soil and water; and third, the environment serves a variety of other functions to humankind, such as life support (for example, the atmosphere, biodiversity), health, amenity and so on.[54]

One of the central issues is that in most instances the environment is available 'for free', and because of this it is being overused and degraded and there is a need to evaluate the cost of the environment. The whole concept of 'the user must pay' is receiving serious consideration. Countries are beginning to introduce legislation to apply this concept; for example, Norway has a tax on sulphur pollution, and an environmental tax on pesticides and fertilizers. According to David Pearce, the intellectual battle to change environmental policy has largely been won; the task now is to develop practical policies.[55]

Industry and consumers It has been shown in earlier sections of this chapter that industry plays an important role in the environment, using natural resources to make products for the consumer, and in so doing causes degradation and pollution. It is the industrialization of the North, with its emission of greenhouse gases which is largely responsible for the threat of global warming and its implications. Industry has the ability by developing new technologies to minimize this harmful impact on the environment, but so far has not seen the need to do so. There is, however, a growing awareness in the business community of the importance of environmental issues. Major environmental disasters such as Bhopal have made companies think about their environmental policies. Consumers have been campaigning for 'green' products for years, and now there is the additional force of the green investor. The increasing pressure from these quarters, together with the threat posed by imminent and possible future environmental legislation, is influencing business people, who are beginning to realize the value of producing environmentally friendly goods. The adoption of less environmentally damaging production

processes and the greater use of recycling are also receiving attention, and even featuring in advertising. Some countries are more advanced in these respects. Germany has a well-established consumer guarantee by the Federal Environment Agency, whereas in other countries, such as Britain, there is a flood of green products on the market, many of which are making false claims as to their environmental friendliness.

It is important to consider the contrasting positions of the North and South. The pattern of consumption varies between developed and developing countries, with the developed countries consuming far more and producing more waste (see Diagram 2.15). Poor people use little energy, and thus contribute little to the damage caused by mobilizing it. The average Bangladeshi is not surrounded by plastic gadgets, the average Bolivian does not fly in jet aircraft, the average Kenyan farmer uses neither a tractor nor pick-up truck, the average Chinese has no air conditioning or central heating. Comprising less than one-quarter of the world's population, citizens of rich nations control some four-fifths of its resources. They, and their technologies which they have spread around the world, are largely responsible for the depletion of soils and groundwater, and have played a major role in causing the destruction of biodiversity, both within their national territories and elsewhere.[56] Other problems arise from the practice of companies from the developed countries taking advantage of the less rigid industrial and tax regulations in the developing countries to set up factories which pollute and damage the environment and seriously affect the health of the workforce they employ. This is also manifested in the dumping of toxic waste and in the implications of possible developments in biotechnology (see Pollution; Biotechnology).

Future industrial development is likely to involve the extra cost of environmentally sound technologies. This will be particularly difficult for developing countries, and their position with regard to technology transfer and financial resources will need to be taken into account in any future global environmental agreements.

A narrowly environmental approach leads to technical fixes for the rich and paternalism for the poor. The developing countries are worried not only about the paternalism, but also about the technical fixes. The techniques which need to be fixed were by and large developed in the North, but the South was told that they were the ingredients of the development it ought to be pursuing. It accepted this argument and after long efforts mastered the techniques, only to be told that they are no longer acceptable and that it must adopt new methods which, of course, belong once again to the North.[57]

There is a North-South dimension to the environmental crisis. We are faced with this crisis because since the 19th century the world has been running a race to deplete the world's natural resources.

The economic model applied until now stresses productivity and consumption over frugality, saving and recycling. What is needed now is a new model for the economy, for development, that makes a different, judicious use of natural resources.[58]

The debt crisis The more obvious effects of the debt crisis on the livelihood of the people have been widely recognized since the early 1980s, but only recently has attention been focused on the environmental impact.

In order to pay their debts, many developing countries are exploiting their natural resources, such as tropical hardwoods, to export to industrialized countries. The trade in tropical hardwoods is one of the major causes of deforestation (see Defores-

DIAGRAM 2.15

GALLOPING CONSUMPTION

The rich North consumes 80% of the world's global resources, while three-quarters of the world's population who live in the poor South share what is left.[1]

In one year, the average person in the West is likely to:[2]

● consume more than 264 lbs of paper, compared to an average consumption of just 17.6 lbs per person in the Third World.

● consume over 990 lbs of steel compared with 94.6 lbs in the Third World.

● consume 57.2 lbs of other metals compared with 4.4 lbs in the Third World.

● purchase energy equivalent to almost 6 tons of coal compared with 0.5 tons in the Third World.

THROWAWAY WORLD

Westerners produce more waste than any other society in history. But as the Third World countries industrialize they are beginning to catch up.

	Annual domestic waste ('000 tons)	Equivalent per person (lbs)
1. US	200,000	1,925
2. Australia	10,000	1,496
3. Canada	12,600	1,155
4. Aotearoa	1,528	1,073
5. Norway	1,700	913
6. Denmark	2,046	878
15. U K	15,816	620

● As examples of waste in the industrializing Third World here is the amount thrown away per person per year in three major cities: Singapore 538 lbs; Mexico City 321 lbs; and Jakarta 305 lbs.[5]

SQUANDERING ENERGY

Most energy comes from non-renewable sources; the West cannot sustain its current levels of energy consumption.

● The US has just 6% of the world's population but consumes 30% of the world's energy – compared with India where 20% of the global population use only 2% of the world's energy.[5]

● Private cars use about 7% of the world's non-industrial energy or 17% of the oil used annually.[7]

● Specially designed houses can cut energy costs by 75 per cent.

Energy consumed in the home per year measured as barrels of oil

Barrels of oil per person

North America	22.0
Australasia	16.5
Scandinavia	13.5
Europe	9.8
Japan	8.5

Source: New Internationalist

tation). Ghana is an example of a country where the government, backed by the donor institutions, is exploiting its timber reserves as one way out of the debt crisis. From 1984 to 1988, the total forest felled rose from 578,000 cubic metres to 1.15 million cubic metres annually.[59]

Countries with mineral resources have increased mining and refining activities, which have led to uncontrolled pollution. This has affected the productivity of the land and water and the health of the people. For example, copper mining in the Philippines has polluted the coastal area, disrupting the ecosystem and affecting the livelihood of 14,000 local fishermen and their families. The Philippines government (which now owns the mine) is in desperate need of the foreign exchange earned from the copper exports, and this is an important factor in official resistance to demands for a reduction of the pollution.[60]

Greater emphasis on cash crop production for export has also had an impact on the environment. Displaced farmers are forced on to land which cannot support their farming practices, and this leads to land degradation.

In Brazil, millions of small peasant families have been displaced from arable land in the south of the country to make way for large, highly mechanized farms. These farms produce huge harvests of soybeans, now Brazil's leading agricultural product. Many of the evicted peasant families are those who have been taken to Amazonia where, without the knowledge necessary to manage the fragile rainforest soils, they have created vast barren wastelands in the search for land for their subsistence.[61]

Another link between the debt crisis and the environment is the presence of large projects involving the construction of dams, highways, roads, and so on. It was, in fact, loans, for the implementation of such projects, provided by the commercial banks in the 1970s that set the debt crisis in motion. The World Bank and its regional counterparts also played a significant role and these institutions' environmental policies have been much criticized by organizations such as the Sierra Club.[62] A prime example of these projects is the Narmada Valley Dam in India which has been the subject of wide condemnation by environmentalists and

DEBT-FOR-NATURE SWAPS

Debt-for-nature swaps were first proposed by WWF (World Wide Fund for Nature) in 1984. Conservation organizations acquire title to debt, either by direct donation from a bank, or by raising the cash to buy it, and then negotiate with the debtor countries to obtain debt repayment in local currency at a favourable conversion rate, or to secure conservation measures/activities.

Alternatively, a conservation organization in the creditor country can donate an acquired debt to a partner in the debtor country, or the creditor country organization may donate the necessary funds for the debtor country organization to directly acquire the debt. In effect, the debt is available at a discount.

Conversion of the debt can involve issuing local currency bonds, measures to protect environmentally sensitive areas, purchase, legislation, cash payment in redemption of debt, or any combination of these. The final step is the agreed-on conservation programme. Debtor countries which have so far participated in this system include the Philippines, Costa Rica, Bolivia, Ecuador, Madagascar and Zambia.

WWF, Tropical Forests

active protests by the peasants and indigenous people who will be seriously affected.

The World Bank and government agencies are now working more closely with NGOs. According to a World Bank publication,[63] discussion between the Bank and NGOs in general has improved mutual understanding and influenced Bank policy, notably regarding the environment and poverty. Environmental NGOs helped to sensitize public opinion and development practitioners, including the Bank, to the importance of environmental issues in developmental projects.

In a country undergoing an economic crisis and forced to make cuts in its spending, items such as conservation programmes are among the first to suffer. The quality of the social environment is also affected as less money is available for government services and infrastructure. One way to stop the destruction and protect the environment is by the exchange of debt for nature, in the form of Debt-for-Nature Swaps (see Box on preceding page).

However, beyond the safeguarding of plant and animal species other questions need to be posed. Humanity long ago left the stage of primary consumption, and modern society as it presently stands is dependent on industrial progress which is based on increased exploitation of the natural resources of our planet. The use of recycled resources is still not being fully exploited. The problem is to find a new economic concept which will spare the environment. It is urgent to draw up a new philosophical and ethical development model in which the preservation of nature is guaranteed. It is not only consumption patterns that must be addressed, but also the tragic waste of raw materials and natural resources.[64]

The role of governments The role of national governments is crucial in achieving the goal of sustainable development and a healthy and improving environment. This cannot be achieved solely by the efforts of organizations and individuals.

According to the Brundtland Report, critical objectives for environment and development policies that follow from the concept of sustainable development include:

- reviving economic growth;
- changing the quality of economic growth;
- meeting the essential needs for jobs, food, energy, water, and sanitation;
- ensuring a sustainable level of population;
- conserving and enhancing the resource base;
- reorienting technology and managing risk;
- merging environment and economics in decision making.[65]

Many governments, including those in developing countries, have already responded to the Brundtland Report with statements and commitments. Countries will also submit national reports to the 1992 Conference on Environment and Development; these are to provide information on the interactions between development processes and the environment.

Government representatives are good at making speeches and signing protocols, but what is important is what these same speakers and signers actually do. Processes are now underway towards the agreement of a global convention on climate change, to be followed by one on biodiversity. If these are to be successful, the needs of all countries must be taken into account and it is important that there is responsible action by governments in working to safeguard the planet and its people.

1 Natural Environment Research Council, UK (1989) *Our Future World*, London; Unesco/UNEP (1985) International Environmental Education Programme, Environment Education Series no. 9 *Environment Education Module for Pre-service Training of Social Science Teachers and Supervisors for Secondary Schools*, Paris, Unesco.
2 WMO/UNEP (1990) *Scientific Assessment of Climate Change*, Policy-makers Summary of the Report of Working Group 1 to the Intergovernmental Panel on Climate Change, Geneva, World Metereological Organization.
3 WWF (nd) *Report on Climate Change*, Gland, Switzerland, World Wide Fund for Nature International.
4 Commonwealth Group of Experts (1989) *Climate Change: Meeting the Challenge*, London, Commonwealth Secretariat; FOE/ICCE (1989) *Blowing Our Cover* (audio-visual education pack), Cheltenham, UK, International Centre for Conservation Education; TVE (1988) *Bulletin*, September, London, Television Trust for the Environment; UNEP/GEMS (1987) Environment Library 1, *The Greenhouse Gases*, Nairobi, United Nations Environment Programme; WMO/ICSU (1989) *Global Climate Change*, Geneva, World Meteorological Organization.
5 FOE/ICCE (1989) op.cit.; UNEP (1989) *Action on Ozone*, Nairobi, United Nations Environment Programme; UNEP/GEMS (1989) Environment Library no. 2, *The Ozone Layer*, Nairobi, United Nations Environment Programme; WMO (1990) *Global Ozone Observing System* (fact sheet), Geneva, World Meteorological Organization.
6 WWF (nd) *The Importance of Biological Diversity*, Gland, Switzerland, World Wide Fund for Nature International.
7 Ibid.
8 Ibid.
9 Reid, Walter V. and Kenton R. Miller (1989) *Keeping Options Alive: the Scientific Basis for Conserving Biodiversity*, WRI Publications Brief, New York, World Resources Institute.
10 Speth, James Gustave (1989) *Issues and Ideas*, WRI Publications Brief, New York, World Resources Institute; UNEP (1988) *The United Nations System Wide Medium Term Environment Programme 1990-1995 (SWMTEP)*, Nairobi, United Nations Environment Programme.
11 Macfarlane, Ron (1990) *Biotechnology: Perils and Possibilities*, Consumer Lifelines, July, Penang, Malaysia, International Organization of Consumer Unions.
12 Walgate, Robert (1990) *Miracle or Menance: Biotechnology and the Third World*, London, Panos Institute.
13 NGLS (1990) *E&D File 1992* no. 9 (fact sheet), Geneva, United Nations Non-governmental Liaison Service.
14 IUCN (1990) unpublished report
15 UNEP (1987) UNEP Environmental Briefs – *The Disappearing Forest* Nairobi, United Nations Environment Programme.
16 Lefort, René (1990) 'Seeing the Forest for the Trees', *Unesco Sources*, October, Paris, Unesco.
17 UNEP (1988) *SWMTEP* op.cit.
18 Ibid.
19 FAO (1985) *Tropical Forest Action Plan*, Rome, Food and Agriculture Organization of the United Nations; Sawyer, Jacquline, 'Deforestation: a Global Problem', unpublished paper, Unesco (1989) *The Courier*, January, Paris, Unesco, UNEP, *The Disappearing Forest*, Environment Brief no. 3, Nairobi, United Nations Environment Programme; WWF (1990) *Tropical Forests*, Gland, Switzerland, World Wide Fund for Nature International; WWF (nd) *Tropical Forest Conservation*, Position Paper no. 3, Gland, Switzerland, World Wide Fund for Nature International.
20 Hare, F. Kenneth (1985) *Climate Variations, Drought and Desertification*, Geneva, World Meteorological Organization.
21 OXFAM (1990) *OXFAM News*, Spring, Oxford, OXFAM UK, UNEP, *Deserts on the Move* (fact sheet), Nairobi, United Nations Environment Programme; UNEP (1982) *People on Earth*, Nairobi, United Nations Environment Programme.
22 UNESCO (1990), *Unesco Sources*, March, Paris, Unesco.
23 UNEP/WHO (1988) Global Environment Monitoring System, *Assessment of Freshwater Quality*, Nairobi, United Nations Environment Programme, Geneva, World Health Organization, World Meteorological Organization, Geneva. Department of Hydrology and Water Resources (personal communication).
24 UNDRO (1990) *UNDRO News*, Jan./Feb., Geneva, Disaster Relief Organization, United Nations.
25 Whittow, John (1979) *Disasters*, Georgia, USA, University of Georgia Press; Wijkman, Anders, and Lloyd Timberlake (1984) *Natural Disasters, Acts of God or Acts of Man*, London, Earthscan Publications, League of Red Cross and Red Crescent/SIDA Books.
26 ILO (1987) *Linking Energy with Survival*, Geneva, International Labour Organization; Unesco/UNEP (1986) Environment Education Series, no. 11, *Energy: an Interdisciplinary Theme for Environmental Education*, Paris, Unesco; UNEP (1988) *SWMTEP* op. cit.; UNEP (1982) *World Environment 1972–1982* Chapter 12: Energy and the Environment, Nairobi, United Nations Environment Programme.
27 UNEP (1988) *SWMTEP* op.cit.
28 Speth, James Gustave (1988) *Environmental Pollution: a Long-term Perspective*, New York, World Resources Institute, (reprinted from *EARTH 88*, Changing Geographic Perspectives, National Geographic Society, Washington, UNESCO/UNEP (1985) Environment Education Series no. 10, op. cit.; UNEP (1986) *State of the Environment*, Nairobi, United Nations Environment Programme; UNEP (1987) *State of the Environment*, Nairobi, United Nations Environment Programme; UNEP/WHO (1988) Global Environment Monitoring System, op. cit.
29 UNESCO (1988), Man and the Biosphere Programme, *Man Belongs to the Earth*, Paris, Unesco
30 UNFPA (1986) *The State of the World Population 1986*, New York, United Nations Population Fund.
31 Ministry of Foreign Affairs, The Netherlands (nd) *Environment and Development*, The Hague. Directorate-General for International Cooperation of the Ministry of Foreign Affairs.
32 UNFPA (1986) op. cit.
33 WHO/UNEP (1986) *Pollution and Health*, Geneva, World Health Organization.
34 WHO (1989) *Our Planet Our Health*, Geneva, World Health Organization.
35 UN (1990) Report. Achievements of the International Drinking Water Supply and Sanitation Decade (unpublished report).
36 UNEP (1986) *State of the Environment*, op.cit.
37 Legar Sivard, Ruth (1989) *World Military and Social Expenditures*, Washington, World Priorities.
38 Fischer, Dietrich (1984) *Preventing War in the Nuclear Age*, New Jersey, Rowman & Allenheld.
39 UN (1984) *Disarmament*, a Periodic Review by the United Nations: The Nuclear Winter Issue, vol. VII no. 3, Autumn 1984, New York, United Nations.
40 Arkin, William M. and Joshua Handler (1985) *Naval Accidents 1945-1988*, Neptune Paper no. 3, Greenpeace.
41 Bertell, Rosalie (1985) *No Immediate Danger – Prognosis for a Radioactive Earth*, London, The Women's Press.
42 Gordon, Janet (1990) 'Testimony from the Nevada Test

Site', in *Health and Environmental Consequences of Nuclear Radiation from Weapons Production and Testing*, Geneva, Women's International League of Peace and Freedom.

43 May, John (1989) *The Greenpeace Book of the Nuclear Age*. Toronto. McClelland & Stewart.

44 Legar Sivard, Ruth (1989) op. cit.

45 Ibid.

46 UNFPA (1990) *State of the World Population 1990*, New York, United Nations Population Fund.

47 Ibid.

48 Falkenmark, Malin (1990) Population Growth and Water Supplies: an Emerging Crisis, in *Earthwatch*, no. 1, supplement in *People*, London, International Planned Parenthood Federation (IPPF).

49 IUCN (1990) unpublished report.

50 UNFPA (1990) op.cit.

51 Ibid.

52 IUCN (1990) *Case Studies in Population and Natural Resources,* Gland, Switzerland, World Conservation Union.

53 Pearce, David, Anil Markandya, and Edward B. Barbier (1989) *Blueprint for a Green Economy*, London, Earthscan Publications.

54 ODI (1990) 'Environment, Markets and Development' (briefing paper), London, Overseas Development Institute.

55 Pearce, David in *The Guardian*, 6 December 1990.

56 Erlich, Paul R, and Anne H. Erlich (1989) 'Too Many Rich Folks', *Populi* vol. 16 no: 3, New York, United Nations Population Fund.

57 Dommen, Edward (1990) 'ECO '92 Whose Voices Will Be Heard?', *Trocaire Development Review*, Ireland.

58 Sayages, Mercedes (1990) World Food Programme, Rome, personal communication.

59 ICFTU (1989) *The African Development Challenge*, Pan-African Conference Report, Brussels, International Confederation of Free Trade Unions.

60 Cleary, Seamus (1989) *Renewing the Earth*, London, CAFOD.

61 Branford, Sue (1989) 'Debt Crisis, Where Now?', *TRF Times Spring 1989*, London, Friends of the Earth.

62 Sierre Club (1986) *Bankrolling Disasters*, Washington.

63 World Bank (1990) *How the World Bank Works with Non-governmental Organizations* Washington

64 Bittencourt, Berenice (1989) 'The Impact of the Debt Crisis on the Environment, presentation at YWCA conference People and the Debt Crisis, Geneva, November 1989.

65 World Commission on Environment and Development (1987) *Our Common Future* (Bruntdland Report), Oxford and New York, Oxford University Press.

3 THE ROLE OF WOMEN

Ecological ways of knowing nature are necessarily participatory. Nature herself is the experiment and women, as sylviculturalists, agriculturists and water resource managers, the traditional natural scientists. Their knowledge is ecological and plural, reflecting both the diversity of natural ecosystems and the diversity in cultures that nature-based living gives rise to.

VANDANA SHIVA, *STAYING ALIVE* *

WOMEN AS USERS ☐ As users, many women in developing countries have direct contact with the natural environment as they collect essential items for their everyday needs. There are also women consumers or purchasers whose link with the environment is less direct, but whose actions can have a bearing on its future.

COLLECTORS OF FUEL, FOOD AND FODDER ☐ In the developing countries, women have always had a close relationship with the trees and the forest. Traditionally women have gathered products from the trees and other plants, products which have provided them with the basic three 'Fs' of fuel, food and fodder, and for a variety of other uses. Whereas men consider the forest more in terms of commercial possibilities, women see it as a source of basic domestic needs.

The source of most of the domestic energy used in developing countries is provided by the burning of biomass and it is the women who are mainly responsible for its collection. (In Nepal, one study showed that women and girls collected 84 per cent of the fuel.) To do so, the women walk long distances and carry heavy loads. The time spent will depend on the availability of the supply. In Bangladesh, rural women and children spend an average of three to five hours daily,[1] while a study in the Himalayas found that the search for firewood involves a daily walk of five kilometres up-hill and the average time spent each day by each household is 7.2 hours.[2] The term 'fuelwood' includes a wide variety of materials used for burning: twigs, leaves, brushwood, grass, straw and animal dung.

Fuelwood collection is often referred to as a cause of deforestation. However, as women mostly collect dead wood, which is easier to cut, their work does not damage the trees. Below is a description of women collecting fuelwood in Burkino Faso.

In Burkino Faso, the cutting of live wood has been forbidden since 1984, and local committees ensure this decree is respected. Kalsaka's women used to get wood close to their compounds. The village committee has banned this so now they walk for about 5 km into the hills that form a backdrop to the village, where erosion, crusting and years of low rainfall have killed off many of the trees.

To see exactly what the job is like, we went out with the women on one expedition. We set out at 7.30. The women had already been to the wells twice for water. I used to imagine wood gathering was merely a matter of picking up sticks lying around. In fact it is a complex and energy consuming operation. On arrival at their destination, the women split up in all directions.

Branches are attacked with machetes and hoes. As these are not very sharp, it can take a long time to hack through a single branch. Stumps are too thick to cut through. Usually the women leave them till the following year, when they are rotted enough to be prised loose. This is done by flinging as big a stone as they can lift at the top of the stump, then shaking until it comes out of the soil.

* Delhi, Kali and London, Zed Books, 1988, p. 41.

48

The women work with energy and considerable courage. Small babies are carried along, and shaken at every blow of the machete. Young girls come along to help. The fittest women climb up trees, scramble steep slopes of sharp scree, often in bare feet, and wrestle with shrubs perched on the edge of cliffs. Falls and injuries from cutting tools and stones are common.

The whole trip took almost four hours. The women do it two or three times a week.[3]

In developing countries, wood is the main fuel used in the towns. Women collect and sell fuelwood, often as a sole means of livelihood. They leave their homes in the urban areas early, and return with heavy loads, often not before nightfall. In India several million women cut wood illegally in order to ensure the survival of their families. Thus, many tribal women who had traditionally learnt to live in harmony with their environment are today collecting as much as possible from the forest before it is sold to logging contractors.[4] In Addis Ababa, Ethiopia, about 73,000 women and children earn their livelihood by collecting and selling fuelwood in the city. They collect the wood illegally from protected forests. In this way women are forced into damaging the environment through their own desperate circumstances and need for survival.

In addition to collecting the fuel, women are involved in its cutting and drying, but not usually in charcoal-making, which is generally the men's work, and is a more commercially oriented activity. More women are, however, making charcoal to sell in the towns. Women are the fuel burners, and traditional methods of cooking often consume extravagant quantities of fuel, but the use of more efficient stoves, which use less fuel, is being encouraged.

These stoves will not only help conserve the forests, but as the cooking will be quicker, allow more time to be spent on such tasks as growing food crops. Yet, according to Ceselski,[5] after years of improved stoves programmes, there is little to show in most countries beyond some laboratory models. Even where some thousands of stoves have been distributed, it is not certain whether they are actually saving fuel. New approaches are being tried which place improved stoves in the wider context of household fuel planning and cooking efficiency, and which take account of women's needs, preferences and purchasing power.

Fire serves many purposes in addition to cooking: for boiling drinking water and to heat washing water; fish and meat are smoked above it; a fire provides light at night; and heat to dry a wet harvest. It may also be used to cure tobacco, boil water to extract natural medicines from leaves and bark, and to make dyes. The smoke from fires also helps keep insects away. In countries where the temperature falls steeply at night livestock are kept by household fires. Fires also have many social and ritual uses, particularly as the focal centre for evening conversations.[6]

The forests are also valued as a source of food supply. Men hunt forest animals and women collect a variety of foods such as fruit, nuts, leaves, bark, roots, fungi, honey and beetle larvae. These foods rarely form the basic diet, but are important as supplementary foods, and of particular benefit at times of seasonal deficiency in food production.

For many people fruit is sometimes part of the regular diet, but trees provide many other forms of nutrition. Nuts high in both calories and protein are an obvious example. Cashew nuts, in particular, are highly prized in many African countries. And the staple food of the Kalahari Bushmen comes from the mongongo tree which provides

FUEL GATHERERS OF ADDIS ABABA

Addis Ababa, the capital of Ethiopia, depends primarily on biomass for 80% of its total energy consumption. This is mainly supplied from eucalyptus coppice forests within a 20km radius around the city.

The fuelwood carriers consist of a large number (10,000–70,000) of women and children who depend on fuelwood carrying and sale for their livelihood. They belong to the poorest section of society, 60% of the women are heads of households. They are mostly unorganised, and do not participate in development policy planning structures. They live in slum areas, often in a single 'multi-purpose' room or in a small rented space in a private house.

The fuelwood carriers commute several times each week to the forests, where they harvest small diameter twigs and leaves. The fuelwood is stacked into bundles weighing between 15 and 50 kilograms, carried on the back, and transported 10–15 km to be sold to individual households or at urban markets. Despite the fact that women fuelwood carriers have few economic alternatives to their present occupation and that they contribute substantially to the energy supply of the city, their activities are illegal. Given the large number of people involved and the hundreds of access tracks to the forest, guarding and prosecution have not been effective, but have severe consequences for individuals that are intercepted. Harassment by forest guards through beatings, confiscation of fuelwood and extortion are routine; rape

has also been reported by many women. The demanding of bribes to avoid prosecution is very common. Some women must pay bribes several times during a single trip to the forest.

Since June 1988 the International Labour Organisation (ILO) in collaboration with the National Urban Planning Institute, with financial assistance from IDRC, Canada, has been implementing a research project on women fuelwood carriers in Addis Ababa. This is designed to find ways to reconcile economic, social and environmental concerns, through the involvement of women's self-help groups and to consider the creation of alternative employment opportunities, and the integration of women fuelwood carriers into a sustained yield management of the forests. The research project has gained the confidence of the carriers, and has succeeded in organising 140 women into four groups in three *kabeles*. These groups have received some initial training in group formation and organisation, and have embarked on income-generating activities identified by the women themselves. Activities already started include soap making and mat making, and other options and activities identified by the women will be explored.

The project contributes to creating a balance between the basic needs of the women fuelwood carriers, the sustainable management of the forest resource, and the urban fuelwood demand and supply.

ILO Project Document, 1990

both a fruit and a nut. The leaves, seeds, pods, sap and bark of trees form part of the diet of many rural people. The leaves of the baobab tree, rich in vitamins, are a major ingredient in the sauces served with starchy foods in some African countries; the vitamin-rich fruit from the same tree is known as monkey bread. The seeds from locust trees (Parkia species) are cooked like beans, or fermented and added to sauces; this food, rich in protein and fats, is known as *dawa dawa* in one African country and is much used in soup. In West Africa palm wine is made from the sap of palm trees; the seeds of other palms can be crushed to extract an oil that is important in providing energy and vitamin A. In the many parts of the south-west Pacific, the pith of the sago palm is processed into a basic food, high in starch.

Trees can also be said to provide food in a number of indirect ways: rural people use nearby forests as an important source of both honey and edible fungi, for example. A study in north-east Zambia found that what was classified as useless forest land was actually a major source of leafy wild vegetables, mushrooms and edible caterpillars. These three items were major sources of protein and cash income; collecting all three is women's responsibility, and they are processed or sold by women.[7]

The collection of animal fodder is also usually the responsibility of the women. They gather grass, branches, leaves and fruit to feed small domestic animals such as goats, rabbits, pigs and poultry which are kept for their milk and meat. Fodder is also needed for the draught animals; in India and Nepal, women and girls are responsible for finding the large quantities of grass and leaves needed to feed the buffalo. Fodder is particularly important at the end of the dry season when grazing is limited.

Women also utilize forest products for a variety of household uses. Items such as bowls, spoons, brushes, mats, baskets and twine are made from wood and fibres, and many plants are widely used in personal hygiene and for medicinal purposes.

Women have often been overlooked in forestry projects, but according to FAO this is changing and women are playing a major role in tree planting and tree management. In the hills of Nepal and Himalayan India women are active managers of forest land, and in South-East Asia women are also involved in planting and managing trees, for fruit and fodder, in gardens and on field boundaries. There is considerable potential to involve women in a wide range of forestry activities if their site-specific roles and needs are properly taken into account by the planners.[8] Many women are involved in both protecting existing trees and in tree planting, as is exemplified by the work of the Chipko Movement in India and the Greenbelt Movement in Kenya (see Chapter 5).

WOMEN AS WATER COLLECTORS AND CARRIERS ☐ In developing countries women play a vital role as both water suppliers and water managers. It is the women who have knowledge of the location, reliability and quality of the local water sources. They are responsible for collecting water and for controlling its use; they also oversee the sanitary arrangements. Water is needed by the family for drinking, domestic purposes, personal hygiene and sanitation, as well as for uses on the farm and the many processes involved in food production and craftwork.

Collecting water can be a tiring and arduous task that usually needs to be undertaken several times each day. The nearest source may entail walking several kilometres in the dry season; paths to springs and other sources may be steep and treacherous, or women may have to wade thigh deep in mud to reach clear water. The water is heavy; some women carry 20 kilograms or more, in containers balanced on their heads or in cans strapped to their backs. Kikuyu women in Kenya, for example:

Almost as soon as they can walk, small girls go with their mothers and older sisters to the well or river. The tin they carry grows bigger as they get older, starting out no larger than a fruit juice can and ending with the four-gallon earthenware jars or brass pots of their mothers. Carrying water is so integral to their lives that it is scarcely something to grumble about. Yet in some parts of Africa women spend eight hours a day collecting water. The journey is exhausting, eating into the time and energy they have for other things. And the continual water bearing can distort the pelvis of young girls, making the recurrent cycles of pregnancy and childbirth more dangerous.'

In addition to the burden of carrying water,

PHOTO: JEAN-LUC RAY/AGA KHAN FOUNDATION

A DAY IN THE LIFE OF ALING MARING

A village woman in the Philippines

Aling Maring gets up quickly as she sees the sun slowly beginning to rise. It is only 4.00 but she knows she has many tasks to do before the rest of her household wake up.

Aling Maring goes back to the kitchen with a sigh, to get the pail before going out to the door to start the long one-kilometre trek to the village pump. Luckily she was only tenth in line when she got there. The line could sometimes reach over 50 women long.

The village pump is always a meeting place for the women while waiting in line to use the pump. It always takes so long for one to finish collecting enough water. The wooden handle is so long and heavy that it takes all her strength to push it down with enough speed to pump any water out. Also the handle is large and rather high for the average height of the women, making it even more cumbersome to grasp properly.

By the time Aling Maring gets home, her family is awake and hungry. She calls her eldest son to go and gather some firewood which would save her an extra chore. In the meantime, she lights the wood left over from yesterday's fire and sets some water to boil.

After the quick breakfast, the two older children prepare for school. They go off to the outhouse where there is a pail of water for bathing. They use this to clean themselves as best they can. This is also where they defecate, in the nearby latrine. Because there is not enough water, they do not bother to flush the toilet. In the meantime, Aling Maring goes outside to look in her small drum of water for washing. This too is almost empty. She must get this filled up, if she is going to get any chores done. So she asks her daughter to keep an eye on the two younger ones and takes the baby with her, to fetch more water.

This time, the line is longer and she must wait longer too. After washing the breakfast dishes and quickly cleaning up the house, it is time to do the washing of the clothes. Aling Maring does this together with bathing the children. She gathers up the laundry and tells the children to follow her down to the laundry where there is a shallow pool. Already there are some women washing, but she can probably squeeze in at the corner. The children jump into the pool while Aling Maring begins to wash with the tiny bit of soap left over from yesterday's washing . . .

Thus goes the story of Aling Maring, typical of women in rural and urban areas, whose domestic functions put them in constant touch with water.

Marion Maceda-Villanueva, in *Balai* (Asian Journal), no. 10, 1984

women often experience difficulty in obtaining it from its sources. In those areas where water can be pumped women have not been taken into account either in the design or location of the pumps. The handle is often difficult to reach, and heavy to use, and when the pumps break down women are not trained to repair them. The quality of the water is often poor, for example water in a village in the Sahel being described as, 'the filthiest I have ever seen, the colour of clay, with wriggling insects and larvae visibly swimming around in vast numbers'.[10] In urban areas, shanty towns frequently lack public water points, and women either have to go to sources some distance away, or buy water from vendors who deliver it by bucket, donkey cart or, in main streets, large tankers. Water vendors charge a high price, which is difficult for these poor households to afford. The lack of sanitation and the overcrowded conditions in these areas are severe health hazards. Obtaining water is especially difficult during times of drought. For example in Madras City in India in 1983, water was supplied on alternate days, and women and girls would walk two kilometres at night to collect it. In the more prosperous suburbs, women were hired to travel to the city by train to get water, and in the slums women extracted water from holes at the beach. Very few men carried water, although some did escort women to the taps at night; and some men carried water on bicycles and carts as a commercial enterprise.[11]

As managers, women are responsible for storing the water and deciding on its use. They also organize the disposal and reuse of the waste water and are in charge of sanitary arrangements. A study of women in Yemen shows that they use the best quality water, preferably from a spring, for drinking, personal washing, cooking, and cleansing drinking vessels, food and flour-grinding stones. 'Grey' water is saved and used for washing clothes and watering plants. Water that was used for washing clothes is given to poultry and cattle and used to clean floors. Women also have their own personal problems: because of their need for privacy, where ablutions have to be done in the open, it is embarrassing and unhygienic, and the women are also exposed to the advances of men.[12]

Women's expert knowledge of local water conditions is passed on to successive generations. This knowledge not only includes the location and availability of water sources, but also the social aspect, for example, where women have separate arrangements, of water sources and sanitary facilities, and of community needs and customs.

Until the UN Water Conference in 1977, and the International Drinking Water Supply and Sanitation Decade, women's role as providers and managers of water was never considered by project planners either at government or local level. An Inter-agency Task Force on Women has been established by the steering group for the decade and this recognizes the basic role that women play in the sustainability and development of water and sanitation projects. Health education, community organization and training are particularly emphasized. In 1983, UNDP launched an inter-regional project, the Promotion of the Role of Women in Water and Environmental Sanitation Services (PROWWESS), which aims to develop replicable models for involving community women in sustainable, effectively used and environmentally sound drinking water supply and sanitation projects. PROWWESS has worked with governments in 20 countries; a PROWWESS project in Kenya is included as one of the case studies in Chapter 6.

The development agencies are also involving women in their projects. The following extract from the journal of the UK agency, WaterAid, considers the design aspects of village water points from the women's point of view.

WaterAid's philosophy is to involve village communities right from the start of a project, making sure that women have their say about what they actually want. Increasing numbers of Third World women are taking part in the design of their village water points.

Of course the most important characteristic of any waterpoint must be constant availability of safe water, and

for that engineering know-how is essential. But other matters are also important, especially to a woman who may make half a dozen water carrying trips a day.

Has the handpump an adjustable handle? Is there a proper footblock beneath it set at a convenient height? It's possible to have two blocks – one for women and a higher one for children. Is the pump spout – or the outlet pipe from a protected spring – set at the right height for filling a plastic jerrycan without spilling? Nineteen inches is about right. Is there a smooth, flat base on which to rest containers? Do women have to get their feet wet to reach it? Is there a concrete bucket-plinth to help with lifting water? Two level plinths are sometimes preferred. Some women prefer to bring their washing to the water rather than the other way round: are concrete washing slabs provided? If so, do they have sinks – and do the sinks have stoppers? Is the water point fenced against animals? Sharing a pump with a persistent cow can be exasperating as well as unhygienic. What happens to surplus water? Could it be channelled for use in raising vegetables, seedlings or seedling trees? Could pumps be set higher, so as to command more ground for these activities? Are shade trees planted near the water point? Pumping is hot work out in the midday sun. Is the path to the village reasonably dry even in the rainy season? To slip and fall with a jerrycan of water on the head is to risk broken bones. And are steps provided on steep slopes?[13]

WOMEN AS CONSUMERS ☐ The importance of women as consumers is reflected in the way in which they are targeted by the consumer industry.

Women make up the largest group of consumers, buying both for themselves and their families. Although to varying degrees their inferior social and economic status makes them targets of discrimination and unscrupulous marketing practices, their leading role as consumers of goods and services presents far reaching possibilities for organising and effecting change.[14]

Women are continually urged to conform to certain standards of appearance and social behaviour according to the specific products being advertised. This is no longer confined to the industrialized countries, in fact there are examples of specific targeting of women for certain products in developing countries, for example, cigarette advertising in India. Because of women's experiences in managing the household and caring for the family, they are mostly discerning consumers, being critical of the goods and services available, with an acute awareness of what is needed.

The health and sustainability of environment involves the recognition of both a 'consumer right' and a 'consumer responsibility', as shown overleaf.

Increasingly, consumers no longer judge products solely on their desirability, performance or cost. There is a growing awareness of the environmental implications. Labelling and green consumer guides are helping individual consumer to make their own response to the present environmental crisis. By discriminating in favour of goods which do not damage the environment, consumers play an important part in awareness raising and are able to influence the powerful commercial and business sector.

Don't just grin and bear it. As consumers, we have real power to effect change. We can ask questions about supply and manufacture. We can request new and different products. And we can use our ultimate power, voting with our feet and wallets – either buying a product somewhere else or not

CONSUMER RIGHT

HEALTHY ENVIRONMENT

The right to live and work in an environment which is neither threatening nor dangerous and which permits a life of dignity and well-being.

CONSUMER RESPONSIBILITY

ENVIRONMENTAL AWARENESS

The responsibility to understand the environmental consequences of our consumption. We should recognize our individual and social responsibility to conserve natural resources and protect the earth for future generations.

Source: IOCU, Consumer Lifelines

buying at all. People's voices are being heard on these issues, and they are getting louder. We are beginning to see real changes. We are seeing changes not only in the products which appear on the supermarket shelves but also in the ways in which they are sold.[15]

Women have been particularly active in consumer groups and other organizations in their efforts to bring environmental issues to the fore. For example, Anita Roddick founded the Body Shop Ltd., which now has branches in 37 countries, retailing cosmetics and health products based on natural ingredients. She was awarded a UNEP Global 500 award in 1989.

In developing countries, too, women are becoming more involved in consumer group activities. The International Organisation of Consumer Unions (IOCU)

Regional Office for Latin America and the Caribbean established a programme on women and consumer issues, which addresses the need to understand the complexity of the relationships of women with consumer matters.[16] In Thailand, the Voluntary Group for Consumers of Thailand has been holding weekend workshops for rural women. These aim to bring consumer awareness to rural women. They are taught to be discriminating in their buying, to look at advertising with a critical eye, and to avoid chemicals in their food.[17]

WOMEN AS CONSUMERS OF THE NATURAL ENVIRONMENT Although women form the largest group of consumers, it is not always easy to consider them separately from the consumer body as a whole. This section highlights some of the areas in which women consumers' actions have specific relevance to the environment.

Women the world over are consumers of products and services which originated from the environment. In the household, women are consumers of energy and water, either directly or by the use of cookers, washing machines, refrigerators, and other domestic appliances. As household managers, women can control the use of the machines to minimize the· consumption of fuel and water; as purchasers, they can select appliances which are more economical of energy and water.

Women are consumers of a wide range of goods made from forest products. In many countries, they have the option of choosing furniture made from wood from sustainable forests, and products such as toilet tissue made from recycled paper.

Fashions in the past, especially those relating to women's clothes and ornamentation, were responsible for the exploitation of certain species. For example, the animals that were trapped for their furs and skins, and products such as ivory and tortoiseshell. In some cases the exploitation

---

Washing powders have a bewildering mixture of ingredients which are damaging to the environment.

- *Surfactants* make water more efficient as a cleansing agent. Those made from petrochemicals probably take longer to biodegrade than those made from natural ingredients.
- *Phosphates* soften the water and make it more alkaline. They usually constitute around a quarter of the weight of most washing powders and a higher proportion of dishwasher powders. A large amount of phosphate in rivers strips the water of oxygen and poisons fish.
- *NTA* or *EDTA* are used instead of phosphates, but both pollute drinking water and food by combining with toxic metals already in the environment.
- *Bleaches* Sodium perborate and sodium percarbonate are used in washing powders to remove stains. The former results in boron contamination of rivers, while the latter can only be used with a stabilizer like EDTA, which also pollutes food and water.
- *Enzymes* digest stains, and are thought to give allergies to workers who handle them.
- *Optical brighteners* are used to make washed clothes look whiter. They convert invisible ultraviolet light into visible blue light; they are thought to lead to allergies.
- *Preservatives* are usually made from petrochemical ingredients which have to be manufactured.
- *Plastic packaging* is mostly non-biodegradable and best avoided.[18]

In some countries, detergents containing fewer of these substances are available as an alternative.

---

almost led to the animals' extinction. Consuming products made from endangered species is still an issue today, although not necessarily related to the demands of women; often the objection is on the grounds of cruelty. Consumer campaigns have been successful, for example, whale products are no longer used in cosmetics, although oil from an endangered species of shark still is.

Many products used in modern society

have been found to be harmful to and even responsible for the destruction of the environment, for example, those containing CFCs, (see Chapter 2 Ozone depletion). Selective purchasing of products containing propellants less damaging to the environment has already influenced manufacturers. Many household products, however, contain chemicals which, when discharged, damage the environment. Phosphates in detergents remain in the water and cause algae bloom which kills many species of aquatic life. Non-biodegradable substances, such as certain plastics, used in packaging are less environmentally desirable than those made from biodegradable paper and cardboard.

Certain products used by women not only have environmental implications but are also known to be harmful to health, for example, sanitary towels and tampons which contain harmful dioxins, formed as by-products of the bleaching process. Dioxins in the effluent from paper and pulp mills kill fish and other wildlife and build up in the food chain, whilst dioxin-contaminated tampons and sanitary towels come into intimate contact with the body. Sanitary towels and tampons biodegrade over time but dioxins and plastic liners do not, and they persist in the environment.[19] The same reservations apply to the widespread use in the industrialized countries of disposable nappies. These have come to dominate the nappy market only since the 1970s. The need for these products can be questioned.

Some cosmetics can also be harmful, in particular skin lightening creams, which contain toxic mercury and hydroquinine. These have been banned in most countries, but there are reports of them still being on sale in parts of Africa and Asia. According to *Utusan Konsomer* (the Malaysian consumer paper), 'face creams containing mercury are still being sold to unsuspecting consumers. The Consumer Association of Penang (CAP) tested six brands of face cream and found four of them to contain mercury above the permissible levels'.[20]

Another important issue of direct concern to women is that of the use of powdered baby milk formulae in developing countries. When the bottle feeding trend was spread by massive advertising campaigns from industrialized countries to developing countries, the consequences were devastating to infant health. Aside from the natural benefits of breast milk, the absence of safe drinking water, failure (often due to illiteracy or misunderstanding) to comply with instructions, inadequate sterilizing precautions, and the inability to afford sufficient supplies were responsible for causing infant diarrhoea and led to under- and malnourishment. In response to the unethical nature of the marketing campaigns, a boycott was launched against the Nestlé corporation. This was followed by the adoption by WHO of the International Code on Breast Milk Substitutes. According to the International Baby Food Action Network (IBFAN), compared to the natural process of breast feeding, bottle feeding is in itself a non-environmental practice, using water, and energy to boil it.[21]

The above are some examples of how women as consumers have an influence on the environment. In developed, industrialized countries in particular, where there is a wide consumer choice, women, by their actions as discerning consumers are able to influence the business and industrial sectors to produce truly environmentally friendly products and to use environmentally sound technologies. All women consumers need to be aware of the environmental implications of the products available to them. In this respect, the work being done in the field of consumer education, by consumer organizations and women's groups, in developed and developing countries is particularly important.

WOMEN AS PRODUCERS □ Women

as producers can be involved in sustainable management of the, environment or in its degradation. Women farmers work to produce basic food and crops for export, and their role is therefore crucial to the sustainable use of the land. Other women workers in the formal and informal sector are often engaged in production processes which have an impact on the environment.

WOMEN AS FARMERS AND FARMWORKERS

Women make a considerable contribution to agricultural production in Africa, Asia and Latin America, although the extent of their participation has been underestimated. Women workers in farming may be classified as: unpaid family labour: self-employed own-account workers; and wage labourers on farms or plantations. The distinction between these three categories is not always clear-cut. In Africa, generally the men have the right to the land and control the farming. The women are allocated land on which they grow food crops, the produce is theirs and they may sell any that is surplus to the family's needs; in this way, they may earn cash even though they are unpaid workers. Also there is often a mutual arrangement with the men to exchange labour with women, so that the women are paid in kind if not in cash.

In Africa, 70 per cent of the food is grown by women, in Asia the figure is 50–60 per cent and in Latin America 30 per cent.[22] In many societies in subsistence agriculture, the men clear the land and turn the soil, and the women plant, hoe, weed, harvest, store and process the crops. They are also mostly responsible for marketing the agricultural produce. In many areas, women traditionally care for the livestock, which may involve collecting fodder for domesticated animals, keeping poultry, tending the goats, or milking the cows. Women's responsibilities vary according to the customs of different regions. In Pakis-

tan, for example, women are responsible for 60–80 per cent of the feeding and milking of the cattle.[23] Women's work, however, is not confined to the production of food crops, as they are becoming increasingly involved in the production of cash crops, especially in those areas where men seek jobs away from the farms, in the mines, or in the towns.

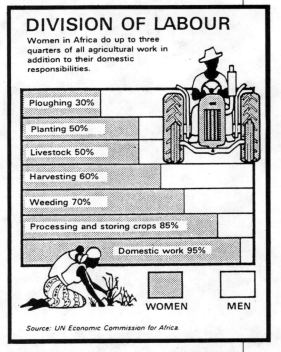

DIVISION OF LABOUR

Women in Africa do up to three quarters of all agricultural work in addition to their domestic responsibilities.

Ploughing 30%

Planting 50%

Livestock 50%

Harvesting 60%

Weeding 70%

Processing and storing crops 85%

Domestic work 95%

WOMEN   MEN

Source: UN Economic Commission for Africa.

In Zimbabwe, for example, women are traditionally allocated a plot of land by their husbands on which they can grow what are termed 'women's crops', such as groundnuts, sweet potatoes and millet. On this plot (which is decreasing in size every year due to cash-cropping attractions) women can decide what to plant, but decisions on planting the remainder of the land are made by the husband who, in most cases, are in the urban area. Having decided what to plant, the woman procures the necessary inputs with financial assistance from her husband; caring for the crop is her

responsibility. The man appears at harvest time to make decisions on how much to store. Once that is done, the woman seeks transport to take the crop to the marketing depots and then waits until the money comes from the marketing board when, again, the man makes decisions about how the money should be spent.

In general, little money is invested in the farm. The woman gets something with which to buy family necessities, the remainder being spent at the man's discretion, often to pay his expenses in the city.[24]

Women's traditional roles are being affected by changes in social patterns and the introduction of technology. As more men have left home to work in the towns, mines or on plantations, women's responsibilities and workload have increased (see chapter 4). Women are now more involved in cash crop production and are taking on jobs that were previously done by men. In Swaziland, women now do 59 per cent of the ploughing, and in Kenya 60 per cent of rural households are headed by women.[25] In spite of this, however, women generally have no land rights and may not make changes to land use without their husbands' permission. Furthermore, the role of women is not considered at the planning stages in development projects and it is the men who have access to training, credit and new technology.

A report on women in sub-Saharan Africa cites an example in Gambia, where, in designing a large irrigated rice project, the planners overlooked certain essential factors. Their assumption was that rice-growers were the male farmers, who were approached and encouraged to turn over their land and cultivate all-year-round irrigated rice for national consumption. Cheap credits, inputs and assured markets came with the package. All access to inputs, finance and labour was made available solely to the male head of household. What the planners did not realize was that tradi-

tionally it was women who grew rice for household consumption and exchange. By establishing this project for the men, the women were forced out to inferior, scattered plots of land. The irony of the situation is that the region now imports more rice for local consumption than it did prior to the project. The report concludes that evidence points to the fact that if women farmers were to receive the same kind of assistance and incentives as men, their agricultural productivity would increase dramatically.[26] It was as a response to this situation that a project was launched to improve rice farming in Gambia (see Chapter 5).

In India, women's traditional jobs in agriculture are to transplant, sow, weed, harvest, winnow and thresh. But there have been many changes, for example, increased male migration means women are doing more work on the farm. The Green Revolution and the introduction of high-yielding varieties has led to the employment of more women as casual labour. In areas where mechanization has been introduced, however, the demand for female labour has fallen; the use of herbicides to control weeds has had a similar effect.[27]

WOMEN AS WAGE LABOURERS Overall, the increased use of land for commercial agriculture and international agro-business has led to an increase in landlessness, causing more women to seek work as paid agricultural labour. In Latin American countries, female labour is widely used for labour-intensive tasks such as coffee picking, and the selection and sorting of beans. Women are thought to be well suited to such tasks, which require nimble fingers and a sense of dedication to tedious, repetitive work. In India, transplanting rice is done almost entirely by women, who work continuously from 10.30 am to 6.00 pm for a statutory minimum wage. In South-east Asian countries, such as Indonesia, women are also very active in rice cultivation. Working as tea leaf pluckers, rubber tappers or casual workers, women in Malaysia and Sri Lanka make up more than half the labour force on plantations, but receive lower wages than men.[28]

Women plantation workers are generally employed in the lowest paid jobs, such as weeding, spraying and harvesting. This can involve tiring and heavy work and, in the case of spraying, the danger of exposure to harmful chemicals. In Malaysia, women form 63 per cent of the labour force on rubber plantations; a rubber tapper's work starts at 6.00 am and in order to tap the required number of trees, approximately 500, a ladder is needed which the woman has to carry from tree to tree. Work finishes at 2.00 pm, and many women then work on other plantations in the afternoon.[29]

On tea plantations women pluck the leaves into large baskets carried on their backs. A description of a plantation in Tanzania refers to working conditions as extremely unpleasant, the women having to pick in heat and rain without any protective clothing. The baskets become very heavy and the plucking process itself exerts stress on shoulder and back muscles. Women complained of disease and wounds on their feet caused by standing in mud, and sometimes human waste, as there are no sanitary facilities in the fields.[30]

Many women plantation workers come into contact with toxic chemicals. The following quotation describes the use of the toxic herbicide paraquat on plantations in Malaysia.

Each day for eight hours women ranging from their teens to their fifties are exposed to this highly toxic chemical. The women are normally not provided with proper equipment to handle the chemical when they dilute it, nor are they provided with protective clothing. Women who dilute the chemical are then required to shoulder it in containers strung on a pole to be distributed to the sprayers at different points on the plantation. Very often water from the streams and monsoon drains is used for dilution and for the washing of containers. This has resulted in contamination of the streams.

The women themselves are often splashed with the paraquat solution as they carry the half exposed containers to and fro about 20 times a day. The sprayers who receive the paraquat solution then pour it into their respective pumps which weigh as much as 25 kg each. They are often not provided with protective clothing. Pregnant workers are sometimes also required to carry a pump on their back to spray paraquat. Cases of miscarriages are therefore on the increase.

Female plantation workers are largely uninformed of the dangers inherent in the chemical which they use so regularly. They therefore do not understand the toxicity of the paraquat. Even where warnings and instructions are labelled these are inadequate or useless since most of the women are illiterate.[31]

Living conditions for plantation workers are often of a poor standard. According to an ILO report, women interviewed on a plantation in Sri Lanka complained of lack of space and the problem of poor water supply.

On average 30–35 people would be using one tap, in many cases there was no water and women had to carry it, either because the piping was damaged or because it was stolen. Other problems were poor sanitation conditions, smell from the latrines, holes in the walls, leaking roofs, and broken doors and windows.[32]

A DAY'S WORK FOR THE DAILY BREAD

Maize grinding is almost a full time job for the women of Dalocha, Ethiopia. A recently installed diesel mill could release their time and energy.

Life for the women (particularly those from the villages) is an endless round of grain grinding, water carrying, firewood collection, infant care, vegetable gardening and childbirth! The most burdensome of the daily duties is grinding grain.

The staple diet of people in this area is a sour tasting bread, *torocho*, made from maize flour. This is usually served with a dollop of boiled kale, *amile*, one of the few vegetables grown in the district. The kale may be cooked with butter, salt and chilli (if the family is wealthy), or simply boiled with chilli in water. The work involved each day to produce this very basic meal is staggering. Lakatch Tsgaye, from the village of Kuteyo Sabolla, talked about her daily task of food preparation . . .

'First I must strip the maize grains from the cob. Next, the grains are ground, a handful at a time, between two stones. The larger stone is slightly dish-shaped and remains stationary. I kneel next to it and with the smaller stone, push brusquely backwards and forwards over the maize. After a great deal of hard work, the grains are reduced to particles the size of coarse sand. But then I must do a second grinding, until a handful of smooth white powder sits on the dish-shaped stone. For the third and last grinding, I mix the flour with water.

There are six people in my family and we use about five kilos of flour daily. It takes me up to four hours of tiring work to grind this amount – and I'm still not finished! The maize flour mixed with water forms a dough, which I wrap in the waxy leaves of the false banana tree and cook over an open fire in the centre of my house. After cooking for half an hour, the bread is at last ready to eat.'

All this hard work results in backache, badly bruised hands and knees, and exhaustion, leaves little time even for other chores, and produces a meal which is neither nutritious nor satisfying. This could soon change, however. A diesel-powered grainmill has been installed by ActionAid in Kuteyo Sabolla. It has the potential to grind more than 2,500 kilos per day – enough to meet the needs of more than 500 households.

Mechanised grinding will significantly reduce the women's workload, releasing time and energy for income generating activities. Along with other ideas, the women have expressed an interest in growing vegetables other than the unexciting *amile*. Although not accustomed to varieties such as carrot, beetroot, lettuce and tomato, they are eager to try them. Such an innovation could furnish the women with not only a source of income but also a more nutritious diet for their families.

Vikki McLean, ActionAid, *Common Cause*, Winter 1989

Women are also employed in agricultural work other than on the large plantations. In Colombia, women form 70 per cent of the paid workers in the horticulture industry on the fertile area surrounding Bogotá. Their work of caring for and cultivating the flowers involves spending much time in enclosed greenhouses. Not only are the very humid conditions unhealthy, but the women are exposed to toxic chemicals, as well as to allergy-inducing pollen and fungal spores.[33] In India, migrant women are employed on farms as seasonal workers, while in Mexico peasant women often work alongside their husbands as labourers on larger farms as more and more men migrate to the towns and are now doing tasks that were once considered men's work.

Many women who work on a large farm or plantation also have their own small plot or garden where they grow the food for their families.

TIME AND TECHNOLOGY Whether on the small family farm or on a plantation, rural women have a long and arduous working day. Most rural women carry out the basic tasks of collecting fuel and water and producing food. They do this in addition to their work in managing the household and caring for the children. Not only is some of the work strenuous, it is also time consuming and, most importantly, this work is largely unrecognized and unpaid.

The further women must walk to collect firewood and water the less time they have to cultivate the land and care for the family (see Chapter 4). One way of saving time is to introduce the use of milling machines that relieve women of the task of pounding grain by hand. In Gambia, where mills have been provided by UNIFEM, the women described how they made good use of the time now freed for other activities. One woman explained that the time and energy she would have spent in pounding she now spends in the fields, weeding and growing more. She has planted maize and beans some of which she sells, and this has given her a cash income for the first time in her life.

Another woman in the village said she grows groundnuts and rice in the extra time she now has available. She sells the groundnuts and can earn almost Gambian DL2000 (around US$150 in 1988 figures), a considerable sum in rural Gambia. In another village which also has a mill, the women have expanded their vegetable garden to grow more nutritious food, including cabbages, onions, tomatoes, sorrel (African spinach), carrots, peppers and aubergines. In this village the mill is used by members of the 500-strong women's group and also by women from nine surrounding villages, and even by women who come over the border from Senegal, some ten kilometres away.[34] (See Box on preceding page.)

Other examples of simple technologies to reduce workloads include improved fuel-saving stoves, fish smokers, and improved access to water, as well as larger-scale energy-saving projects such as biogas production.

When introducing such labour-saving devices, it is important to ensure that the technology is appropriate, as inappropriate technology often results in the failure of many projects (see Chapter 5, Constraints). Another important factor is control of the technology: in many cases women have been provided with items such as carts to carry water or wood, and men have taken them for their own use.

Rural women have an extensive indigenous knowledge of their natural environment, which has been taught from generation to generation. They know the best trees for fuelwood, which plants have medicinal uses, where to find water in the dry season, and the best conditions for growing local crops. It is the women who are the invisible managers and practitioners of the environment. Women in their role as managers of natural resources are considered in detail later in this chapter.

WOMEN AS WORKERS IN THE FORMAL AND INFORMAL SECTORS ☐

This section does not attempt to cover all aspects of women workers, but includes examples of how, in developing countries,

women workers have a link with the environment. In many cases they are involved with the environment directly, for example, they may make use of the natural environment for raw materials and energy, and women working on construction projects are involved in its modification. On the other hand, factories where women work may cause environmental damage and expose the workers to harmful products.

FOOD PROCESSING AND COTTAGE INDUSTRIES Food processing in many forms is widespread, and is a natural extension of women's work as food producers. Although much of the produce is for family use some will be sold in the market or in the street. Preparation of basic food, such as husking and polishing rice, is mainly done as unpaid labour, and therefore women who perform these tasks commercially will earn only a very low wage in order to be competitive. Women earn money from baking, making preserves, drying and smoking food, and brewing beer from palm, rice or maize.

In Ghana, and many other countries, women are involved in processing palm oil which is used for cooking. The traditional method of boiling the fruit, then pounding it to extract the oil which must then be boiled again for the oil to separate, has been largely replaced by modern methods using a press and distillation tank. The women sell drums of oil in the markets, mostly to agents, although some is sold in smaller quantities. Local food products made from ground corn which are eaten with fried fish are also sold at the market.[35]

An example of food processing that uses large quantities of fuel from the environment is fish smoking. This an important activity in West African coastal villages. In Sierra Leone women spend 60–80 hours a week processing fish which they buy from the fishermen. The centre of activity is the beach, where the fish are cleaned, pro-

cessed and marketed. Traditionally, fish are smoked on a banda fish-smoking stove: a rectangular wooden platform covered by wooden poles which is placed in a banda-house, usually a mud hut with a thatched roof. The entire process is time consuming and labour intensive and uses a large quantity of fuelwood. The more efficient Chorker smoker ovens, originally developed in Ghana, are also being introduced in this area.[36]

Many women make items from materials they collect or grow to sell at the local markets. In India a variety of products can be seen at the weekly village bazaar, or shandy. According to a UNESCO study, at one such bazaar, one woman sells little balls made from a mixture of crushed onions, garlic, mustard, urud dal, curry leaves and oil. These are the essential ingredients used in the seasoning of Indian curries. Another young girl, hardly 20, deserted and with a two-year-old baby, makes beautiful pot holders from ropes. Another woman, together with her husband, makes and sells wooden combs.[37] Women who are unable to afford the rent for market stalls often trade as hawkers and vendors. In Lima, Peru, more than half the hawkers are women.[38]

Handicrafts and cottage industries are also important. Local materials, especially those from the forest are used to make products such as baskets and mats. Women as home-based producers are involved in making clothes, small items of furniture, footwear and lace and beedis (a kind of cheroot).

The beedi is a small, cheap cigarette made from tendu leaves wrapped round a small amount of tobacco, sewn up with thread and baked. In India alone, some 2.5 million people were involved in beedi making in the 1970s – and there are probably more now. About 90 per cent of beedi producers are landless women, mostly working from home, and

mostly working long hours – typically, 7 hours a day for 285 days a year. Beedi production is one of the few sources of income for these women since it requires only their labour. In spite of the income earned from beedi making, most beedi producers live in extreme poverty: regulations passed to improve working conditions have proved impossible to enforce.

The beedi industry encompasses not only those who make the cigarettes but also those who collect the leaves. More than 350,000 tonnes of leaves are harvested annually by some 600,000 women and children. Many women illegally harvest tendu leaves which are sold to traders who commission the beedi making and make large profits. Attempts by the forestry service in Bihar to cut out the middle men led to bloodshed: riots ensued, forestry offices were burned to the ground and people killed. Tendu harvesting and beedi making are examples of forest based small scale enterprises that benefit millions of Asian women. Improving conditions for these women will, however, be difficult because of the informal nature of the business.[39]

THE CONSTRUCTION INDUSTRY In many developing countries, women work in the construction industry, and this work often has a link to the environment, for example, building dams. An International Labour Organisation (ILO) programme involves the implementation of labour intensive work schemes to promote employment and rural development. These schemes involve work in activities such as afforestation, irrigation, flood protection and land rehabilitation, as well as the construction of schools, health centres, roads and so on. Women's participation is often fairly high, for example 43 per cent in Burkino Fasso

and 50 per cent in Uganda and Burundi.

Women benefit directly from projects which bring about an improvement in the forest and water resources, and the opening up and maintaining of tracks and paths enables them to have easier and quicker access to markets and other facilities such as clinics. The money earned by the women themselves is an important benefit. If they are married, they tend to spend it to satisfy domestic needs, particularly to improve the family diet.

Unmarried women may purchase such items as clothing and soap. Women who do not participate directly in the work also benefit. For example, the increased purchasing power available to the men working on the schemes enables the women to sell products generated by small commercial activities, by selling food and drink on the work sites or in the market. The reduction in the rate of male emigration and the improved diet and, consequently, health of the children are additional benefits.[40]

Many women are also employed through food-for-work projects. Women are generally more interested than men in working for food which provides a benefit that women can control more directly than money. In India, Bangladesh and Lesotho, from 50 to 90 per cent of the workers in World Food Programme – assisted food-for-work projects – are women. Many are landless peasants unable to find other employment during the slack season.

EXPORT PROCESSING ZONES Women form the larger part of the workforce in the Export Processing Zones (EPZ). In these zones goods can be imported and exported free of customs duties, and they have been set up in many developing countries to enable them to attract foreign investment to help meet their debt obligations. The transnational corporations have set up labour intensive part-processing concerns in sectors such as textiles, clothing, food processing, and electronic assembly. These are mainly in South-East Asia, Mexico, the Caribbean and Brazil.[41]

The establishment of these enterprises frequently damages the environment, through their initial construction and their production processes, including the discharge of waste. The workers, mainly women, are often exposed to working conditions potentially harmful to their health. The women employed are mostly between 15 and 25 years old, who have migrated from rural areas and must either live in overcrowded dormitories or travel in from some distance away.

Nora lives in a fishing village along the foreshore of Penang, Malaysia. A few years ago the sea bed in front of the village was filled in to make way for the development of the area through the construction of business and tourist facilities. Nora's husband, a fisherman, lost his livelihood and Nora went to work in a textile factory in the newly opened Free Trade Zone some miles down shore. She is a widow now with four young children. Her wages are insufficient to buy the basic necessities for her family so she has had to place her three eldest children in an orphanage. A neighbour cares for her baby while she is at work.

Because of the noise and the fibre dust in the factory, Nora suffers temporary hearing difficulties when she leaves the plant, as well as respiratory ailments. After spending eight hours on her feet in the factory, she returns home to several more hours of work, fetching water and fuel, preparing food and washing clothes. The squatter village where she lives has no running water or electricity. Nora suffers from chronic fatigue, but she cannot afford to take a day off to rest. She is paid only for the days she works.[42]

The subject of women as workers, including the working environment and the contribution of trade unions and other organizations, will be dealt with in a future book (*Women and Work*) in this series.

WOMEN AS MANAGERS ☐ It has already been noted that many women are involved in some form of environmental management. In this section women as managers are considered with reference to population and natural resources. Women are key agents in the balance between population and the environment, as they can play a vital part in the control of population growth. Women as managers of natural resources are the subject of the final part of this chapter. This section is written by Colette Dehlot, an expert on the subject, who has the additional advantage of personal knowledge of women's indigenous use of natural resources in her own country, Congo.

WOMEN AND POPULATION ☐ Women, through family planning, can make a contribution to a reduction in the rate of population growth. And as population pressure is a key factor in environmental degradation, it is to be assumed that a reduction in population would benefit the environment. Fewer births will benefit the women, enabling them to be more efficient in their role as environmental managers.

WOMEN'S TRADITIONAL ROLE In many societies, a woman's status depends on her bearing many children, especially sons, for which there is an overall preference and who tend to be better cared for.

Discrimination against women and girls begins at birth, when girl children are valued far less than sons. Of 38 nations studied by the World Fertility Survey, in 23 a preference for male children was the norm. Boy children are breast fed longer, given more protein and taken more readily to health services. Girls begin their female 'chores' at a very young age and soon their adolescence falls victim to highly prized virginity. A girl passes from child to woman on the

day of her first menstrual cycle. Often married before her body is fully formed, the risks of pregnancy and motherhood are multiple. Bearing children too early, too often, and too late undermines the health and strength of millions of women.[43]

Women in developing countries marry when they are young. According to the World Fertility Survey figures, those married by the age of 18 years are 50 per cent for Africa, 40 per cent for Asia and 30 per cent for Latin America. In Bangladesh the average age for girls to marry is 11.6 years and in Sierra Leone it is 15.7 years.[44] From this early age the women set out on a reproductive treadmill, having many children with insufficient birth spacing.

There are several reasons why people want many children; to offset the high infant mortality rate, to maintain an ample supply of labour, in the continual hope for a son, and, in the case of polygamous families, an important factor is the privilege and inheritance value of being the wife with the most children.

This reproductive treadmill endangers the health of the women and of their children. In the developing countries there is a high rate of maternal mortality. In Africa one out of 21 women dies as a result of pregnancy or childbirth; the figures for Asia and South America are one in 38 and one in 90 respectively. The youngest and oldest mothers are at most risk, the main cause of maternal death being post-partum haemorrhage, which is most common in women who have already had several, closely spaced pregnancies.[45] Many women die or are badly affected by non-medical abortions. Another health problem is the cycle of malnutrition, in which insufficient birth spacing leads to less robust children, and this is one factor in high infant mortality rates.

Apart from the effect on women them-selves, there is also an indirect effect on the environment. Where women's ability to work is affected by illness due to pregnancy, and much time is spent caring for small children, the environment will be neglected, as there will be less time available to look after the land and make careful use of natural resources.

WOMEN AND FAMILY PLANNING For women the availability of family planning methods is important as this gives them the right to choose the size of their families and allows them access to wider sexual options. With regard to world population, family planning is necessary if population targets are to be attained. According to the UN, the world population at the end of the twentieth century will be about 6.25 billion, and by 2025 about 8.5 billion. It may stop growing at 10 billion, about double its present size, in the late twenty-first century.

This projection is quite optimistic: it assumes that fertility in the developing world as a whole will drop by one-third in the next 30–40 years. This in turn assumes that a very large number of women in developing countries will start to use family planning methods in the next two decades. To secure the projected drop in fertility, the number of women in developing countries practising family planning must rise to 730 million (58 per cent) in 2000 and finally to 1.218 billion (71 per cent) (or the present level in industrialized countries) by 2025. In sub-Saharan Africa this would mean a ten-fold increase in family planning by 2025.[46]

According to the World Fertility Survey, of the 38 countries included, 23 showed that more than one-quarter of the women would prefer smaller families, and up to a half of women aged 40–49 did not want their last pregnancy.

There are several reasons why all women do not have access to family planning. One is the difficulty in getting to the clinics,

UNFPA

THE OPPORTUNITY

If women who wanted no more children had the choice there would be a be a 38% reduction in births and a 29% drop in maternal deaths worldwide

PERCENT REDUCTION IN ☐ BIRTHS
■ MATERNAL DEATHS

AFRICA

27%

35%

ASIA

33%

35%

LATIN AMERICA

35%

33%

UNFPA

THE UNMET NEED

An African woman is 200 times as likely to die in childbirth as her European counterpart. But millions of Third World women are denied family planning.

● In 60 per cent of developing countries half the population does not have easy access to family planning.

● In Latin America 75% of women not planning their families would like to do so. The figure is 43% in Asia and 27% in Africa.

LATIN AMERICA 75%

ASIA 43%

AFRICA 27%

● In 10 African countries up to 90% of women have not heard of modern methods of contraception.

especially in terms of the time factor. Rural women cannot afford the time to walk long distances to get supplies of contraceptives. The cost involved in travelling to the clinic may be another factor. In many cases cultural barriers have to be overcome. There is a need to find suitable methods, and to gain the general acceptance of the men. Overall, 60 per cent of the population of developing countries have ready and easy access to at least one modern method of contraception, that is, they can obtain supplies without spending more than two hours per month, or more than 1 per cent of their wages. But the proportion varies widely between regions. Some 95 per cent of people in East Asia have this level of access, 57 per cent in South-East Asia and Latin America, and 54 per cent in South Asia. But in the Muslim world the proportion falls to 13–25 per cent, and in sub-Saharan Africa to a mere 9 per cent. Obviously the rank order for use of contraception is exactly the same.[47]

Worknesh Tesfamariam, who lives just outside Addis Ababa, Ethiopia, is working to educate the women of Africa in family planning.

She says of herself:

I have come a long way since I started as an extension worker. I am now a field supervisor and a trainer as well. I have seen myself develop in many areas, learning new skills and enriching my own life. And what I have learnt I have shared with the women in the different villages. In 1987 the Family Guidance Association of Ethiopia gave me training in family planning information and motivational work. In Africa, you're not a woman if you do not have children. So when we talk of family planning it has to be from a health rationale. Women play a key role in ensuring child survival and the wellbeing of their children. But when women introduce appropriate technology and apply the home

economics and health education that they have learnt to their every day lives, this is not enough. They must learn to space and limit their family size. But I am sad to say that many hundreds of women still have to walk up to 20 km to get their contraceptives. We need more help to make family planning available in our villages.[48]

LOOKING TO THE FUTURE The UN State of the World Population Report 1989 had the title *Investing in Women: the Focus of the Nineties*.[49] In this report the director of UNFPA, Dr Nafis Sadik, explained that women are the key to development and are crucial to the goal of sustainable development. Investing in women means widening their choice of strategies and reducing their dependence on children for status and support. Family planning is one of the most important investments because it represents the freedom from which other freedoms flow. Besides family planning, investment in women should also include access to health services and education, their rights to land and credit, rewards of employment, as well as personal and political rights.

The report made the following recommendations: that women should have equality of status and that their contribution to development should be documented and publicized; there should be an increase in women's productivity, and a reduction in their double burden of household and outside work; women should be provided with family planning methods and improved access to health and education.

There are many examples of progress and changing attitudes. In the West African Sahel women working to control desertification are aware of the negative effect of population growth.

There is a new feeling towards children emerging nearly everywhere: the size of a family no longer gives a sure guarantee for its parents in the countryside: the departure or rebellion of the young has demonstrated this. Furthermore,

women want fewer children, better fed, properly cared for, properly dressed and educated. But the women also consider it essential to involve the men in any attempt to raise awareness, as it is the men who are most reticent and who have the power to decide. Legislation has been introduced but implementation is often hampered by religious objections and the attitude of the men. New family health projects are not meeting women's needs, especially in rural areas.[50]

In India, the National Family Planning campaign has changed its approach so that women are able to choose contraception for themselves. India's strategy is predicated on the belief that only by elevating the status of women, especially in the rural economy, will the nation succeed in stabilizing its population and achieving its economic potential. More specifically, the plan is to integrate family planning with services aimed directly towards women; maternity and child care, literacy and occupational training. Talking about the prospects for stabilizing India's population, S. K. Alok, a health ministry official who heads the national family planning programme, says, 'It is no longer a question of national will. It is a question of women's will'.[51]

The importance of women in determining future population growth rates was included in the Amsterdam Declaration.

We the participants of the International Forum on Population in the Twenty-first Century, held in Amsterdam, the Netherlands, from 6 to 9 November 1989, in addressing ourselves to the pressing needs and issues in the field of population:

Recognize that women are at the centre of the development process and that the improvement of their status and the extent to which they are free to make decisions affecting their lives and that of their families will be crucial in determining future population growth rates.[52]

MANAGERS OF NATURAL RESOURCES*

There is little dispute over the importance of women in managing natural resources, particularly in the developing countries. In many recent international fora, recommendations and resolutions have been adopted calling for the involvement of women at all levels in working for sustainable development based on the rational use of natural resources.

The current interest in women and natural resources is growing, but the paucity of knowledge on the linkage involved remains great. The means of identifying the linkage between women's role and natural resources management depends largely on the theoretical framework, policy objectives and mandate for action. In the developing countries there is a need to crystallize perceptions about the crucial issues of social policies, institutions and technical capacity at the national level in order to sharpen the focus of domestic and international policies, if management of natural resources is to be pursued in a meaningful manner.

Natural resources can be grouped under two major categories: renewable and non-renewable. The renewable natural resources are mainly plants and vegetation, animals and humans. These can be increased in quality and quantity. The non-renewable resources are those of water and land (soil). In terms of quantity they are finite, but their quality can be improved under certain bio-conditions and with good management. One major natural resource that is seldom mentioned is time. Time is a constant factor to which the completed cycle of any natural resource is subjected. Although for most natural resources genetic manipulation can modify time in terms of duration; only time will tell whether such manipulation was beneficial or harmful.

* **Colette Dehlot**, Ministry of Health and Social Affairs, Congo

FALLING BARRIERS

Euphemia was lucky to have all the barriers to family planning fall down before her. A short while ago her decision would not have been acceptable. For a start, she has only one son in a culture which prizes boys above girls. Second, she has just three children in a country which remembers that at Independence in 1960 a third of all under fives died. And third, as an Igbo woman she would traditionally be expected to want to bear 10 or 12 children – a feat that would be rewarded by the slaughter of a cow, a big party and entry into an élite association of matrons.

But Nigerians are changing – and the changes are occurring in many parts of their vast and culturally diverse nation. Government policies are partly to thank.

The traditional arch-enemy of Nigerian family planners has been the Nigerian man. But today many men are taking the family planning initiative – though on behalf of their wives. The reasons are usually economic. Average annual incomes slumped from US$860 in 1982 to US$370 in 1989. Inflation is officially running at 51 per cent, and hardship – with the prospect of worse to come – has changed men's attitudes, even in the rural areas where 70 per cent of the population lives.

But for the women in a small village, where large families are still the norm, the pressure to conform remains powerful. If popular opinion condemns family

UNFPA

planning, most women will toe the line.

Traditional rulers have to be co-opted as advocates for government welfare programmes. 'When we enter a village we greet the husbands through the chief. We present them with kola nuts and wine and explain our mission,' says family planning officer Mrs Florence Anyim. 'We have to go through the men otherwise there would be an uproar. But in the past year men's attitudes have changed because of the huge amount of government propaganda – we even had a radio soap opera dealing with the issue here.'

But there remains the problem of reaching women independently of their husbands – so that they can make their own decisions. And of course, there is the problem of having enough government resources to get contraception out to willing villagers.

Elizabeth Ọbadina, *State of World Population*, 1990, UNFPA

Poor countries, which tend to depend heavily on their natural resource base, also have relatively high rates of population growth; yet they are the most vulnerable to the effects of environmental degradation.

This is because shortages of capital and trained woman/man power severely limit their ability to switch to other economic activities when their natural resources can no longer sustain them. In addition, the poorest people in those countries are those who suffer most from environmental degradation.

The range and forms of environmental degradation have already been referred to in Chapter 2. In many developing countries, the most critical environmental problems relate to a complex network of events: overgrazing, commercial logging and fuelwood collection, land clearance, deforestation, burning of crop residues and dung, soil erosion, sedimentation, flooding and salinization. Direct economic consequences include severe reductions in energy for domestic use and in agricultural productivity, the indirect consequences of which have profound and far-reaching effects on human well-being, in particular on women in their multiple roles.

It is generally accepted that population pressure is one of the root causes of poverty and natural resource degradation. Too often, however, the direction of concern is on the population growth in developing countries and the provision of family planning. Population movement and natural resource consumption patterns of the human race are far more damaging to the natural environment than the unborn.

Managerial processes The effects of poor natural resource management are being demonstrated dramatically in many developing countries. Different ecosystems have been and are under constant attack from all sides. For example, in the marine resources, while women process fish, for their family welfare, fishery industries use dynamite to harvest more fish thereby depleting the marine ecosystem of its diver-

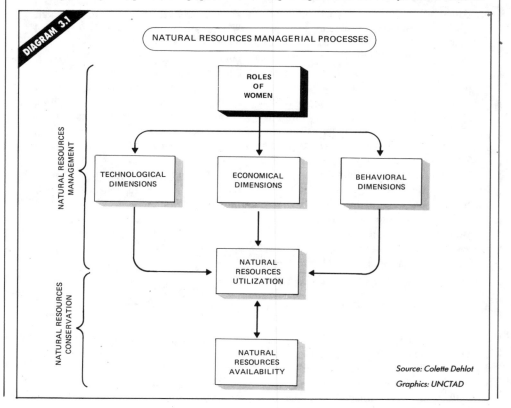

DIAGRAM 3.1

NATURAL RESOURCES MANAGERIAL PROCESSES

ROLES OF WOMEN

NATURAL RESOURCES MANAGEMENT

TECHNOLOGICAL DIMENSIONS

ECONOMICAL DIMENSIONS

BEHAVIORAL DIMENSIONS

NATURAL RESOURCES UTILIZATION

NATURAL RESOURCES CONSERVATION

NATURAL RESOURCES AVAILABILITY

Source: Colette Dehlot

Graphics: UNCTAD

sity of life-forms. While women gather fuel-wood for cooking or meagre home brewing, over-exploitation of industrial logging is exposing the forest canopy to sunrays and is destroying the fragile ecosystem balance. This is more dangerous to the stability of tropical rainforest ecosystems. In the arid lands of Africa, women have organized themselves around desertification for years by means of combining grain storage and livestock for drought survival, drought being a regular phenomenon in arid areas. The Sahel region has been the focus of many national and international pro-grammes that, allegedly, have the answer to controlling desertification by telling women not to graze their livestock, or by giving them marginal lands. When women's acti-vities are flourishing, laws often change, leaving them empty handed and frustrated despite all the efforts they have invested in managing their meagre resources.

In the developing countries, however, there is no doubt about the importance of women as managers of their natural resources. It is how the relationship is linked that is poorly understood. Diagram 3.1 Natural Resources Management Pro-cesses aims to demonstrate such a link. As agents of social change, women in the developing countries operate at three spec-ific levels, or dimensions in the manage-ment of natural resources, as shown in this diagram.

First is the behavioural dimension. There is in every culture a form of environmental behaviour that more or less protects the natural environment. In some parts of Africa, however, for example, it is more overt. Certain trees are specifically 'women' trees, that is, men have no right to whatever resources are gathered from those trees. An example is the karite tree in Mali. In some areas of the tropical forest, certain trees serve specific purposes, and fines are often imposed for trespassing. These are exam-ples of cultural-bound environmental pro-

tection. But also, where women harvest fuelwood it is mainly from dead branches that have fallen from the forest canopy.

Women will seldom cut a green, growing tree, for they know the value it will bring when it reaches maturity. Frequently it is the case of women tuning their behaviour to accord with nature, as they know that to do otherwise means starvation for their family, regardless of whether or not they are head of the household. Worldwide, there has been ample demonstration of women's con-sciousness of the importance of protecting the natural environment. Still, however, their opinion is not sought when it comes to introducing environmental and natural resource management programmes.

Second are the economic dimensions. The subject has been covered in many international fora where it has been recog-nized that women in general form the 'Fifth World', as they are the poorest of the poor. It seems, however, that developers, plan-ners, bilateral and multilateral organizations are especially concerned to work against Third World women's productive capacity. From the introduction of cash crop mono-culture to chemical fertilizers it is the women who may not understand the mech-anism, but are nonetheless asked to repair the deteriorating effects. Arable lands are exploited for monocropping from which women have not yet seen the benefits. On the other hand, women reduced to use whatever natural resources are available do so from the perspective of housekeeper or income earner, especially the latter. As women are responsible for a large part of agricultural production, obviously natural resource management is very important to them and they can offer valuable advice and information, provided their opinion is asked.

Then there are the technical dimensions. Environmental technology tends to operate on a crisis basis rather than as a preventive measure. Most environmental technology is developed in laboratory settings with little or no reproduction of the real environment into which it will be transferred. In the developing countries women are asked to implement such technology regardless of whether or not it is appropriate for the area and social conditions (see Chapter 5). When some agencies claim the relevance of their technology for women, it usually correlates with the profit that it will accrue (though not for the women) rather than the alleviation of their burden or improvement of their income-generating activities.

Yet in many instances, women, especially in Africa, have employed trial and error systems involving intercropping, multicropping, agro-forestry, soil regeneration and so on. However rudimentary, these techniques have enabled their families to survive. Unfortunately these methods are no longer tenable in the present world economic situation. The greater demand on natural resources and their exploitation, together with the increase in population density have overshadowed the women's efforts. And too, regrettably, their contribution to the conservation of the biodiversity of the natural environment has gone largely unrecognized.

Women as natural resource managers

To date, women have not really been perceived to be part of the natural environment conservation scene. They are often seen as part of the problem, seldom as part of the solution. But because of the various roles women play in food processing, farming, agricultural management and family health, it is crucial that their understanding of environmental issues should be increased and their knowledge and skills taken into account in the conservation strategy of natural resources.

It is important that women are well-informed on the cost and benefits of the sustainable use of natural resources, and these must be equally distributed among all

users. It must be seen that technologies developed to utilize natural resources are steered towards meeting women's needs, developing their local capacity and enhancing community self-reliance. It is important, therefore, to see these women as key agents in maintaining and improving the quality and stock of natural resources through a development path which is both sustainable and profitable for them and their families welfare.

People's participation in the management of natural resources is crucial. All too often excluded from the decision-making levels, women have developed their own informal approaches to solving problems. Grass-root village groups represent the first level of the institutional framework needed to ensure bottom-up development processes. These groups, in which women have an important role, are the platform for peoples' perceived development requirements and source of traditional know-how. Both of these are vital inputs to activities involved in the sustainable use of natural resources. Thus, within the framework of community participation and institution-building it is important to highlight the role of women, emphasizing their multiple tasks in maximizing the family economic opportunities.

In almost all countries, women's networks consitute a natural mechanism for community-based actions. Often it is the women's organizations, large or small, that are finding the new solutions women need. Likewise, grass-root organizations serving the poor in the countryside and city slums have few links with the formal national development systems; they nevertheless carry on some development activities on their own initiative. The special characteristics of these organizations make them a key factor in community involvement and ideal for natural resource management and conservation activities. Examples of such activities are included in chapters 5 and 6.

Socio-economic processes associated with

poverty are deeply intertwined with environmental degradation. For example, in developing countries, rural women are often forced by pressing needs for their family survival to make over-intensive use of natural resources such as the land and forests. At the same time, women's lack of access to appropriate technology, inputs and credits can lead them to environmentally unsound farming practices. The resulting strong linkage between poverty and environment assumes a form of vicious circle. Another factor is that while it is the poor who suffer directly from environmental degradation, it is often the rich who cause it. Many women in rural areas are at the centre of this poverty and degradation cycle of the unsustainable use of the natural environment.

Concerning technology, many of the environmental techniques women apply are traditional, but some have been developed more recently, in response to the rapid deterioration of the environment. These involve the selection of drought and pest resistant tree species, the conservation of genetic diversity and species of nutritional, medicinal and economic value. The saving of energy and the use of wastes are also important. Other techniques include measures to conserve soil and water by terracing, and using methods of planting and mulching to trap ephemeral stream water. For example, in Mali, women are involved in improved methods of vegetable production. Three-brick high walls, or murets, are built around the vegetable beds, inside which the soil is prepared by mixing sand, earth and organic matter. The murets allow the conservation of water and prevent erosion.

In technology development, the use and maintenance of the resource base and the problems identified by women are generally neglected. The wealth of women's traditional local knowledge on sound resource management is ignored/forgotten. But this knowledge needs to be incorporated into project development design and implementation activities. There is clearly a need for a greater understanding of the nature, dynamics and severity of natural resource degradation in the light of economic and social criteria, including the welfare of vulnerable groups, such as women, and of the future generations. More work needs to be done on the underlying causes of degradation, both human and natural, and the possible appropriate economic, social and institutional policy interventions.

Policy issues at local, national and international levels have direct consequences on women's productive capacity, and appropriate legislature taking women into consideration is crucial. However, the impact that changes in policy decisions have, especially on women in rural areas, is often difficult to fully understand. Thus policy makers should be constantly informed about the issues in order to improve their understanding of the impacts of policy decisions on the rural poor. It should be possible for natural resources management to be integrated directly into economic and social policy. For example, investment in programmes that support environmental and natural resource objectives. Also through economic, social and institutional policies, incentives can influence the environmental-related activities and attitudes of government agencies, major resource users and small-scale income-generating resource using activities.

As far as research challenges are concerned, further enquiries are needed on the extent of interdependence between human activities and natural resource systems. Effort should be made to quantify the impacts at each stage of the interlinked ecological and economic system in physical or monetary terms in order to determine the points in the system at which it would be most socially profitable to intervene with explicit policy measures. One of the essential elements of this exercise would be to separate out natural events, which, when compounded by human activities, may dwarf environmental damage caused by human activities alone. Based on research findings, guidelines need to be developed to direct the formulation of specific projects/ programmes involving women and the management of natural resources, especially where there is no sustainability in the use of the natural environment.

Programme policies If project and policy measures are to be viable, they should be based on a sound understanding of not only the physical linkages among events, but also the equally complex economic, financial, social, and institutional linkages that parallel them. Much work needs to be done in these areas. There is a profusion of literature on natural resource degradation, but relatively little attention has been given to the point at which individual and/or institutional behaviour plays a key role and at which policy interventions might be feasible.

At the local level:
- Women's participation in selection, design, implementation, control and evaluation of environmental conservation requirements in natural resources management programmes.
- Direct benefits for developing-country women and their families from more effective resource management, in terms of income-generating, community and self-help development.
- Greater sharing of conservation practices between and among women and their organizations.

- Extension of appropriate environmental technology to women and their organizations.
- Institution building and resource development, especially of women's organizations.
- Training of trainers and extension workers in natural resource management activities.

At the national level:
- Information-communication-education (ICE) about national natural resource sectors.
- Establishment of systems for surveillance of natural resources to prevent depletion and maintain conservation requirements.
- Assistance to community members, especially women, to develop project/ programme proposals for natural conservation requirements and for community benefits.

At the international level:
- Definition of the operational mechanism to implement locally the global strategies for the sustainable use of natural resources.
- Contribution to the practical approaches to conservation of the natural environment, with particular attention to women's roles and needs.
- Dissemination of information upon which continued awareness-raising can proceed, so that women are involved fully in natural resources management and development efforts.
- Establishment of a database information system and network directory of women and organizations involved in relevant issues.

1 FAO/SIDA (1987) *Restoring the Balance: Women and Forest Resources*, Rome, Food and Agricultural Organization of the United Nations, Stockholm, Swedish International Development Agency.

2 *The State of India's Environment 1984–85* The Second Citizen's Report, Centre for Science and Environment, New Delhi, India.

3 Harrison, Paul (1988) 'Inside the Sahel' in *Earthwatch*, no. 33, supplement in *People*, London, International Planned Parenthood Federation (IPPF).

4 *The State of India's Environment 1984–85*, op. cit.

5 ILO (1987) *Linking Energy with Survival*, Geneva, International Labour Office.

6 FAO/SIDA (1987), opt. cit.

7 Ibid.

8 FAO, Secretariat note on Women and Forestry, Committee on Forestry, September, 1990.

9 New Internationalist Calendar 1989,

10 Harrison, Paul, op.cit.

11 *The State of India's Environment 1984–85*, op. cit.

12 Ansell, Christine, quoted in Van Wijk-Sijbesma (1985) *Participation of Women in Water Supply and Sanitation – roles and realities*, The Hague, The Netherlands, International Reference Centre for Community Water Supply and Sanitation.

13 WaterAid (1990) article in *Oasis*, Spring, London.

14 *IOCU Newsletter* August 1989 The Hague, International Organization of Consumer Unions.

15 Elkington, John and Julia Hailes (1989) *The Green Consumer Guide*, London, Victor Gollancz Ltd.

16 *The Consumer Educator* (1989) no. 11, Women as Consumers. Consumer Educators Network Penang, Malaysia.

17 IOCU (1990) *Consumer Lifelines* September, Penang, Malaysia, International Organization of Consumer Unions.

18 *New Internationalist* (January 1990) Oxford, New Internationalist Publications Ltd.

19 *The Ethical Consumer* (July/August 1990) Manchester ECRA Publishing Ltd.

20 *Utusan Konsumer* (January 1990) Consumers' Association of Penang, Malaysia.

21 IBFAN (1989) *Fighting for Infant Survival*, information kit. Geneva, International Baby Food Action Network.

22 Black, Maggie (1988) 'Mothers of the Earth', *Earthwatch* 32, supplement in *People*, London, International Planned Parenthood Federation (IPPF).

23 FAO (1990) *Women in Agricultural Development*, Rome, Food and Agricultural Organization of the United Nations.

24 *Ecoforum* (October 1988) vol. 13, no. 2, Nairobi, Environment Liaison Centre International (ELCI).

25 FAO/SIDA (1987), op. cit.

26 Ivan-Smith, Edda, Nidhi Tandon, and Jane Connors (1988) *Women in Sub Saharan Africa*, Minority Rights Group Report no. 77, London.

27 *The State of India's Environment 1984–85*, op. cit.

28 ICFTU (1985) *World Economic Review*, Brussels, International Confederation of Free Trade Unions.

29 Suara Wanita no. 2 (1989) reproduced in *Women in Action*, December, Rome, ISIS International.

30 Mbilinji, Marjorie (1989) 'Plight of Women Plantation Workers', *Tanzania Women's Magazine*, September, Tanzania Media Women's Association.

31 Yohe Ling, Chee (1989) 'The Malaysian Experience', *Women, Environment, Development*, Seminar Report, London, Women's Environmental Network.

32 Karian, Rachel (1981) 'The Position of Women Workers in the Plantation Sector in Sri Lanka', paper for Rural Employment Policy Research Programme, International Labour Office, Geneva.

33 FAO (1984) *Ideas and Action – Rural Women*, Rome, Food and Agricultural Organization of the United Nations.

34 Kanu, James (1988) 'Organizing for More Food' *International Agricultural Development*, September/October 1988, Reading, UK.

35 Okine, Vicky T. 'Impact of the Informal Sector on the Economy', unpublished paper, Unesco.

36 Hammer, Margareth, (March 1988) 'The Day Revolves Round the Banda', *Gate*, German Agency for Technical Cooperation.

37 M.A. Singamma Sreenivasan Foundation, Bangalore, India, 'Integrating Women in Development Planning: the role of traditional wisdom', unpublished paper, Unesco

38 ICFTU (1989) *Organising Women in the Informal Sector*, Brussels, International Confederation of Free Trade Unions.

39 FAO, SIDA (1987) op. cit.

40 Carle, I. (1990) unpublished paper, International Labour Office.

41 ICFTU (1985) *World Economic Review*, op. cit.

42 JUNIC/NGO Programme Group on Women and Development (1984) *The Key to Development*, Development Education Kit, Vienna, UN Division for the Advancement for Women

43 Lajali, Malika and Perdita Huston (1990) 'Listen to Women First', *Earthwatch* no. 1, Supplementing *People*, London, International Planned Parenthood Federation (IPPF).

44 UNFPA (1989) *State of the World Population*, New York, United Nations Population Fund.

45 Ibid.

46 UNFPA (1990) *State of the World Population*, New York, United Nations Population Fund.

47 Ibid.

48 Population Concern (1989) Annual Report, London.

49 UNFPA (1989) op cit.

50 Monimart, Marie, *Women in the Fight Against Desertification*, Paris, OECD.

51 Popline (March 1990) *Open File*, June 1990, London, International Planned Parenthood Federation.

52 UNFPA (1990) *Amsterdam Declaration. A Better Life for Future Generations*, New York, United Nations Population Fund.

Deforestation: Habila refugee settlement near El Geneina.

THE EFFECTS OF ENVIRONMENTAL DEGRADATION

Probably no other group is more affected by environmental destruction than poor village women. Every dawn brings with it a long march in search of fuel, fodder and water. It does not matter if the women are old, young or pregnant: crucial household needs have to be met day after weary day. As ecological conditions worsen, the long march becomes ever longer and more tiresome. Caught between poverty and environmental destruction, poor rural women in India could well be reaching the limits of physical endurance.

The specific difficulties that women face – their extraordinary work burden or lack of access to health care, for instance – do not arise out of ecological deterioration per se. They are located in the sexual division of labour, marked by a double work burden (at home and outside) and by the specific nature of the tasks they do, and in the unequal distribution of resources like food within the household, which stems from women's inferior status in the household and from a lack of control over cash and productive resources like land. But given this situation, environmental destruction exacerbates women's already acute problems in a way very different from those of men.[1]

THE ABOVE EXTRACT FROM *The State of India's Environment* illustrates the importance of the effect of environmental degra-
dation on Third World women, whose way of life is intrinsically linked with the environment. These women bear the brunt of the environment's destruction and, for reasons beyond their control, poor women frequently become the agents of their own resource depletion as they struggle to ensure their families' survival.[2]

BASIC NEEDS IN RURAL ENVIRON-MENTS ☐ In rural areas the depletion of natural resources by environmental degradation has a significant effect on the daily life of a woman and the well-being of her family. As more people are competing for diminishing resources, women find that each day they must walk further from their homes in search of water, fuelwood and other forest products for their basic needs. This extra distance not only adds to their physical burden, but also means that there is less time for looking after the family and for the production and preparation of food.

Deforestation and desertification result in a reduction in the variety and amount of biomass material available for fuel, fodder and supplementary foods. Lack of the traditional source of fuelwood causes many problems. In order to be able to cook, an alternative source of fuel has to be found and a different wood, or other biomass material, may take longer to burn and produce less heat. In India, women collect roadside weeds, try to dig out tree roots, or use cowdung as a fuel (the latter is reported to produce highly polluting smoke).[3] Crop residues such as cassava stalks are also used as a substitute for fuelwood, but, like dung, they are needed in large quantities to be effective, and their use as fuel makes them unavailable for fertilizer. Some 800 million people rely on residues of some kind for at least some of their energy needs.[4]

Less efficient fuel makes cooking more time-consuming, and the need to search for fuel sources also leaves less time for other tasks. Consequently women may be forced

REFUGEE WOMEN AND FUELWOOD

It is a cruel irony of nature and politics that a large part of the world's refugee population is concentrated in some of the most environmentally vulnerable areas. And as if to make this irony more bitter, the refugees' efforts to gain a living from the land can contribute further to the steady process of ecological degradation.

Over 900,000 refugees from Mozambique have made their temporary homes in Malawi. The impact on already scarce natural timber resources in the border-area has been devastating. It is women, both refugees and Malawians, who will bear the greatest hardship resulting from these depleted forests. Their traditional responsibility for collection of firewood now requires them to make longer and longer journeys, often into mined areas, and, out of desperation, into forest reserves. Wild foods which traditionally supplement the family diet are increasingly scarce, and the physical energy expended by women in looking for them places even greater demands on their health.

A pilot project has been developed which hopefully will reduce some of this burden, both on women and on the environment. Forests in areas of Malawi not impacted by refugees will be scientifically culled, and the much needed firewood transported to refugee camps for distribution.

As this example illustrates, the influx of large numbers of refugees can often affect the delicate balance of nature. Organizations working with refugees must identify, with them, means of leaving the natural resources of their country of asylum in as good or better condition as when they arrived.

UNHCR

---

to cook less frequently, or to change the traditional diet (see Women's Health).

Baking and fish smoking, for example, also need fuel, and a reduction in these activities means that less food is available. Also these activities, and others dependent on fuel supplies, are often practised for the purpose of income generation, and, therefore, this too is restricted by dwindling fuel supplies. The quantities of fuel needed are quite large: for example, pottery-making in Tanzania uses one cubic metre of wood for 100 large clay pots, which is nearly equivalent to the annual average per capita rural consumption in Africa; fish-smoking uses 0.8 cubic metres per tonne; and brick-making uses five cubic metres to build a two-roomed house.[5]

Alejandra lives in a village outside Pisac, about

40km from Cusco, in the high sierra of Peru. At this altitude of 3500 to 4000 metres, both agriculture and livestock are important for survival. These days there are few tree branches to collect from the ground to cook with. Alejandra has seen the landscape changing. Now, there are hardly any old (native) trees left, and the eucalyptus trees that were planted as part of a reforestation campaign just before she was born (21 years ago) on both communal and private land are slowly disappearing. Not only did hardly anyone plant new trees, but also the 'commerciantes' (traders) come more and more often to the village to buy whole trees for about 3000–5000 soles (less than 1$ US) to sell to the many restaurants and bakeries in Cusco.[6]

DIAGRAM 4.1

LINKAGES BETWEEN THE FOREST, FUELWOOD, WOMEN'S LABOUR AND HOUSEHOLD NUTRITION

WOMEN WORK HARDER

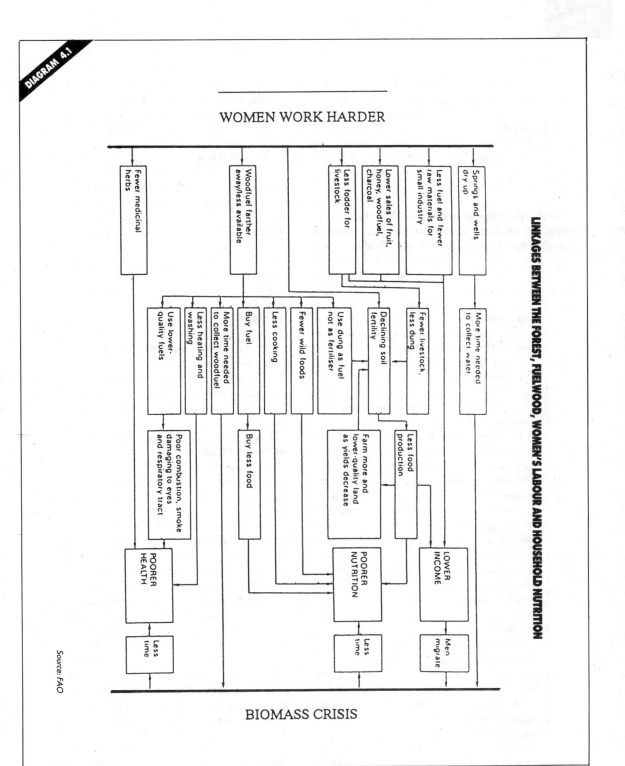

BIOMASS CRISIS

Source: FAO

Where fuel is difficult to find, women may have no option but to buy from traders, with money which could have been spent on other basic needs. They are now paying for a product which they used to gather for free, largely due to the activity of traders who are more ruthless in the extraction of the wood from the forest.

> **I hate this village! There is nothing here for us now. We have to go to Malia (the neighbouring town) to buy everything including fuelwood and even fodder sometimes.**
> **INDIAN VILLAGE WOMAN**[7]

The diminishing amount and variety of foods available from wild plants tends to lead to a poorer quality diet with less diversity and a greater reliance on purchased foods. For example, in the African Sahel the severe reduction in the amount of supplementary food products to be gathered in the bush has affected traditional products such as vegetable butter (*soumbala*).[8]

Fish supplies are becoming diminished as a result of environmental degradation and large-scale commercial fishing methods. Fishing is generally done by the men, but in some areas it is an important part of the women's work. Many women are involved in fishing in the shallow waters of low-lying coastal areas and their activities will be affected by any rise in sea level resulting from climate change. In southern Nigeria, where many rural women are involved in fishing and farming, the rivers and creeks are being polluted by the oil industry;[9] and in Sierra Leone, local ponds fished by women are silting up. Women's income-generating work of processing and preparing fish is also affected by reduced fish supplies.

Most food is obtained from the people's farms. Women farmers of the Third World are responsible for producing food for their families, and increasingly they face the problems of the degradation and reduced availability of cultivable land. With the greater emphasis on cash crop production, the cultivation of food crops by women is being relegated to poor, marginal land. The women find themselves working harder to produce food from increasingly overworked land, and, unlike the men growing cash crops, they have limited access to fertilizers or modern farming techniques. Insufficient access to and control over the vital resource of land is a central issue in understanding the relationship between land degradation and the position of women. It is stated that in the deeply degraded areas of Northern India, women's suicide rates are higher than those of men, and this is possibly related to the deterioration of the natural resource base.[10]

In areas of traditional livestock herding, milk production is largely the responsibility of the women. Traditional herders are dependent on their animals for meat and milk, but land available for nomadic herding is increasingly lost to settled farmers and other forms of development. Pressure on the land leads to over-grazing and eventually to desertification and the destruction of the rangelands. The search for water and fodder is also becoming more and more arduous.

For many women the daily task of obtaining safe water for the family is their most pressing problem. As water sources dry up, become choked with silt or contaminated by pollution, the provision of this essential basic resource bcomes increasingly difficult. Not only do women have to walk further, and wait longer at the water points, but also the return journey, carrying the heavy load, can damage their health. Research has shown that this task can absorb a quarter or more of the daily food intake, so there are nutritional implications, as well as the danger of physical deformation.[11] To save time, nearer, unsuitable sources may be used, such as ponds where children bathe and clothes are washed, or irrigation ditches polluted by agricultural chemicals.

In Papua New Guinea for example, previously clean sources of water have been polluted and blocked by sediments as a result of logging and mining activities, so money has to be spent on iron water catchments, roofs and galvanized tanks, which rust within five years.[12]

In India, there was a dramatic increase in irrigated sugar cane cultivation in the early 1980s. As more water was consumed by this cash crop, however, women in a nearby village found their water supply diminishing. In 1981 a new well was dug, but in a year it was dry. Three more wells were then dug, but they also went dry, as did another the following year. Eventually water for the village had to be brought a distance of 15 kilometres by a water tanker.[13]

Children's health is most at risk from lack of clean drinking water, but adult women are more exposed to hazards of polluted water than are men. They are the primary water carriers; they wash clothes and utensils; and when children are sick, women who must nurse them are more likely to succumb to the infection than are men. Clearly, poorer households suffer most, as they have less access to clean water sources and are less likely to have help in domestic chores.[14]

Environmental degradation also denies women other basic needs. The reduced number of species means that plants and so on, which provide raw materials for household items, are becoming more difficult to find. The basic construction of the family dwelling is usually men's responsibility, but women are often involved in the finishing processes and repair work. Plants that provide framework and thatching material become more difficult to find as the processes of deforestation and desertification take their toll. Scarcity of water is a problem where mud is needed for the walls.

Women use many natural products in their craftwork. Water is needed to make clay for pottery and for mixing dyes; canes and fibres are needed to make baskets. The loss of medicinal plants is particularly serious, especially in places where other medical care is not easily available. The depletion of these raw materials not only increases the demand on women's time as they search for alternatives, but also means spending money to buy products previously obtained for free, and, too, denying them a source of cash income.

BASIC NEEDS IN URBAN ENVIRONMENTS □ Women in urban areas may not have the same close relationship with the natural environment as do those in rural areas, but they are still affected by its degradation, being faced with problems such as poor housing, overcrowding and inadequate water supply and sanitation.

The number of women in urban areas is increasing as more migrate from the countryside; of particular note is the increase in the number of women-headed households. Many women have to live in the poor, urban squatter settlements, located on unsuitable land, such as steep slopes susceptible to landslides, badly drained, frequently flooded lowlands, land dissected by gulleys and ravines or, as at Bhopal, land which is dangerously close to potential industrial hazards.

Poor, urban women face great difficulties in obtaining access to land and building materials to provide some sort of shelter for their family. They need income-generating work to enable them to buy food and water, but this is difficult to find near to home.

The following example illustrates the difficulties in obtaining basic needs (in this case, shelter), in a settlement in a mangrove swamp in Guayaquil, Ecuador. The families were motivated to settle as a means of acquiring land and owning their own home instead of having to pay prohibitive rents.

Plots were not always occupied immediately when acquired but were held as a future investment to be occupied when infrastructure had reached the area. The distance from the city centre, lack of electricity, running water, sewerage and above all roads, deterred families from living on their plots. Women were most reluctant to move because of the dangers to children of the perilous system of catwalks, the considerable additional burden of domestic labour under such primitive conditions and the very real fear of loneliness. It was the men, generally less concerned with issues such as these, who persuaded the family to move. But it was the women who bore the brunt, and the distress experienced by many in the early months and years should not be underestimated. Initially, walking on catwalks was so frightening that many crawled on hands and feet, venturing out as infrequently as possible. Acquiring water from the tanker or food from the shops up to a mile away, was costly, time-consuming and physically gruelling, with women recounting hazardous stories of wading miles through mud to acquire necessary provisions.

It was the struggle for survival in a situation where even water was a scarce and valuable commodity, which forced women to develop and retain friendships with their neighbours, and gradually resulted in an increasing awareness among women of the need to try and improve the situation. Although women became aware of their common suffering, this experience itself did not always provide sufficient motivation for common action. Women did not question the fact that their responsibility for the domestic arena, which they saw as natural, made them the primary sufferers.[15]

Many women living in the urban areas make use of the environment around the city, in fact some women depend on it for their survival. These women will be affected by the degradation of this land which, through force of circumstances, they are often helping to destroy.

Aidenaire is one among the many millions in the world who have abandoned their rural homes to move to the cities.

Adenaire Carm lives in the slums of Haiti's capital, Port-au-Prince, cheek-by-jowl with thousands of other people in their thrown-together homes. She sells bananas in the market for a living, if you can call it that. She is a widow with four children.

As evening comes she makes her way through the debris of a day's buying and selling, back to the shack that is home: one room for the five of them. She can smell the charcoal smoke, the bananas cooking and the rotting garbage. The noise is awesome – blaring radios, people shouting, dogs barking.[16]

ENVIRONMENTAL DISASTERS Disasters can devastate the environment, urban and rural (see chapter 2). All members of a community are affected as farmlands and settlements are destroyed and people's livelihood is lost, but the women are still responsible for feeding the family and caring for the children, often under impossible circumstances. According to the World Food Programme, the organization which channels roughly half of the world's emergency food assistance in response to sudden disasters, when disaster strikes, the most vulnerable are women and children.

In 1988, 25 million people were left homeless and two million hectares of crops were damaged by floods that covered 85 per cent of Bangladesh. It was the women in particular who were affected, as a large proportion of the poor households are headed by women, so many men having died during the independence war.

The impact of natural disasters on women is illustrated by the following comments from women in Peru, after the earthquake in May 1990.

We had an adobe house (explains Maria Fernandez Olivar). We built it little by little, over the years. We lost everything overnight. The earth even swallowed up the land. I don't know what is going to happen because my husband is out of work and my children have nothing to eat.

As of the night of the earthquake three families have been sharing each tent. Imagine the mess. And this isn't all. Looting has broken out and we are afraid for our few remaining possessions (a sobbing resident of Rioja explains). My husband went to look for work because he said that now with all the damaged buildings there may be more construction work.[17]

WOMEN'S HEALTH* □ In their book, *Women in the World*, S. Jovelan *et al.* state that 'for women there are no developed countries'.[18] Implied in this statement is the truth that women everywhere work longer hours than men, are less well-nourished and in poor health. This section will examine how this comes about, with particular reference to the condition of poor, rural and fringe urban women who comprise a large segment of the world's population, carry the heaviest burdens, and in whose situation is most clearly visible the structural patterns which operate detrimentally to women's health and well-being, and incidentally to those of their families. The focus of this section is on social factors which generate health hazards for all, but which expose women to additional or particular environmentally related risk due to their socio-economic status and reproductive capability.

The extent of the health impact on women in relationship to the environment is most pronounced in the rural areas of the developing world. There women have few choices about lifestyle and fewer opportunities to change unsatisfactory conditions and improve their own and their family's health

* Jacqueline Sims

status. This is due to the multiple roles performed by the majority of women in developing countries, and by all women in the poorer sectors. Juggling the triple roles of home-manager, economic provider and reproducer generates health problems and hazards in a number of categories, some derived from women's socio-cultural status, some from their reproductive role. These risks tend to reinforce each other to the detriment of their overall health status.

Conditions and factors that have negative health implications for women can be categorized as: those of the immediate environment (the household and the land immediately surrounding it); the local environment (the village, town or district); and the wider environment (the region or country and their policies).

IMMEDIATE ENVIRONMENT The state of health of human beings is determined to a great extent by the properties of the environment in which they live and by their behaviour and lifestyle in that environment (WHO 1987). In the immediate environment, shelter is therefore a strong health determinant. If the shelter available is inadequate in size, design, or robustness, then it is hazardous to health. In 1985, 30 per cent of all households in the world were headed by women, and in urban areas of Africa and Latin America the proportion rises to 50 per cent. Should this trend persist, it is estimated that by the year 2000 the majority of all poor people may be in women-headed households. Due to lack of access to resources, women alone are condemned to the poorest, least adequate types of housing and the increased health risks they bring.[19] These include a high accident rate, overcrowding, increased risk of infections, such as tuberculosis, mental stress, inadequate water supply and sanitation, noise pollution, indoor air pollution from cooking and heating fires, and intra-familial violence.

Insufficient food intake by women is also a health threat of the home environment; depending on factors such as status of females relative to males, a woman's or female child's food intake may be less than that of male members of the family in circumstances of general insufficiency. Women may be so fatigued by their double day that they neglect their own nourishment. Food taboos add to women's nutritional deficiency in some societies by prohibiting high protein sources such as fish, eggs and chicken during pregnancy and lactation.[20] Nutritional deficiency is reinforced by the custom in many traditional societies of women eating what is left after men and boys have finished. These factors combine to reduce women's nutritional reserves in times of food insufficiency. Pregnancy depletes the reserves still further, and malnourished mothers may experience problems with breast-feeding. A vicious circle of under-nutrition, ill-health and infection can develop, as lowered resistance makes women increasingly vulnerable to disease.

LOCAL ENVIRONMENT In the vicinity of the household, women have an active inter-relationship with the local environment. In rural areas, women are predominantly responsible for fetching water and fuel for household use, and often for providing animals with fodder and water. The women fuel-carriers in Addis Ababa suffer frequent falls, bone fractures, eye problems, headaches, rheumatism, anaemia, chest, back and internal disorders, and heart failure. The low status of this work and those who perform it militates against the problem being addressed at national level.[21]

The fuelwood crisis also has implications for health as can be seen in reduced energy use. Energy may be saved by preparing foods which require shorter cooking times than some nutritious staples, or by cooking less frequently. A close correlation has been noted between per capita food consumption and that of fuel use. In India more rice is being consumed as it is quicker and easier to cook than millet or maize, but its nutritional value is lower. Having fewer cooked meals can be harmful as people are not able to consume sufficient food in one meal to provide them with the nutrition they need. Health may be affected through reduced heating in winter, and through reluctance to use fuel to boil safe drinking water, cook food, or heat water for personal hygiene. Fuel may have to be purchased with scarce cash resources, and the overall standards of living fall as a result, directly affecting health status.[22] In this context, the Latin American proverb '*Cuando la comida es poca, a la nina no le toca*' has relevance: When food is scarce, young girls get none.[23]

At the same time, biomass fuel is a double-edged sword; although it can be gathered at no financial cost, prolonged exposure to the smoke from these fuels can lead to respiratory disorders, such as chronic obstructive lung disease in adults and acute respiratory infections in children, and is a contributory cause of nasopharyngeal cancers. In developing countries, exposure to biomass fuel emissions is probably one of the most significant occupational hazards for women, due to their role as cooks and home managers.[24] National health policies have not yet adequately acknowledged or responded to this major threat to women's health.

Lack of water and sanitation, other grave causes of morbidity and mortality in the developing world, affect women disproportionately as they are the prime procurers and users of water in most communities, and are often solely responsible for waste management and sanitation training, home and family hygiene. For these reasons they are at significantly higher risk of exposure to water and sanitation-related diseases, and

PHOTO: J. COURTIN/UNHCR

general poor health, than are men.[25] Some of these include amoebic dysentery and other diarrhoeas, hepatitis, typhoid, cholera, tapeworm, hookworm, guinea-worm, schistosomiasis, trachoma, malaria, filariasis, onchocerciasis, dengue haemorrhagic fever, and yellow fever.[26]

With either a rural or urban lifestyle in which time is such a precious commodity and the workday so long, taking time off to visit a doctor, nurse a sick child, remain at home should a woman fall sick herself, visit the nearest health clinic to vaccinate children, and generally maintain the health of the family is highly problematic. Lack of time and lack of mobility are therefore direct health threats to the majority of poor women. It is a fallacy to assume that households have a primary male wage earner, and that the wife's role is domestic or as the provider of secondary income. Even when family composition includes males, these may be unemployed, permanently or temporarily absent through out-migration, or generate too small an income for household survival. It is the multiple roles performed by women, at cost to their own health, which keep families intact.[27 28]

Wherever women work, they are exposed to hazards both because of the nature of the work and their reproductive capability. Excessive exposure to noise, light, heat, toxic chemicals, radioactive or other harmful substances causes chronic and acute illnesses and may affect a woman's reproductive capacity. Pesticide residues or other potentially toxic substances may be ingested from breast milk by a nursing infant. Accidents impair women's ability to care and provide for the family. In Latin America, accidents were among the top five causes of death for mid-life women in 11 out of 18 countries surveyed.[29] The heavy agricultural chores which are part of many rural women's daily lives also place them at risk from prolonged exposure to wind, rain and sun. Female plantation workers typi-

cally suffer from high levels of respiratory and bowel diseases.[30] Market vendors in Lima, as in many other cities, work in insanitary conditions with no garbage removal facilities, latrines or first-aid facilities, and insufficient water space to ensure cleanliness. Symptoms such as kidney trouble, varicose veins, bronchitis and internal disorders are commonplace; and, if medical assistance is sought, debts are incurred as these women habitually earn too little to support any additional unforeseen expenditure.[31]

Breast-feeding infants for as long or as often as desirable is often difficult due to women's working responsibilities in either town or country. This accentuates the difficulties of providing safe and nourishing weaning foods under home conditions where adequate fuel and water supplies cannot be guaranteed.

WIDER ENVIRONMENT The term 'wider environment' is here used to refer to the policies that influence women's health. At the regional or national levels, health and related policy is made which affects, for better or for worse, the condition of women. It is at these levels that sanction, overt or covert, is given to the position occupied by women, frequently through the lack of specific policies in areas of concern to them.

A combination of national policy and social pressure educates fewer girls for fewer years than boys in many developing countries (see Chapter 5) and this forces women into insecure and low-paying employment. Not only is there a direct correlation between health status and level of education, but women's economic insecurity directly affects their access to health care. Poor women may forgo medical treatment altogether or seek it exclusively from traditional practitioners who charge less or are more easily accessible, but cannot effectively treat all health problems.

4 The Effects of
Environmental
Degradation

The triple role performed by women is nowhere sufficiently acknowledged by the provision of infrastructural services to ease the burdens which threaten their health. Motivation to change prevailing social norms is low, and the difficulties are exacerbated by the low level of political power wielded by women at any level. Women's lack of voice in national processes of priority setting and decision-making is reflected in the continued existence of national policies which disadvantage them at all levels and enhance health vulnerability. Only recently has it become routine to include gender in the categories into which health data are broken down. If this is not done, the factors affecting women's health are rendered less visible and difficult to define.[32]

The root of environmentally derived health hazards to women is not, therefore, so much the environmental factors themselves, but rather the social forces which determine women's exposure to such hazards, coupled with the vulnerability of their biological function as reproducers. These forces can be summarized in two words: marginalization and powerlessness.

For poor women, the greatest symptom of their marginalization and powerlessness is lack of time, not only to perform their tasks but to ensure sufficient leisure time to maintain health. The reasons for lack of time have already been explored (see Chapter 3); lack of leisure, however, has particular health implications, namely the effects of incessant drudgery as a restraint on women's creative thinking and an impediment to better organization of their lives, even within existing constraints. Drudgery, in other words, forms an effective means of social control over women and at the same time ensures additional leisure and a higher standard of living for men.[33] Women also suffer from persistent sleep deprivation. In Sri Lanka, a study of women in the rural household concluded that they perform their multiple roles only at the expense of leisure and sleep. Women with small children have further disturbances to the little sleep they can get.[34]

The task of increasing the perceived value of women's work and status, and thereby their health and access to health care, is enormous and results will be slow to appear. Improvements in education, and

THE ENVIRONMENT, THE MILITARY AND WOMEN'S HEALTH

As human beings, our health and well-being depends upon a number of factors, not least of which is a healthy environment. When the environment becomes contaminated with toxic substances, it can have a serious impact on the health of nearby populations. This has been the case in French Polynesia where, since 1963, not less than 167 nuclear weapons tests have been conducted on the atolls of Moruroa and Fangataufa. Of these tests, forty-four were conducted in the atmosphere, subjecting the region to significant quantities of nuclear fall-out. Although testing has been conducted underground since 1974, dangers to health, to the environment, and to the socio-economic well-being of the Polynesians persist. As with other areas of the world where nuclear tests have been conducted, few reliable statistics are available as evidence of the grave impact that nuclear activities have had on the environment and, through extension, on human health. Publication of public health records was suspended soon after testing began. Although there is no *statistical proof*, the people of Moruroa know that there are too many miscarriages, too many stillbirths and 'jellyfish' babies, too many birth defects, too many cancers and illnesses . . . ▶

Military activity is often overlooked as a source of environmental degradation and, by extension, the deterioration of human health. The following story illustrates the impact that one form of military activity, nuclear testing, has had upon the people of French Polynesia. This is one woman's story—this is Tiare's story:

In 1974, Tiare, a Tahitian woman now in her early 30s, fell in love with a young man, Peni, of the same age. In the Polynesian way, she went to live with Peni in his parents' home and soon became pregnant, eventually giving birth to a well-shaped and healthy daughter named Tina. But life was already becoming difficult for all Tahitians, due to the arrival of more than 15,000 French troops and settlers. Peni began looking for a job to pay a share of the rapidly increasing living costs of the family.

The only well paid job he could find was as an unskilled civilian worker on the nuclear test site at Moruroa atoll, 1,200 kilometres from Tahiti. The only opportunities he had to see his family from then on was during the two to three days leave that all the Polynesian workers at Moruroa were entitled to each month.

Peni's work consisted of collecting garbage of all kinds, including contaminated clothing shed by the technicians at the test site and the dead fish that would float in the lagoon after each nuclear test. Often, after having burnt the garbage in a pit, he had to climb down into the pit to clean it, barefoot, with no gloves or protective clothing.

During the following ten years, Tiare gave birth to four more children. Her second daughter Moana, born in 1977, was in poor health from birth but it was not until she was five months old that the

doctor discovered that she had an enlarged liver. In 1979, she had her first boy, Nui. He suffered from meningitis and despite medical treatment he suffered mental instability.

A year later, Tiare was pregnant again. Prenatal problems lasted for five months, until a premature baby was born. The hospital nurse told her that the child was alive, but when Tiare and Peni, very naturally, wanted to see their child, they were told by the French doctors that it had died and were only shown a photograph of a foetus. In January 1986, Tiare gave birth to another boy, Manu, who seemed to be in good health but was born without an anus. Tiare has been sent with Manu several times to France for surgery. She had her last child, a daughter, in 1987.

It was a terrible period of problems, worries and suffering for Tiare and Peni. By 1987, Peni, who had worked for eleven years at the Moruroa nuclear test site, asked to be transferred to the army camp in Tahiti, so he could look after his family better, especially when his wife was absent with Manu in France. Manu is now 4½ years old and is once again in France for extended medical treatment. He hopes that he will soon be able to return to Tahiti and begin school, as he is no longer urinating all the time which, up to now, has made it necessary for him to wear diapers.

This is a true accounting of one family's tragic experience with the effects of nuclear radiation on human health. They do not represent a 'statistical glitch'. Their story is not unique, it is replicated to a lesser or greater extent in many families in French Polynesia.

Note: The names of the family members have been changed to protect them from reprisals.

Women's International League for Peace and Freedom

increased access to income, together with a reduction in the work burdens generated by women's environmental and social circumstances, will raise the health and status of the whole family.

While the amelioration of social conditions affecting women is an immense task, it is encouraging to note a few signs that social change is not inevitably negative. Fahey notes that young women in a Papua New Guinean village repudiated attempts made by older men to control them through the 'female pollution' principle. These men claimed that through the purchase and use of sanitary pads the women were attempting to disguise the times at which they were 'dangerous' to men. During menstruation, the young women broke the taboo related to food and served food to the men, who suffered no ill effects.[35] But this demonstration of a taboo's invalidity was possible only because the women understood that it was inappropriate and unnecessary for the kind of lives they now led. When women achieve this conviction over the whole question of their rights and status, traditional patterns of social control may be revised more quickly.

SOCIO-ECONOMIC IMPLICATIONS □

Women, in their central role, play a vital part in the adjustment and adaptation to the changes in lifestyle.

THE IMPACT OF COMMERCIAL DEVELOPMENT ON DOMESTIC LIFE

Traditionally, a subsistence economy involves the whole family, with the women playing the major role, working together to provide the daily needs. This way of life is dependent on the surrounding environment for the free supply of natural resources. The introduction of commercial development into a locality can have a considerable impact, with far-reaching implications for the women. In Papua New Guinea, commercial logging activities have meant that women are not only having to find alternative sources of fuel and water, but are also faced with the disruption of the traditional family life, as there is a tendency for the breakdown of customary methods of subsistence. The men, who usually have a major role in the initial clearing of the garden, find very low-waged employment with the loggers. The lure of easy money easily entices the young girls to the all-male logging camps. With an increase in mosquito-breeding sites caused by water in wheel-tracks and potholes in roads, outbreaks of malaria generally reach an epidemic scale once logging starts in a new area. With the sudden input of money into the community from wages and royalties, alcohol begins to have its usual anti-social effects. Diet quickly becomes degraded from a variety of home-grown staples, vegetables, fruits, hunted sources of protein, and fish, to be limited to white rice and tinned fish. With the excitement of strange machinery in the area and the logging boats anchored close by, school attendance suffers.[36]

In Sarawak, logging is completely destroying the way of life of the indigenous forest dwellers as they are solely dependent on the forest for their survival and way of life (see Box, p.94).

In India, mining developments have had a devastating effect on the women, not only by destroying the forests which were a source of fuel and fodder, but also by taking their land. Wherever rehabilitation is considered, whether by giving employment to the displaced, by settling them on land elsewhere, or paying them compensation, women are never even mentioned. Plots of land are given, according to uncodified Hindu law, only to men. When displacement takes place in tribal areas in the eastern part of India, men usually migrate in search of employment, while women try to survive on forest produce or work in large numbers on roads and dam construction sites.[37]

THE PENAN OF SARAWAK

For thousands of years the Penan have lived in harmony with the forest, harvesting and not destroying the forest which sustains their survival. This is a society where women and men participate equally in maintaining the communal life in the forest.

In March 1987, thousands of indigenous people in Sarawak, Malaysia, formed human barricades across logging roads in the deep interior of the tropical rainforest. For more than 20 years, their forest has been ripped apart for logs which are predominantly exported to Japan.

Entire villages walked for days across the mountains to the logging roads which traverse their lands. While the men set up wooden fences and built rest shelters, the women wove leaves for roof thatch and organised food supplies. Breastfeeding mothers, old women, young children and men stood in vigil, stopping logging operations for almost seven months. The police and army forcibly dismantled the blockades and arrested some of the men. Blockades were set up again at the end of 1988, and in early January 1989, more than 100 Penan men were arrested under a newly created offence designed to criminalise the Penans' battle for their legitimate land rights. The women take over the responsibilities of the villages, seeking food and water supplies. Many have to stand by helplessly while their children have less and less to eat and polluted water causes diseases to increase.

The struggle of the Penan to maintain their culture and way of life is dismissed as 'primitive'. They are urged to join the mainstream and be 'developed'. But the reality is that no alternative is offered for the deprivation of their forest resources. Where resettlement has taken place in other native communities, the effects have been negative, leading to a breakdown in the community itself and a dependency on the cash economy.

Meanwhile arrests and intimidations continue, but the Penan refuse to give up. As the forest dwindles, the Penan have to walk for days to seek food and clean water. The land is their life. 'If we don't do something to protect the little that is left, there will be nothing for our children. Until we die we will block this road.'

Edited from Chee Yoke Ling, Friends of the Earth, Malaysia, Women, Environment, Development Seminar, Women's Environmental Network, March 1989

The loss of farmland to large-scale developments such as mining, road construction and inundation following dam construction will affect women who will have to cope with the loss of their farming land, as well as the problems of the family in adjusting to resettlement. Often, insufficient attention is given to the needs of women in the planning stages of resettlement schemes. In many cases changes in land tenure do not favour women, and women have little representation on committees that are set up.

The failure of a scheme to satisfy the needs of the settlers can lead to further migration as was the case with the Volta Dam resettlement scheme in Ghana. People displaced from the site when a dam is built find work for a short time during its construction, but then have no alternative but to migrate to the cities.

For Vandana Shiva, it is the images like those of tribal women uprooted from their homeland that have transformed her life. She refers to a song that women displaced by a dam in India sing:

**As I build this dam
I bury my life.
The dawn breaks
There is no flour in the grinding stone.**

**I collect yesterday's husk for today's
    meal
The sun rises
And my spirit sinks
Hiding my baby under a basket
And hiding my tears
I go to build this dam.**

**The dam is ready
It feeds their sugar cane fields
Making the crop lush and juicy.
But I walk miles through forests
In search of a drop of drinking water
I water the vegetation with drops of my
    sweat
As dry leaves fall and fill my parched
    yard.**[38]

MIGRATION The degradation of the environment is leading to vast areas of the world becoming unfit for human habitation. People are being forced to leave their homeland to settle elsewhere – becoming 'environmental refugees'. Though not officially recognized, the number is estimated to be at least ten million and is likely to overtake the number of officially recognized refugees in decades to come.[39]

The processes leading to degradation have already been explained in Chapter 2. The productivity of the land deteriorates gradually, until it is so vulnerable that it is unable to survive extreme drought or intense rains. The people, too, gradually experience more and more hardship, as they produce less and less food, and thus become weaker through malnutrition and illnesses related to this condition. Initially, perhaps one or more of the family migrate for a short time, returning to work at har-

vest time, but the time they are away lengthens until finally the whole family may be forced to leave. Sometimes people move to farm increasingly marginal land, either voluntarily, or because they are forced out by landlords. Increased cultivation of cash crops has led to many women being forced to farm on marginal land. In Northern Nigeria, desertification is causing whole families to migrate southwards. The rate of migration from Sokoto, Katsina and Borno states is increasing annually and inevitably these mass movements are having an impact on the environment in the new areas of abode.[40]

Environmental degradation frequently results in larger-scale male migration, leaving the women solely responsible for the family and the farm. The loss of men from the family and community disrupts the normal social structure. It is the women who carry the burden of poverty and survival, and they have the problem of not knowing where their husbands are or when they will return; they can only wait. Meanwhile, children grow up fatherless, merely waiting to reach the age when they too can leave the home.[41]

Women rarely receive much economic benefit from the migration. The men often have difficulty in finding work, and have to use their meagre wages to pay for their own food and lodging. Any surplus is more likely to be spent on beer rather than being invested in the farm. Even when men are away for short periods, women's workload is increased as they do much of the work formerly done by the men. When particularly heavy work is involved, tasks may be delayed until the men's return. For example, unless the men return at the time when land has to be cleared, crops may be planted late, or there may be longer cropping periods and shorter fallows, leading to declining soil fertility.[42] Women may change to the cultivation of crops which demand less labour, as in Ghana where the cultivation of yams intercropped with vegetables is replaced by cassava, giving an overall reduction in the nutritional value of output from the land.

In Southern Africa, men are away for long periods working in the South African mines. In Botswana, over one-third of all households are headed either permanently or temporarily by women, and in Lesotho almost 60 per cent of all male workers have seasonal jobs in the South African mines.[43] As a result, many women are becoming more involved in the marketing and trading of food crops and more are working on other farms (see Box, p.97).

Many women are also left to sustain the small farms in India, where, with the increasing difficulty of this task, cultivation becomes less intense or is even abandoned. More and more women seek work as labourers on other farms, sometimes as migrant seasonal workers, or they resort to headloading.

In the African Sahel, the increased desertification means that the men are having to migrate further away to countries outside the region, or even to Europe. Here, as in other areas of extreme desertification, the women are also having to leave, with no alternative but to join the masses of other environmental refugees in camps on the outskirts of the towns.[44]

In general, as life in the rural areas becomes increasingly difficult, more and more women are migrating to the towns, either with their husbands or as head of the household. For the illiterate, rural woman accustomed to the village community this can be a difficult and distressing experience.

THE DEBT CRISIS AND POVERTY Many of the problems related to the environment that face women of the Third World have been exacerbated by the debt crisis. In particular, the increased emphasis on timber and cash crop exports has a consider-

able impact, as women are the collectors of timber and the cultivators of staple food crops. Not only do they face the difficulty of finding fuelwood, and relegation to cultivating inferior land, but they are also suffering as a result of changes in farming practices which affect their work patterns and their employment opportunities. In societies where women traditionally help with cash crops grown by men, they may be required to increase their work contribution, while they must still work on their own crops. Although the increase in cash crop agriculture could lead to more women being employed, they are usually employed as temporary labour and are more likely to be exploited. Additionally, the widespread introduction of mechanization and modern technology can lead to the displacement of women labourers.

Women are also affected by economies in government spending. Often cuts are made in maintenance of equipment such as water pumps. Reductions in health and education services particularly affect women. According to the 1989 UN World Survey on the Role of Women in Development, education and health expenditure have borne the brunt of reductions in government spending in many countries. Almost half of the African countries in the study sample and more than 70 per cent of the Latin American countries experienced reductions in the share of public expenditure devoted to health and education.[45] Women are especially affected by any lowering of the quality of health services, as they need access to these services because of their reproductive role. In societies that traditionally place a higher value on male children, or on educating and training boys rather than girls, a reduction in access to education or to health is likely to affect female more than male children.

In developing countries, women now form a larger proportion of the country's poor; female-headed households, due in

WIDOWS OF MIGRATION

For twelve years Mopota Maseuroane has lived alone with her three young children in a village a few kilometres outside Maseru, the capital of Lesotho.

Every day she cooks, cleans the house and then, when her 'women's chores' are finished, she starts the 'man's work'. Mopota, like thousands of Basutu women, is a grass-widow. Her husband works hundreds of kilometres away in the South African goldmines and she has become sole head of her family. For 12 years she has seen him once a year, when he comes home on leave. She never knows when he might arrive, but she always knows when he will go again. 'I feel very much alone. I dream that one day my husband will find a job in Lesotho so he can help me bring up the children, share my fears and worries about them and do all the heavy jobs.'

A large percentage of the country's women are in the same boat as Mopota. The main source of strength for such women is often the support they give and receive from each other. In Mopota's village, for example, they hold regular village meetings. These meetings were particularly important during the violent strike period of 1987 when there was no way of knowing your husband was alive until he came home on leave—or didn't.

Mopota shows her children pictures of their father and regales them with stories about him in an effort to keep his memory alive for them. The loneliness—and the fear of infidelity—are, she says, one of the most painful emotional side-effects of her husband's absence. But there are other problems. Traditionally, a black woman in rural Lesotho defers absolutely to her husband's wishes. She

may only see him once a year, but this still holds true.

So even though she may be keeping goats and cattle (as well as a family) in a remote, virtually inaccessible mountain region she will have to consult him before making important decisions. If one of her children falls ill and needs urgent medical treatment the mother has to get permission from her husband before she sells a cow to raise money. As most of these remote communities are either semi-literate or illiterate this can mean waiting until next he comes home.

Often the wife will not know where her husband is. South Africa itself seems very far away. She seldom knows which mine he is working in or even what town. One woman did not realise that her husband had died in a car crash on his way back to Johannesburg after his annual leave, until she heard the news two years later by way of an erratic social grapevine.

Over 40% of grass-widows see no money from their husbands. This is often because the women are living too far away from towns for the men to bother to send money home. To collect money, the women would have to travel to the capital which often takes several hours by car and is virtually impossible on foot.

The 'widow's poverty is compounded by the number of mouths she has to feed. Rigid social codes governing fertility only make matters worse. A husband will come under great pressure from his parents and in-laws to impregnate his wife every time he comes home. This means that the woman has the double burden of having no control over her own fertility but at the same time not having her man at home to help.

Edited from article by Charlotte Bauer, UNFPA, 1989

part to male migration, are generally among the poorest. Female-headed households are often neglected by government services. For example, according to a study in Tanzania, female-headed households had fewer visits from the advisory extension workers and adopted fewer recommended innovations, because they were poorer, had smaller farms, farmed fewer acres on their farms and produced less for consumption and sale than did male-headed households. Adapting policies and programmes is especially important because female-headed farms have often been found to be as efficient as those headed by males.[46]

It is now widely recognized that women are becoming increasingly the poorest of the poor. The 'feminization of poverty' is a reality, and the degradation of the land and its natural resources, and the deterioration of the living and working environments of the poor, are in part responsible for, and certainly exacerbate, the problem.

1 *The State of India's Environment 1984–85*, Centre for Science and Environment, New Delhi, India.
2 *IDOC Internazionale* (March 1989) Rome.
3 *The State of India's Environment 1984–85*, op.cit.
4 FAO (1987) *Restoring the Balance: Women and Forest Resources*, Rome, Food and Agriculture Organization of the United Nations.
5 ILO (1987) *Linking Energy with Survival*, Geneva, International Labour Office.
6 ISIS, *Women's World*, no. 10, Rome, ISIS International.
7 *Women, Environment, Development* (1989) seminar report, London, Women's Environmental Network.
8 Monimart, Marie (1989) *Women in the Fight Against Desertification*, Paris, Organization for Economic Cooperation and Development (OECD).
9 Muduka, J. (nd) 'The Better Life Programme', unpublished paper, Nigeria.
10 Van Dijk, Natasha (1990) 'Both Ends', unpublished paper, The Netherlands.
11 Ministry of Foreign Affairs, The Netherlands (1989) *Women, Water and Sanitation*, Directorate–General for International Cooperation of the Ministry of Foreign Affairs, The Hague.
12 Rooney, Nahau (1989) 'The impact of logging on women', South Asian Workshop, Asia Pacific Development Corporation.
13 Shiva, Vandana (1985) 'Women and the water crisis', *Ecoforum*, Nairobi, Environment Liaison Centre International.
14 *The State of India's Environment 1984–85*, op.cit.
15 OECD (1989) seminar report, *Focus on the Future: Women and Environment*, London, International Institute for Environment and Development.
16 Wells, Troth, and Foo Gaik Sim (1987) *Till They Have Faces – Women as Consumers*, Penang, Malaysia International Union of Consumer Unions, and Rome ISIS.
17 League of Red Cross and Red Crescent Societies (August 1990) *Spotlight*, newsletter, Geneva.
18 Seager, J. and A. Olson (1986) *Women in the World: an International Atlas*, London/Sydney, Pan Books.
19 Jordan, S., R.S. Jordan, C.S. Cook and F. Wagner (1989) 'What Price Poverty? Women in Development: Water Supply and Sanitation', paper at the Regional Seminar on Women in Human Settlements, Buenos Aires.
20 Huston, P. (1979) *Third World Women Speak Out*, New York, Praeger Publishers.
21 WHO (1990) *World Health* Magazine, Geneva, World Health Organization.
22 Munslow, B., with Y. Katere, A. Ferf and P. O'Keefe (1988) *The Fuelwood Trap: A Study of SADCC Region*, London, Earthscan Publications.
23 WHO, *World Health*, magazine, op.cit.
24 WHO (1984) Biomass Fuel Combustion and Health, EFP/84.64, Geneva, World Health Organization.
25 Jordan, S. *et al.*, op.cit.
26 WHO (nd) *Women, Water and Sanitation*, Geneva, World Health Organization.
27 Jordan, S. *et al.*, op.cit.
28 Sims, J. (1987) 'The Inter-relationship of Gender and Class in the Deprivation of Women', unpublished paper.
29 WHO, *World Health*, magazine, op.cit.
30 Samarrasinghe, V. (1989) 'Access of Female Plantation Workers in Sri Lanka to Basic Needs Provisions', unpublished paper.
31 Buvinic, M., M.A. Lycette and P. McGreevy (1983) *Women and Poverty in the Third World*, USA, Johns Hopkins University Press.
32 WHO (1980) Health and the Status of Women, FHE/80.1, Geneva, World Health Organization.
33 Leghorn, K. and A. Parker (1981) *Women's Worth*, Boston, Routledge, & Kegan Paul.
34 Wickramasinghe, A. (1989) 'Women's Role in the Rural Household and Agriculture in Sri Lanka', unpublished paper.
35 Fahey, S. (1989) 'The Intersection of Emerging Class and Gender Relations; Theory, Method and a Case Study from Papua New Guinea', unpublished paper.
36 Rooney, Nahau (1989) op.cit.
37 *The State of India's Environment 1984–85*, op.cit.
38 Shiva, Vandana (1989) 'Looking to the Seventh Generation: Women, Development and Ecology', *Focus on the Future: Women and Environment* (1989), op.cit.
39 Jacobson, Jodi L. (1989) 'Environmental Refugees: Nature's Warning System', *Populi* no. 1, New York, United Nations Population Fund.
40 Maduka, J. op.cit.
41 Monimart, Marie (1989) op.cit.
42 Day, Jennie (1984) *Women in Food Production and Agriculture in Africa*, Rome, Food and Agriculture Organization of the United Nations.
43 Ivan-Smith, Edda, Nidhi Tandon and Jane Connors (1988) *Women in Sub Saharan Africa*, London, The Minority Rights Group Report no. 77.
44 Monimart, Marie (1989) op.cit.
45 United Nations (1989) *World Survey on the Role of Women in Development*, New York.
46 Ibid.

5 WOMEN AS AGENTS OF CHANGE: AN INFLUENTIAL FORCE

The Green Belt Movement in Kenya has mobilised women to take charge of their environment and meet their needs and that of their families. The success has given women a positive image of themselves. They have gained economic power which has enabled them to raise standards of living for themselves and their families and consequently that of the nation.
WANJIRU KAMAU, AT A WORKSHOP AT IUCN, MARCH 1990

UNDERLYING THE PREVIOUS CHAPTERS has been the fact that women are often seen as innocent victims due to the many constraints to their advancement and their overall status. It is therefore of particular significance that despite these limitations, women are playing an important role as agents of change, and are at the centre of the environmental movement. In all societies women have clearly recognized and distinct roles.

In Diagram 5.1, Colette Dehlot sets out the multi-disciplinary roles of women. According to Dehlot, women's roles as wife, mother, housekeeper and income earner are the most well-known and agreed upon worldwide and have been thoroughly researched in many academic areas. Those roles in Group II (community organizer and family and kinship maintainer) have been the subject of research mainly by anthropologists, but are rarely considered by governments and planners when introducing new programmes in the community. Most developers, especially those with patriarchal – patrilineal influence, tend to address themselves to their male counterparts. Even professional women working in the rural community neglect these two roles which have been the essence of social maintenance.

Women as agents of social change are beginning to be recognized in the international forum. Dr Nafis Sadik, Executive Director of UNFPA, has acknowledged this with reference to the great potentiality of reducing maternal and child mortality and the strengthening of family planning programmes. In fact, the avenues of this overall role are seemingly limitless, yet in most development programmes women are regarded as passive recipients rather than as the active elements in introducing change into the community. This role is crucial for the future of the environment and to the economies of the developing countries.[1]

This chapter first details the main areas of constraint to women's progress and then focuses on their contribution to the environment, as agents of change, through their role as communicators and by their practical involvement at the grass-roots level.

CONSTRAINTS TO WOMEN'S PROGRESS ☐ Although women are central to the issues in environment and development, they are prevented from participating fully by constraints which limit their opportunities. This section sets out the main areas of constraint that affect women's progress and their overall status.

SOCIAL AND POLITICAL CONSTRAINTS
In many societies women's position in the family and the community is determined by traditional practices and customs, and the

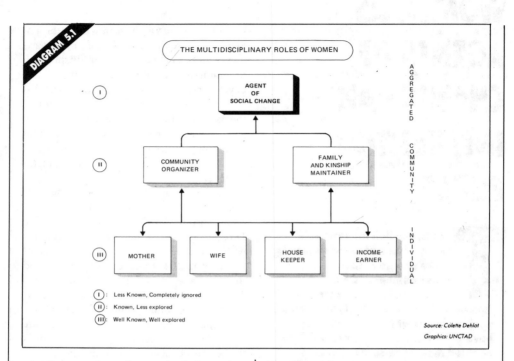

DIAGRAM 5.1

THE MULTIDISCIPLINARY ROLES OF WOMEN

AGGREGATED COMMUNITY, INDIVIDUAL

(I) AGENT
OF
SOCIAL CHANGE

(II) COMMUNITY
ORGANIZER

FAMILY
AND KINSHIP
MAINTAINER

(III) MOTHER — WIFE — HOUSE KEEPER — INCOME EARNER

(I): Less Known, Completely ignored
(II): Known, Less explored
(III): Well Known, Well explored

Source: Colette Dehlot
Graphics: UNCTAD

overall constraints of a patriarchal system. In certain societies, women are restricted by cultural codes and religious practices which may be enforced by law as, for example, Muslim women in certain countries, especially in rural areas. The practice of protecting women from the outside world, known as purdah, is symbolized by the wearing of the veil. 'The women's sphere is defined as private, whereas the men's is public, (although the community well is regarded as the women's realm). The poor, however, especially in rural areas, cannot afford not to make use of women's labour, so that often purdah becomes synonymous with social status.' In some parts of northwest Pakistan where 'life is strictly governed by a rigid code of tribal beliefs, an indiscreet word with a member of the opposite sex to whom one is neither married nor betrothed will result in swift death of both man and woman'. 'One rarely sees a girl of over six or seven years old either in the countryside or the urban centres.'[2] In Northern Nigeria, which contains 80 per cent of the country's Muslim population, it is said that

the plight of women is one of perpetual silence and immobility. The houses are built in such a way that women and children are housed in separate quarters from the men.[3]

There is a general absence of political participation by women. The political scene is invariably dominated by men. Women are rarely represented at the local level on the village committees, and therefore have no access to the political process, and their needs are not met, as men are not aware of them. In most cases, the legal framework exists, but the women themselves are unaware of this; they lack the necessary information and are not 'politically educated'. In countries where women have equal voting rights, few women are represented in government, and consequently are not being involved in the planning or decision-making processes.[4]

EDUCATIONAL CONSTRAINTS Education is the key to women's future, as it enables them to widen their horizons beyond child-bearing and household drudgery. Educated women tend to marry later and have fewer, widely spaced births. They can find satisfying, well-paid employment which can be of benefit to them and their families. Educated women can play a full and active role in development projects and are better equipped to manage the environment. They are also more effective in educating their children in issues such as health and the environment.

Women make up two-thirds of illiterate adults in developing countries; in 1985 only 51 per cent of women could read, against 72 per cent of men.[5] Parents in many developing countries still give preference to boys' education and fail to appreciate the value of education for girls. Instead, they see the value of girls' labour in the house and in collecting firewood and water, and fear that education may damage their daughters' marriage prospects. Consequently few girls continue into secondary education.

In 1986, the enrolment of girls in the Third World in secondary education was highest in Latin America, yet even there it was only 53 per cent. In the Arab states the rate was 39 per cent, in Asia 33 per cent, and in Africa a mere 21 per cent. Even at primary level, female enrolment is lower than that for males. At secondary level the differentials widen: in Africa the girls' secondary enrolment rate is only 55 per cent that of boys; in Asia and the Arab countries it is 70 per cent. In Latin America the roles are reversed and more girls than boys are enrolled.[6]

THE RIGHT TO LAND AND PROPERTY For women, lack of the right to land is a major problem. Although the situation varies, in many countries the law discriminates against women, and they are dependent on their husbands for access to land.

In Africa, the women may have the right to produce food on the land, but it is the male head of household who maintains the control over the land. Legal rights and inheritance laws sometimes prevent women from inheriting land from deceased relatives, but countries are introducing new land legislation giving more rights to women. Sometimes local customs can be very influential and can contradict the law. In Zimbabwe, a law was passed allowing women the right to own property, but traditional attitudes in rural areas still reserve land ownership for a woman's father or son.[7]

Asian women's rights vary according to the country in which they live. In Vietnam and China, the main issue is women's access to labour and employment within systems of collective ownership and management of land. In other countries, settlement schemes discriminate against women. A review of settlement schemes in Indonesia, Malaysia, Sri Lanka and Papua New Guinea showed that while women have a considerable role in agriculture, settlement scheme services are designed, and provided, for men. Land reforms, such as India's, tend to assign land titles to male heads of household. Where land reform has improved women's legal title to land and access to production services, traditional values and practices still make it difficult for them to enjoy their rights in full. They may still be excluded from decision making and deprived of the income from their labour in agriculture.[8]

Women also experience discrimination with regard to the right to property in urban areas, whether it is as an owner or tenant. Although the details of women's access to urban land are undocumented, there is sufficient evidence to demonstrate that women suffer disproportionately from the diminishing availability of low-cost land. In squatter settlements, women's legal status is often ill-defined, and research shows that statutory land allocation tends to favour male-headed households.[9]

ACCESS TO CREDIT Women face great difficulty in obtaining access to credit, whether to buy tools for the farm or for down-payment for housing. They generally lack the collateral required by the banks for loans. For example, in Africa the main forms of collateral for agricultural credit are land title, ownership of cattle or membership of a co-operative. Another factor is the usually low level of education, which together with a lack of information, undermines the women's ability to cope with the lengthy and complex processes of financial institutions. As a result, women must often resort to borrowing from unscrupulous money lenders. Yet women are likely to be more careful borrowers than men, as with the concerns of their families uppermost, they are less likely to take risks.

ACCESS TO TECHNOLOGY For women farmers, the lack of credit also denies them access to technology. They cannot afford to buy tools, equipment and fertilizers to improve their farm output and save them time.

Changes in African cassava processing provide an illustration. In order for it to be edible this staple food must first be processed by grating to reduce its cyanide content. To grate cassava by hand is labour intensive, women's work. In Nigeria, in the 1960s the first mechanized graters were introduced; women could then take their cassava to a machine to be grated, thus saving time and energy. But women themselves lacked the capital to buy the grating equipment, so what was traditionally a women's industry began to move into men's hands. In 75 per cent of cases, the graters are owned by men who hire female labour

to operate them; men also cultivate the cassava and sell it to women to process. Women cannot afford to buy the mechanized graters because the profits of their labour are so small they cannot accumulate sufficient capital, and access to credit is difficult. Men therefore control the means of production – land, raw crop and mechanized processor, while women have only their labour to put on the market.[10]

Women who work on large commercial farms are also at a disadvantage, as the introduction of technology favours men. Jobs formerly done by women, such as harvesting and weeding, are now being done by machines operated by a small team of men.

Women's access to technology is also limited because it is often inappropriate, as women were not consulted in the planning and design process. It may be a simple design fault, so that women are unable to operate the equipment, for example, being unable to reach the handle of a pump at a well, or stoves being unsuitable for the type of cooking pot used. Local customs are not always taken into account, as in the case of pedal-powered technologies being created for women who are not permitted to sit astride. Solar cookers were thought to be an answer to the fuelwood shortage, but they need constant turning during the daylight hours when the women are working in the fields; cooking is done in the evening.[11]

CONSTRAINTS TO EMPLOYMENT
Women in developing countries have less access to employment than do men because of their limited education and their restricted availability due to family and domestic responsibilities. In these circumstances, many women can find work only in the informal sector.

In agriculture, on plantations, women are mostly employed as unskilled workers on a temporary basis, whereas the permanent jobs are for men. In many cases women are neither hired nor paid in their own right, but as part of a family team subject to contracts agreed with the male head of family.

In industry, compared with male occupational distribution, women are concentrated in a limited number of sectors. They work in a narrow range of low-skilled, low-income jobs in poor working conditions, with inadequate safety measures and a lack of job security. Traditional values discourage women from full participation in the education system and from career-advancement, and women are therefore ill-equipped to enter the industrial market. Where special industrial training programmes are provided these are usually targeted to males. In some countries women with some education are employed in the export processing zones (EPZs), but under exploitative working conditions.[12]

Women are also treated unequally as far as wages are concerned, and get less pay even for the same job. According to the *State of the World Population* 1990,[13] in Brazil, in 1980, the average woman worker had one-third more education than the average man, but earned one-third his wage. One study in Santiago, in Chile, found that the discrepancy was even greater further up the occupational ladder. Primary-school educated men and those who had never been to school were paid 71 per cent more than women with the same education; those with secondary education received 84 per cent more; while male graduates took home almost three times as much money as women with the same qualifications.

The following example illustrates the difficulties that can be experienced by women in rural areas. Khadija is 17-years-old and is a seasonal wage-labourer in Morocco. She is illiterate and has never been to school. Her work on nearby farms, often private ones, is irregular. In answer to the question of how she finds work she replied:

That's the problem. You see, you can't go to the big farms and ask for work. They chase you away; they don't want to hire you; they only hire those they know. You have to be called to work. You stay in the village and wait to be called.

That's our problem. As the village is not visible from the main road, as it is hidden, the big employers, who have trucks for collecting workers, don't come over here. They prefer to inform the villagers who are on the road or go straight to the Placement Office where a large number of people are registered and available. As for us, we are forgotten. We have to be satisfied with the neighbouring farms that we can get to by foot, one or two kilometres away. They inform us the night before, and we get going in the morning. If nobody comes to inform us, we stay in the village and wait.[14]

EDUCATION AND COMMUNICATION*

☐ Women, as environmental educators, communicators and information specialists, are key agents of change in the evolution process leading to a more sustainable development of the planet. Women are traditionally environmental conservationists. In 1989, a world survey on public attitudes on the environment sponsored by the United Nations Environment Programme (UNEP) showed that women, as compared to men, are more likely to choose a lower standard of living with fewer health risks rather than a higher standard of living with more health risks. When they are placed in impoverished emergency situations, however, they are forced to apply survival strategies, which usually imply environmental degradation, in order to provide food and energy to their families. There can be no real advance towards a more environmentally sustainable world society without

---

* Contributed by the UN International Research and Training Institute for the Advancement of Women (INSTRAW). The views expressed are those of the author, **Elisabeth Massollier** and do not necessarily represent those of INSTRAW.

addressing the problem of gross inequity and absolute poverty which is affecting most women and children.

The role of women as key players in the application of sustainable development values and techniques can be reinforced by providing them with appropriate environmental training and information, and employment opportunities. This would lead to a more equitable and sustainable development of the planet as well as a healthier environment.

WOMEN AS EDUCATORS, COMMUNICATORS AND INFORMATION SPECIALISTS

The following definitions of information, communication and education are used here:

- Information consists of knowledge or data.

- Communication is the transfer of information. It is also a social process by which information is transferred from a sender to a receiver in order to influence knowledge, opinion, attitudes and/or behaviour. Senders and receivers can be individuals, groups, organizations or other collectivities.

- Education is the use of information and communications systems to teach in a given matter or field using a structured approach and applying it in a formal or an informal setting in order to improve the knowledge and understanding of others.

Women as environmental educators, communicators, and information specialists have been and continue to be key agents of change in our society. They are influencing the whole world from the family circle to the decision makers. Women influence the entire family circle, and especially children, in their environmental perceptions, values and attitudes and in ethical considerations, as well as in the use of natural resources,

energy consumption, and in waste and recycling. International organizations such as UNICEF developed training and development projects in silviculture on community lands, efficient cooking stoves, biogas plants and water mills. Those projects are capitalizing on women's natural conservationist attitudes and are promoting sustainable development, self-sufficiency and a better environment in which to live.

As has been explained in previous chapters, in many parts of the world, women are the sole providers of the 'domestic' services that is, fetching water, food and fuel. Since women are more knowledgeable about water than men, they should play a leading role in advising and educating on sustainable water development. An African organization, the African Water Network, dedicated to ensuring sustainable water development throughout Africa, intends to achieve this by increasing the participation of women at every level of water development projects. It has 50 representatives in 17 African countries.

Women as environmental specialists and leaders have raised environmental issues with a feminine touch. They have not only been presenting blunt facts, but also reaching people's hearts. Their thinking and actions have led the way to the concept of sustainable development and its applications. Rachel Carson (1907–64), a pioneering American ecologist, in her book *Silent Spring*, single-handedly alerted people throughout the world to the misuse of chemicals in pest control. The book was published in 1962, long before the creation of many of the agencies and institutions designed to protect the earth. The World Commission on Environment and Development, driven by the energy of its chairperson, Gro Harlem Brundtland, recognized officially the importance of the concept of sustainable development and defined it for the world in *Our Common Future*. This publication also paid tribute to Rachel Carson by promoting as a development strategy for the world, 'Thinking globally and acting locally'.

The participation of knowledgeable women in think-tanks and in environmental training activities is now allowing women to educate the public and policy-makers about the vital linkages between women, natural resources and sustainable development. It is also an important factor in changing the roles of women and exposing them to new opportunities, even in societies where women's roles are dictated by cultural norms and traditions. The Senior Women's Advisory Group on Sustainable Development to UNEP is one of those think-tanks. Some women's groups have as their goal the education of other women on sustainable development issues, for example the Women and Environment Group in Nepal.

Women usually tend to have a regard for others and pass on their acquired knowledge. Many female environmental specialists have been applying their research findings in a formal or an informal educational extension side-project. For example, Any Chaves, director of the Central American Sea Turtle Programme, based at the University of Costa Rica, is recruiting local poachers of sea turtle eggs and transforming them into environmental conservationists. Sea turtles are an endangered species, and she explains to the poachers that their activity can be sustainable only if some entire clutches of eggs are left untouched. One of the goals of her project is to define the optimal level of permissive harvesting; the poachers are recruited to help in this task.

Women have easier access to local women's environmental knowledge and concerns than do men. Consequently, they are better able to identify, convey and include local women's concerns and knowledge in development projects. Therefore it is of fundamental importance to include women in the planning, implementation and monitoring phases of the development projects. Women are interested in many environmental issues, such as water supply and sanitation, energy, sustainable development of resources for future generations and stability of the productive ecosystems. As women have little access to technology and credit they produce and store food in traditional ways. They are the repositories of vast knowledge on the different seed strains, and on seed conservation techniques. However, one international institution is promoting this knowledge at the regional and country levels and contributing to its inclusion in the planning process. The United Nations International Research and Training Institute for the Advancement of Women (INSTRAW) has a mandate to carry out research, training and information activities worldwide to ensure the integration of women as key agents of development.

Women, Water Supply and Sanitation as well as Women and New and Renewable Sources of Energy are two of the sectoral issues in which INSTRAW has been particularly active. The Institute produced a multimedia training package of seven modules on Women, Water Supply and Sanitation as well as a sensitization and training programme in energy. Planners and project managers, who need to develop sensitivity and awareness of women's roles and potential, together with the leaders of women's organizations, who can play a significant role in motivating and catalysing the promotion of women's involvement, are the main target groups. INSTRAW training materials have been used worldwide in regional and national seminars.

Women as information specialists have been promoting general environmental values and issues as well as their own specific environmental concerns and interests. Public opinion is a strong force in shaping the world, and international public opinion depends on communication. Through radio and television, the whole world can be linked almost instantaneously. Popular organizations have a first-hand knowledge of the impact of environmental degradation on their communities. The media can play a leading role in increasing environmental awareness using local and regional examples provided by these organizations, not only in quantitative but also in qualitative terms. Women environmental reporters are particularly good at this. Leading women reporters, such as the late Barbara d'Achille, have raised environmental awareness within their country and around the world. This Peruvian journalist established herself by presenting accurate information, accessible to the general public, on environmental issues and sustainable development projects. She said:

Public opinion cannot be manipulated with impunity; therefore, it is important to provide accurate information that is scientifically correct and without exaggeration.

When shoemakers, gardeners, butchers, bakers

and housewives understand, when students know, when professionals consider that this world is renewable only as we let it renew itself, then we will have public opinion obliging governments to have an environmental policy.

She wrote extensively about the Amazon forest and the Andes, where she died in an ambush while reporting on a UN-supported sustainable development project.

Yanina Rovinski, a Costa Rican journalist who specializes in science and natural resources, wrote about environment issues related to the Costa Rican pipeline. Her action was crucial in informing public opinion and in the final rejection of the project. Associations of women journalists have also been reporting on the environment, especially in Africa. For example, the Tanzanian Media Women's Organization, a group of women journalists, is 'dedicated to capture the voices of women who have not been heard'.

Conferences sponsored or hosted by recognized organizations which present women's concerns for the environment at the international, regional and national levels also serve to attract attention and inform the public. At the World Conference to Review and Appraise the Achievements of the UN Decade for Women, in Nairobi, women's environmental concerns and priorities figured among items at the top of the agenda.

More than 1,500 journalists attended this Conference and publicized women's views and concerns related to their own situation and their environment. Decisions endorsed by the 167 countries represented at this Conference were made available in the Nairobi Forward Looking Strategies for the Advancement of Women. These strategies affirm the importance of energy and environmental considerations to women's health, incomes, work, social facilities and general well-being. Among the environmental issues presented at the Conference, two especially were addressed: the effects of energy and environment on women's work; and the participation of women in energy and environmental management.

The 1991 International Conference on Women and the Environment, in Miami, organized by WorldWIDE and UNEP, will provide an opportunity for women to prioritize and address environmental issues of special interest to them prior to the 1992 World Conference on Environment and Development. INSTRAW is initiating a research programme on women, environment and sustainable development, and this includes three regional case studies developed by local organizations.

Another development has been the building up of information networks, such as WorldWIDE and the recently formed WEDNET at the Environmental Liaison Centre in Nairobi. Women and environ-

ment professional rosters are organized, for example, the WorldWIDE Directory of Women in the Environment, the women's roster of the International Union for the Conservation of Nature and the INSTRAW Roster of Experts in Environment.

Women are also using their networks to reach out and involve other women in environment and development issues and activities. It is essential to identify and involve influential women who have access to, or are part of, the power structure in a community as well as existing women's groups. Media portrayal of women recognized as world environmental authorities and visionaries, such as Rachel Carson, is also an important factor of change in women's perception of themselves as well as the world's perception of women.

ENVIRONMENTAL TRAINING AND INFORMATION Women in developing countries already have a wide knowledge of

---

Many women are communicating through their organizations. This appeal was made by the president of the World Ecologist's organization, Ms Charley Barretto of the Philippines.

A meal for every single man, woman and child on this globe can fit in the

PALM OF YOUR HAND!

The ecological problems of our globe today are so large and so complex that you ask— Where do I begin? What can I do? Asia's "Tree Lady" Charley Barretto of the World Ecologists has a simple answer. Plant a tree!

What can one single tree do, you wonder. Take one mango seed which can fit in the palm of your hand and plant it. When the seedling matures it can produce hundreds of trees every year for decades. Say you took five hundred of its fruits and after enjoying the fruit, you planted the seeds. You would have five hundred new trees. What if you then continued to plant five hundred of the seeds of each tree, and continued for ten generations of trees. How many mangoes would you have? Take a guess. Then look at the staggering figures. You would have one septillion, nine hundred fifty

sextillion, one hundred twenty five quintillion (1,953,125,000,000,000,000,000,000,) mangoes! Enough mangoes to go to the moon and back 456,304,012,377,406 times if laid end to end. Enough mangoes to feed all the children of tomorrow. Enough trees to absorb the carbon dioxide in the atmosphere and clean our air. Enough trees to provide firewood for the energy needs of the future. Enough trees to change the entire ecological balance of our planet. Each seed is the testimony of the abundance of nature—an abundance each person can experience if they just do their share. For the potentials of nature can only become realities through the cooperation of man.

Never ask what one tree can do. Just plant it and see! And the next time someone asks how soon we can solve our ecological problems, ask them, how soon can you plant a tree!

WORLD ECOLOGISTS

W.E. ARE HERE!

PEACE AND PROSPERITY THROUGH ECOLOGY

Source: International Women's News, Vol 84, No. 1, 1989.

their environment: energy quality, the location of water springs, seed selection, gardening and the use of medicinal plants, for example. They are the potential cornerstone of sustainable development programmes and projects, but they need training, in such areas as soil sciences, particularly soil survey and land evaluation and assessment of soil degradation and desertification. Agricultural training needs to include the assessment of land-use potential from an agro-ecological perspective, and evaluation of population-supporting capacities. Other areas where women need to be trained are: forestry management, botany, silviculture, pisciculture, hydrology, land-use planning, management of the aquatic ecosystems, economics and sociology.

Locally, once trained, women farmers can play a key role. As extension workers they could disseminate information to those who need and can use it; training sessions of two to four weeks could be set up. To carry out this work, these women would need adequate teaching aids such as guidebooks, filmstrips and posters, such as men are provided with in recognized extension programmes.

Women with basic knowledge of the environment deserve to be trained in environmental management and in development project design at all levels, including university level, and job opportunities in accordance with training and experience should be made available for them. Efficient training to recognized technical and professional levels would enable women to obtain greater access to responsibilities for designing projects that accord with sustainable development.

It is increasingly realized that, in Africa, any alleviation of the food crisis depends on the productive potential of women farmers. Traditionally, in most African countries, women are responsible for providing food to the family, while the men have been trained by international development agen-

cies to produce cash crops. Consequently, women produce at least 80 per cent of all the food in Africa. Most of Africa's small-scale farmers are women, many of whom do not have the same advantages of legal title and access to credit as do men farmers. The women therefore welcome small-scale schemes that increase profitability and conserve the land. Training for these women also must be based on an integrative approach. While it is necessary to provide them with income-generating skills, enabling them to become self-reliant, it is essential to integrate what is done for women with what is already done by them, particularly as women have usually developed their own strategies to cope with their problems. In some male-dominated rural sectors, the organization of environmental activities for couples might enable women to benefit from activities which otherwise would be attended only by men.

Formal environmental education programmes being developed by many institutions are increasingly accessible to women. Environmental education is a priority for many international agencies, such as UNEP and UNESCO, and UNEP's Governing Council has laid particular emphasis on this. The UNESCO General Conference gave priority to the development of environmental education, notably as part of basic education, including literacy and post-literacy education for young people and adults alike, as well as primary, secondary, technical, vocational and higher education. Other UN organizations have developed training activities for women: the World Food Programme, one of the UN's leading agencies in sustainable development projects in rural areas, is providing women farmers with several training and job opportunities. The International Labour Organization (ILO) has developed relevant training projects for self-reliance in Lesotho, funded by the UN Development Fund for Women (UNIFEM) and the Swedish

International Development Authority (SIDA). One of the interesting features of the projects is that the first target group was local trainers, who would then teach the second target group – women leaders – at grassroots level.

The statement 'Making Common Cause Internationally', originally voiced by the International Council of Voluntary Agencies, has been endorsed by many NGOs involved in international development, environment and population. They affirm the need to maintain the integrity, stability and beauty of the planet's ecosystem as well as the imperative for social justice. Public education, both at the formal and informal levels, is one of the key areas of concern. For example, in India, the Gorakhpur Environmental Action Group is organizing educational workshops in community development and environmental conservation.

Networks, designed by women specifically to focus upon women's environmental concerns, are also being developed. This information is most commonly disseminated by newsletters, for example: WorldWIDE News and the Women's International Network newsletter (WIN News). Others aim to inform about simple methods to foster the economically efficient use of natural resources at the local level, and are also of general interest to women throughout the world.

The whole United Nations system is committed to increasing and improving the quality and extent of environmental information disseminated to the public. The department of Public Information has been selected to co-ordinate a joint communication programme on the environment, which will include women's concerns related to environmental matters. It is to be hoped that this flow of environmental information will contribute to the need for a change in attitudes, as advised in the Brundtland report.

WOMEN WORKING TO IMPROVE THE ENVIRONMENT □ Throughout

the world women are attempting to conserve and improve the state of the environment and to achieve a better quality of life. They are involved in caring for the environment at grassroots level, through activities such as tree planting, fuel saving, water management and more efficient farming. Women's increased participation in the development process has a positive link with the environment. By using labour-saving technologies, women have more time to make better use of the land and to develop sound environmental management practices. By the adaptation of traditional tasks into rural industries women become income earners, and by being involved in community projects, they gain in confidence and status.

CARE AND MANAGEMENT OF THE ENVIRONMENT Women often initiate

movements that have been nationally and internationally recognized. One of the most famous is the Chipko Movement in India, which has been successful in preventing the destruction of large areas of forest.

As well as conserving trees, many women are involved in planting trees in areas where the forest has been destroyed or where desertification has set in. The trees prevent further soil erosion and provide shelter, as well as eventually providing fuel and other resources when they are mature. Women have been involved in forestry work in several FAO programmes. In a project in the Sudan, women leaders working with local extension workers established tree nurseries within their compounds and planted trees around their homes. Some groups of women planted and managed woodlots near their villages.

In Honduras, women took part in a project to replant areas of forest which had been destroyed by a hurricane. The techniques to be used were new to the area,

IDOC INTERNATIONAL, MARCH 1989

THE CHIPKO MOVEMENT

A fight for truth has begun
At Sinsyari Khala
A fight for rights has begun
At Malkot Thano
Sister, it is a fight to protect
Our mountains and forests.
They give us life
Embrace the life of the living trees and
  streams
Clasp them to your hearts
Resist the digging of mountains
That brings death to our forests and
  streams
A fight for life has begun
At Sinsyaru Khala.

Ghanshyam 'Shalland, Chipko poet

India's forests are a critical resource for
the subsistence of the country's rural
peoples because they provide food, fuel
and fodder and stabilise soil and water
resources. As these forests have been
increasingly felled for commerce and
industry, Indian villagers – mainly
women – have sought to protect their
livelihood through the Gandhian method
of *satyagraha*, non-violent resistance. In
the 1970s and 1980s, this resistance to
the destruction of forests spread
throughout India and became known as
the Chipko Movement.

In 1974, village women of the Reni
forests of the Chamoli district in Uttar
Pradesh decided to act against a commercial enterprise about to fell some
2,500 trees. The women were alone; the
menfolk had left home in search of
work. When the contractors arrived, the
women went into the forest, joined
hands and encircled the trees ('Chipko'

means to hug). The women told the
cutters that cut the trees, they would first
have to cut off their heads. The contractors withdrew and the forest was saved.

The movement spread as more and
more villagers throughout the Himalayas
began to fast for the forests, guard them
and wrap themselves around the trees
scheduled to be felled, saving them by
interposing their bodies between them
and all the contractors' axes. In 1980, as
a result, Indira Gandhi issued a 15-year
ban on green felling in the Uttar Pradesh
forests. Since then, the movement has
spread to Himachal Pradesh, Karnataka,
Rajasthan, Bihar and the Vindayas and
generated pressure for a natural resource
policy that is more sensitive to people's
needs and ecological requirements.

The Chipko Movement is the result of
hundreds of decentralised and locally
autonomous initiatives. Its leaders and
activists are primarily village women
acting to save their means of subsistence
and their communities.

Chipko Information Centre, India
IDOC *Internazionale*, March 1989

introducing the idea of terracing and reafforestation rather than the traditional shifting agriculture. The men were distrustful of
these new ideas but agreed to provide plots
of land for the women. Not only did the
women succeed in constructing terraces but
they also grew, harvested and marketed a
series of successful vegetable crops. In reafforestation programmes in Indonesia many
women have begun home gardens which
are said to provide as much as 60 per cent
of the food and fuel that they need.[15]

The Green Belt Movement in Kenya was
established by Professor Wangari Maathai,
through the country's National Council of
Women. It all started in 1977, with the
Save the Land Harambee Movement, in
which participants contributed their labour
rather than money for a national tree-
planting campaign. Later that year, after
the UN conference on Desertification, the
idea of planting trees to prevent the spread
of desertification gained popularity. Small
plots of woodland were planted and the
term 'Green Belt' was used, referring to the
narrow strips which were planted bordering
school compounds. The following year a
tree nursery was established and so the
whole movement began. Women are
involved in rearing the seedlings, planting
and marketing; in addition to becoming
expert foresters, they also earn a cash
income. The Green Belt Movement is not
only restoring the environment, but also
enables women to benefit from environmental education, and to practise professional forestry techniques, while at the
same time they are developing their own
status.[16] (See The Work of the Green Belt
Movement.)

THE WORK OF THE GREEN BELT MOVEMENT*
■■■■■■■■■■■ Wanjiru Kamau

Individuals or groups wishing to participate

in the Green Belt Movement must first
prepare the available land to meet the
Movement's specifications. The land is
inspected and the holes approved before an
application can be filled out. Before the
planter receives any trees, a Green Belt
Promoter discusses the physical demands
and maintenance of new seedlings. Care is
taken to assess a thorough understanding of
the participants' obligation to ensure a high
survival rate for the trees.

The Green Belt Movement, through its
rangers, mounts an extensive follow-up
procedure that promotes success. Visits are
carried out periodically to check progress or
unforeseen problems. When a large green
belt is planned, the organisation arranges a
ceremony with important guests of honor to
emphasise the significance of the event and
to pronounce the community's awareness of
the project. The National Council of
Women of Kenya (NCWK) has the responsibility of distributing the seed and seedlings, monitoring, coordinating and
evaluating, whereas the daily management
of the seed collection, quality control and
payment is in the hands of the women in
their respective organisations.

One of the strategies of the Movement
was to mobilise women to take charge of
their environment and meet their needs and
that of their families. The success has given
women a positive image of themselves.
They have gained economic power which
has enabled them to raise standards of
living for themselves and their families and
consequently that of the nation.

The benefits continue to be reaped and
the undertaking has become a family effort.
Children collect the seed for the mother,
and some men are identifying themselves
with tree planting. Trees are being pruned
and dry wood is being used as firewood. A
total of 91 nurseries were recorded in 1988.

---

* Extract from a paper presented at a workshop at
IUCN, March 1990.

The environment is beginning to resemble that of the days when men and women were not allowed to cut a tree without replacing it. ●

Planting trees can help to control soil erosion. A project in a village in Tanzania helped the women of the village to restore land which had been subject to unsuitable farming practices and was severely degraded with denuded hills and deep erosion gulleys. The area was completely treeless and women were having to walk up to 16 kilometres for firewood. Training in tree nursery management was given to the women, and in 1987 they started to raise seedlings of indigenous trees, which were later planted in communal woodlots, and fruit trees which were planted round homes. Other methods of erosion control included planting trees as wind-breaks and constructing terraces; instruction was also given in contour ploughing. Today the formerly bare hillside is described as being 'a verdant green'. The women did most of the work and within three to five years they will be able to gather their fuelwood from the trees they planted.[17]

Women in the West African Sahel are combating desertification by building banks around the contours to protect the land from erosion. In an experimental project on the Mossi Plateau at Yatanga, women have played a major part, making up 75 per cent of the labour force. The oldest women look after the children in a shady place, close to the mothers, who can then stop to breast-feed in peace. The youngest women carry the stones, and those in the middle age group arrange the stones or prepare meals for the workers. Some of the women have formed women's teams to build stone banks for wages in other people's fields.[18] Women are also taking part in the laborious task of filling up ravines with rocks. This enables the land to soak up the rainwater that previously flowed away down the gulleys; as a

result the water level in the wells is rising.[19]

Women are actively involved in ensuring the provision of a safe water supply and sanitation. They are taking part in various projects from village level to large government schemes. Many of these activities were initiated during the International Drinking Water Supply and Sanitation Decade (1980–90). In Kenya, women have been brought into the decision-making process for the installation of handpumps and are also participating in village schemes (see Chapter 6). In Lesotho, where over one-third of all households are headed by women, village water committees have been encouraged to select women for training as water-minders. A similar programme to promote women as pump-minders has been implemented in Zimbabwe, and in Sri Lankan villages women have been involved in manufacturing water pumps. Rural sanitation programmes incorporating specific roles for women have resulted in a significant drop in the incidence of diarrhoea in the under-fives, and women have been involved in many programmes involving improved latrines, and the installation of household water-closets.[20] In Natal, South Africa, the Associated Country Women of the World has been responsible for the installation of a borehole and waterpump at a nutrition centre. According to the organizer, Wendy Segerius:

Before the installation of the water pump and borehole it was not possible to accommodate so many people at Vezokuhle as the centre was entirely dependent upon rainwater tanks. Now the horizons stretch limitlessly and more and more people are making use of the facilities offered to improve their knowledge of nutrition and health and to lift the quality of their and their children's lives.[21]

An example of an individual working to

THE SWACH PROJECT

Swach means 'clean' in Hindi. It is also an abbreviation for the Integrated Sanitation, Water, Guinea-worm Control and Community Health Project, in Rajasthan, India. In this project, women have not only been allowed to participate, but have consciously been encouraged to come forward at all levels. Apart from being engaged as project staff members, rural women are being trained as village animators, village contact drive members, and as hand-pump mechanics in charge of the operation and maintenance of their own water sources. And this is in spite of the traditional myths prevailing in the male-dominated Indian society as regards women's capabilities in general and in technical fields especially.

In the beginning the emphasis was mainly on drilling wells and the development of hand-pumps, whereas today the support also goes to other areas of importance, such as fighting water-related diseases, giving children a better chance of survival, and providing women with opportunities for taking part in decision making. It is realised how important it is to reach the rural women, as they bear the responsibility of fetching water, preparing meals and seeing to the family's health and hygiene.

Traditionally the maintenance and repair of the pumps has been exclusively the work of men. During 1989, the project initiated an experiment, where 24 village women were trained to maintain and repair the hand-pumps. Many of them are illiterate, but it is apparent that they are fully capable of the task. This represents a big step forward for the women, who had never before earned their own money. It is obviously of greater interest to the women than to the men that the pumps are in working order. Should the pumps break down, it is the women, not the men, who have to walk great distances to fetch water from dirty water sources.

The women are also involved in keeping in daily contact with the other villagers. To this end, the project has recruited village women who have been given training in various relevant areas. They are called animators, or *sachetaks* in Hindi. 'The idea is that there should be one woman for every three to four villages, representing a population of 3000 to 4000 people,' says the project director. 'Each woman should contact five to six households a day and talk with the women about health and hygiene, about the relation of water to health, about women's rights etc. Furthermore, she is to see whether the hand pumps are functioning. If not, she is to inform the hand-pump mechanic. She is also to check on how the women go about fetching water and how they store it at home. In addition they are to inform about any epidemics, especially those arising from water borne diseases.'

The money the women are paid is an important addition to the household income, as there are few opportunities for women in rural areas to earn an income of their own. Women are also being trained to pass on information to other remote villages.

The SWACH project is a good beginning and, if it continues to work well, the concept of integrating hygiene, health care and health education into drinking water programmes can also spread to other parts of India. An important lesson can also be learned from the effectiveness generated by ▶

working together with the people concerned, i.e. the villagers – especially the women and children. The SWACH project is fully supported by the Swedish International Development Authority (SIDA) channelled through UNICEF.

SWACH – Facts on
a SIDA-supported Project

improve the water supply is that of an Indonesian villager, Bu Eroh, who in 1985 led her community in West Java in constructing a water channel across four kilometres of rough mountainside. Three villages benefited from the water supply and increased their rice production. In recognition of her achievements, the Indonesian Government honoured her with the Kalpataru (Tree of Life) award in 1988 and in the following year she received the UNEP Global 500 award.[22]

Some of the most successful projects are those integrated projects that tackle a full range of environmental problems. In Ghana, for example, four villages in different ecological zones have been designated for special help to overcome their ecological problems and become self-sufficient in food and energy within five years. The villages have a range of problems; one suffers from drought and desertification, another from deforestation. Tree planting is common to all villages. In addition, the Women's Action Group for the Environment operates in all villages, establishing its own farms alongside the community farm, providing tree nurseries, food crops and facilities for food processing. In this integrated project, women are involved in the environment, farming, income generation, and discussing health and family planning, although a family planning component has not yet been incorporated into the project:

In Binduri, for example, human beings outnumber natural resources, and the carrying capacity of the land is always crying; there's no period of rest for the land. No matter what we do, if they don't embrace family planning, we'll still have environmental problems. We'll plant all the trees all right, but they'll cut them down because they have to feed themselves.[23]

Some development projects incorporate a range of environmental activities, such as those run by the Bhagavatula Development Trust in India (see below).

WOMEN TAKE THE LEAD IN RURAL DEVELOPMENT PROJECTS
Jenny Pryke

L. Abaddam lives in a village in Andhra Pradesh, South India. In 1984 she was in trouble financially. Her husband was too ill to work and she had to support him, her five children and her mother-in-law. She sold the family's cow and mortgaged their one acre of land. Then the members of the village women's group came to her rescue. They made her join their thrift programme, and helped her get a loan from the programme's thrift fund.

She used the money to buy a cow and grew guinea grass for fodder on the small piece of land outside her house. Then she took part in a training programme in nursery raising run by the Bhagavatula Charitable Trust, a rural development project that works in this area. She raised 20,000 seedlings. With the money she earned from this, and taking an additional loan, she paid off the mortgage on her land and planted saplings. Three years and nine months later she sold the trees. She used the money from the sale to have a well dug and a motor fitted for irrigation. With improved water supply the coconut trees she had planted a year before began to bear fruit. Another training programme in agricultural methods at the BCT demonstration farm, Panchadaria, taught her how to grow chilli, lentils, oil seeds and tobacco in between the trees. Her family is now almost self-sufficient – and with improved nutrition Abaddam's husband is much better and can help his wife.

There are many stories like this one in the villages where the BCT operates. Pressure on land to provide fuel and fodder has led to deforestation. But the women's initiative, combined with expert advice, is transforming lives at the same time as improving the environment.

The BCT did not set out to work with women. It began work in 1976 training young men as village 'animators'. Men were the obvious choice. The women were withdrawn and silent, some even ran away if approached. But some women observed what was going on and asked to be included. So, when a reorientation programme for the young animators was held, some women were asked to participate. During the programme they remained silent. At the final evaluation meeting one old lady gave the reason: 'Sir, do you really expect us to come out with our opinions openly? You are combining old and illiterate women with young educated men. If you are serious about getting our opinions expressed, kindly have programmes separately for women.'

Today the BCT works almost exclusively with women, programmes flourishing and multiplying because of the women's enthusiasm. At first they faced opposition, including physical intimidation, from men. But this has decreased as the men have realised that they gain too from the women's projects.

There are women's groups, or *mahila mandals*, in 29 villages. These operate as thrift societies. The women save a small amount each week and, if they pay up regularly, after six months they are eligible for a loan of double the value of their savings. The loans can be used for numerous income generating schemes. In an area where many people are unemployed for as much as half the year, the extra money makes a real difference to a family's standard of living.

Many of the *mahila mandal* projects help the environment. If a woman takes a loan for a dairy animal, she must also take a course in how to look after it, run by the BCT. This includes instruction on how to grow fodder crops – to improve the milk yield and to stop it feeding on overgrazed land. Many women, like Abaddam, raise seedlings, planting them on common lands, around fields, on road margins. Members are encouraged to use seeds from Panchadaria to start kitchen gardens next to their houses. More vegetables improve the diet, and there is a demand for any surplus in the near-by steel producing town.

In one village, women have taken loans to build bio-gas plants, which use human and animal excrement. The left-over slurry is excellent fertilizer and using the plants saves scarce fuel wood. In the same village, when floods devastated the men's salt pans, the men asked their wives for a loan from the thrift fund to repair them. The men repaid the loans in salt, which the *mahila mandal* then sold. Another BCT training programme showed the villagers how to cultivate prawns in the reservoirs of the pans. All this is in a village where, before, the women, because of their caste, didn't leave their homes.

The most ambitious project is the reafforestation scheme. Inspired by the flourishing Panchadaria Farm, which is on 50 acres of reclaimed land, 198 marginal farmers asked the Trust for help to develop their 58 acres. The project is managed by an all women committee, made up of BCT staff and women's group members. The head of the *mahila mandal* commented: 'We are involving ourselves in the programme. Five of us are on the Board of Directors. The BCT is helping us technically and financially in developing the land. Our men never object to our involvement. Why should they when we're working for their benefit?' ●

Environmental care is not confined to the rural areas—many urban women are working to improve their environment:

In many cities people live on and off the rubbish dumps. To the east of Calcutta, in an area called Dhapa where the city's wastes are dumped, thousands of people live and make their living. They pick over the piles of garbage, collecting rubber, tin, cork, glass, foil and other items which they sell to middlemen for recycling. Others grow vegetables on the piles of rotting humus, which they sell in the city.
The Calcutta Social Project, started by a group of middle-class women in the late sixties to work in some of the slum areas, moved into Dhapa in 1981. They began with literacy and recreational classes for young garbage pickers in an abandoned shed. Then vocational training in carpentry, masonry, and sewing were added. A primary health care clinic now flourishes, with an immunisation programme alongside. Serious flooding in 1984 and 1986 threatened epidemics and mass pollution as sewage channels and effluent from the city's tanneries overflowed. Older students, teachers and health workers teamed up to prevent disaster by disinfecting drinking water, distributing foodstuffs, encouraging inoculations, and teaching about diarrhoea and oral rehydration therapy. Oxfam has assisted with the provision of a deep tube well for the clinic, and a building for the children; and is currently providing funds for staff salaries and vehicle running costs.
OXFAM

IMPROVING RUBBISH DUMPS IN LA PAZ
Up at the top of the city, the refuse trucks are nowhere in sight. Dumps form haphazardly, filling crevices in the eroded landscape, littering wasteland and clogging streams. Kids play on the tips amidst swarms of flies.

One organization of shanty-town women, concerned about the risk to their children's health, did a survey to find out where dumps were located and what they consisted of. The results were disconcerting: many tips were only yards from schools and markets. And one of their main components was human excrement, since few houses have toilets in the poorer zones.

The women set up a project to make cheap, home-built latrines with local materials. While that took shape, they organised a massive dump-clearing campaign, with voluntary teams working in each zone. Pregnant women and grandmothers kept the children entertained with puppet shows at a safe distance from the tips, while others worked together to pile up, burn and bury the rubbish.

The Town Hall, afraid of bad publicity, sent a convoy of refuse trucks around the shanty towns the day before the campaign. But the task of clearing hundreds of tips was too much for them to take on at the last minute.

'We're living on top of a load of trash,' said community leader Nelida, shovel in hand, a handkerchief tied bandit-style over her face against the dirt, smoke and dust. 'We're getting contaminated and our kids are getting sick. We have to deal with the problem ourselves, until the authorities remember we exist.'

Susanna Rance, *New Internationalist*
January 1990

Some of the worst living conditions are to be found in the squatter settlements in the large cities. In Bombay the pavement dwellers are referred to as the as 'wretched of the city', and are not even mentioned as a category in any mobilization programme.

Through the members of the Society for Promotion of Area Resource Centre (SPARC), women are being mobilized to work for better living conditions. Their activities include the designing of possible housing and organizing saving through a

BETTER LIFE FOR THE RURAL WOMAN

Some countries have national programmes enabling women to improve their living conditions and therefore their environment. The following is an example from Nigeria:

In order to improve the living standards of the Nigerian women, especially in the rural areas where the majority of women live, some in abject poverty, Mrs Maryam Babangida, Nigeria's first lady, launched a national programme known as Better Life for the Rural Woman in 1987. This encouraged the formation of the National Commission for Women at the federal level and Directorate of Women's Affairs in all the twenty-one states of the federation.

The objectives of the Better Life Programme include:

- the creating of awareness among the women, of the abundant natural resources in Nigeria and their utilization to their best advantage;
- developing themselves economically without the need to migrate to the urban areas;
- getting themselves actively involved in agricultural and industrial programmes;
- forming part of the decision-making body in their communities and the country at large;
- promoting good health, literacy and political awareness among women.

To be able to achieve these objectives, women have formed themselves into social/economic cooperative movements for agriculture, cottage industries and cultural activities.

The National Commission for Women has identified areas of the impact of human activities on the environment and has recommended solutions. There has also been an appeal for environmental awareness at all ages and levels of education, with participation in the following global environmental issues:

- creating sustainable energy
- raising energy efficiency
- avoiding mass extinction of species
- controlling toxic chemicals
- shifting to renewable energy
- planning the global family
- conserving soil and planning
- investment in environmental security

The pollution of our environment is a result of economic growth, and if women are to play meaningful roles in the development of Nigerian society they must be able to understand fully the implications of certain actions of theirs for the environment. The Better Life Programme is encouraging a greater environmental awareness and is involving women in activities relating to the improvement of the environment.

Joanna Olutunbi Maduka,
Chairperson, project committee,
The Better Life Programme

housing fund.[24]

In one of the poorest environments, in the *comunidades* of Lima, Peru, women celebrated Earthday 1990 by involving the children in their project to plant trees in a new park in the centre of an urban area. One of the women leaders said:

In a comunidad like ours, there is a very clear understanding of what ecology really means: humans establishing a healthy, balanced relationship with other animals and their shared environment. The mothers in Villa El Salvador are very concerned about the well-being of their children; they obviously would rather see their young ones growing up in a clean community than in a neglected polluted one.[25]

WOMEN FARMERS Women farmers, who have often suffered at the expense of cash-crop farming or large-scale logging or irrigation schemes, and who have for so long missed out in the development process, are at last being recognized for their importance as food producers.

Cameroun is one of the few African countries which is self-sufficient in food, yet at the start of the 1980s self-sufficiency in food was less than 80 per cent. The success of the government's policies has been in part due to the involvement of women farmers. In a scheme to test new maize varieties, one-third of the extension workers are women who help the women farmers to introduce the new varieties, and new ideas, including credit facilities. Some women have since formed their own groups, and are so successful in some areas that the men are feeling left behind and have suddenly developed a previously unknown interest in growing food crops.[26]

In Moroba Province in Papua New Guinea, the Women's Association, with the support of the provincial government, has set up the Subsistence Agricultural Programme. This aims to train subsistence farmers in improved farming techniques which can be incorporated with traditional methods, and to introduce stable gardening methods as an alternative to shifting cultivation. The farmers take their produce to sell at food centres; and the programme also includes training in food processing and food preparation.[27] Women in the remote valleys of North Pakistan have formed their own village organizations which enable them to improve their farming and status.

WOMEN IN NORTHERN PAKISTAN
■ Amenah Azam Ali ★

In the remote valleys of Northern Pakistan, women are still, for the most part, illiterate, poorly nourished and trapped in a cycle of drudgery. The Aga Khan Rural Support Programme (AKRSP), which started working with the farmers of the northern areas in 1983, recognised that until women escape their traditional isolation, there could be little hope of bringing them into the development process. Thus the village organisations fostered by AKRSP were intended to provide a vehicle for both men and women to organise themselves and work together in developing their resources. But women are often inhibited in expressing their opinions in front of men. So in nearly 300 villages they have formed their own separate organisations (Women's Organisations) which then present a collective voice to the rest of the village.

In this area there is a high rate of male migration, and women are left alone to shoulder the burden of farmwork. The farming is geared to subsistence production, but improved inputs and techniques could bring about economic changes. After testing various approaches with a few WOs (Women's Organisations) it became clear

★ Project Co-ordinator for Women in Development, AKRSP

PHOTO: JEAN-LUC RAY/AGA KHAN FOUNDATION

that certain 'packages' worked better than others. The most successful have been in vegetable production and home-based poultry.

Vegetable production for home consumption is a traditional activity for the women, but the production was limited in both quality and quantity by low-grade seed and unscientific methods of cultivation. With the increase in productivity and quality made possible by the vegetable package, the women are interested in marketing their produce and thus increasing their income. While women traditionally cultivate vegetables, the heavy work of land preparation is done by the Village Organisation for members. Since women cannot themselves take goods to the market, the VO marketing specialists are responsible for marketing.

The poultry package also builds on a traditional activity – raising backyard poultry for eggs for the home – and increases productivity by introducing high-yield vari-

eties of scavenging poultry, and training in disease prevention. The potential increase in productivity is four or five times that of traditional poultry.

The fact that, at present, a large proportion of the local consumption of vegetables and poultry comes from outside the area means that there is a great potential for indigenously produced goods to replace the imported produce. In some parts the tourism and trekking industry also provide a large and growing seasonal market.

In one village in the remote Ishkoman valley, the women say that before the formation of the WO, they were considered 'no better than a man's shoe', and their labour had no value because it did not earn money for the family. Now, with a cash income, the value of women, and hence status, in the village and at home has increased, giving them a new self-respect and confidence. The formation of the WO played a major role in bringing about this change. As one WO manager puts it: 'Before the formation of the WO, we all used to be alone: we would work alone and bear our burdens alone. Now we work together, plan things together and share our problems. We all look forward to our weekly meetings.'

Apart from the projects currently being offered, there are other possibilities for the future. A pilot project in sustainable forestry is currently being conducted in the Upper Hunza area in collaboration with IUCN, which envisages the participation of women in raising saplings of forest trees, and later will offer training in harvesting forest products. ●

Where women are farming in areas of extreme environmental degradation, they face considerable problems, and many are responding by taking on new activities. In Kenya, the husbands of women environmental refugees migrated when their temporary settlement was affected by drought. The women left behind survived by receiving famine relief. The Council for Human Ecology (CHEK) helped these women to improve their lives by establishing new enterprises, one of which was bee-keeping, traditionally men's work. After some training, the women became successful, and subsequently formed a co-operative producing and selling honey throughout Kenya.[28] The Masai women of Kenya have also suffered greatly as a result of drought, when the wells and streams dried up and there was no pasture for the cattle and goats. One group of women started a self-help group, the Olkinos Women's Group. They were not cultivators, but they started growing vegetables, they learned how to irrigate the land and raised money for the irrigation pipes by starting a handicraft co-operative. At first they worked secretly, without telling the men, but now the men treat them differently. 'The men value women now, because of their knowledge, effort and initiative,' said Kipiku, the group's leader.[29]

In Bogotá, Colombia, women are farming where there is no farming land available, that is in the barrios or squatter settlements. They are successfully growing vegetables by hydroponics.

The vegetable beds can be made from old sticks of wood, and the plastic sheeting to line them is recycled from big flower farms around Bogotá. The plants grow in a mixture of rice husks and coal slag about eight centimetres deep, and need to be watered daily with nutrients. Although the nutrient solution, containing about 15 minerals and other elements, is bought commercially, it represents less than seven per cent of the production cost. Almost all the urban farmers are women. Those with small children can stay at home and earn some money, instead of spending a large chunk of their wages on bus fares to jobs the other side of the city. By the second harvest – lettuces are sold after 80 days – the investment has already paid off; about 40 lettuces can be grown in one square metre.[30]

Women farmers are being trained in ecologically sound agricultural practices to help them protect and make better use of their land. One successful example is a World Food Programme-assisted project in the Dominican Republic, in the central mountain district of La Sierra, where the torrential rain and rapid run-off washes away the topsoil of their tiny plots perched on the steep mountain slopes. The farmers, women and men, are learning techniques such as mixed cropping, and are halting water run-off with small ditches and terraces. The soil is no longer heavily ploughed, and agricultural and animal wastes are used instead of expensive artificial fertilizers. Farmers receive food rations during training and in the first months while they switch to the new techniques and wait for the new crops.

An example of an individual success in

sustainable farming and improvement of the environment is that of Mrs Tabitha Njeri in Kenya who, in partnership with extension officers, has developed her farm, which was ravaged by soil erosion, into a model of sustainable productive agriculture (see Box below).

A major obstacle to women's progress as farmers is their lack of access to credit or its equivalent in land and possessions (see

MRS NJERI'S FARM

Mrs Tabitha Njeri cultivates coffee as the principal cash crop, and maize as the main staple. There is also a significant proportion of the farm set aside for Napier grass, bananas, and fruit trees like avocado, mango and citrus, and also a number of minor crops. Trees grow in abundance amongst the crops and on the field boundaries. Near the living quarters at the top of the slope there is a rudimentary zero-grazing unit for two cattle.

But perhaps most importantly, the farm is very well conserved with a number of soil and water conservation structures and measures. There are retention ditches and fanya juus that reduce the slope and erosion, and aid water retention; there are sacks, stones, trash and live plants to prevent gulley erosion; there are well-maintained bench terraces for the coffee; there are infiltration pits to again slow water flow downhill; and there are many gravillea, mutundu (Croton macro stachys) and black wattle trees which help bind soil with their roots.

Like many other farms in her village, there is extraordinary complexity in the crop–livestock–tree interactions. The cattle eat Napier grass grown on the retention ditches and fanya juus, and paspalum grass grown on the terrace risers. Both grasses also serve to stabilise the soils. The animals also consume maize stalks and stove, banana leaves and stalks, tree leaves and during the times of shortage wild plants such as maegoya, plus sweet potato vines, cassava leaves and tubers.

A number of plants are used as bedding for the cattle and for adding bulk to the manure. These include euphorbia and grevillea. Euphorbia can also be eaten by goats. In return, manures from the cattle are essential for maintaining soil fertility and structure.

Although Mrs Njeri applies inorganic fertilisers, she favours manures. But she does not have sufficient for her requirements. The priority crops for manures are coffee, followed by maize and then Napier grass. The shortage was aptly summarised when she said, 'I wish you could come with a lorry load of manure. It would make me so happy.'

In addition to these finely tuned relationships many of the individual components of her shamba are multipurpose. The squash plants provide food and are a medicine to control cattle intestinal worms. The lima beans supply food and fix nitrogen in the soil.

But perhaps the most diverse are the trees. All have more than one function, acting as sources of fuel, building materials, live-fencing, fruit, fodder, bedding material and shade. The attitude to trees here are expressed by the chief of the village – 'That is a beautiful area', he said, 'just look at all the trees.'

International Agricultural Development,
November/December 1989

Constraints). This having been recognized, the situation is improving as organizations and banks are setting up schemes to allow women access to credit. The UN International Fund for Agriculture and Development (IFAD) has introduced the idea of group lending and group liability for loans, which has removed collateral requirements and opened up an opportunity for a wider range of women to become beneficiaries of credit and agricultural loans. In Nepal, the Production Credit for Rural Women Programme provides loans for livestock and farming, those participating include migrant and landless women. They are motivated to form small groups who elect a leader. More than 1,000 women's credit groups participate in the scheme (see section below).

THE PRODUCTION CREDIT FOR RURAL WOMEN PROGRAMME (PCRW) IN NEPAL*

PCRW was conceived as a pilot project to bridge the gap between the realities of the nature of women's work in the rural household and the lack of services to support her in her endeavours. PCRW's objectives are to enhance the status of women by increasing their income, to establish self-reliant women's groups and to develop a delivery system capable of providing services to rural women. The wider objective of the programme is to integrate women's needs into the overall national development strategies.

PCRW was started in 1982 and primary emphasis was placed on developing an institutional framework for community development and the organization of rural women into groups. No specific performance targets were established for the organization of groups or for the provision of credit to such groups. Initially, work commenced with 100 households and gradually expanded thereafter. The effort concentrated mainly on establishing at least one site in each of the 24 districts to launch the programme. The strategy was to aim for lateral expansion of the programme with a gradual build-up of sites in each district.

By January 1987, 284 credit groups had been formed covering 1,444 members, of which 1,184 had taken loans amounting to NRs 2.9 million ($US 134,300). Some 80% of these loans were granted for livestock, underscoring a strong demand. Loans were given to individuals on the basis of group collateral. The groups, however, are not cohesive and cannot become self-managing. The overall repayment performance of livestock loans has averaged 67% due in part to the problems of livestock mortality, inadequate training of clients and lack of technical support. The repayment of crop and cottage industry loans, on the other hand, has been almost 100%.

PCRW has made a considerable headway in Community Development Programmes (CDP). These are looked upon as a way of freeing women from their daily activities to enable them to participate in a meaningful way in income-generating projects and improve their quality of life. Since inception, a total of 41,403 people have benefited from the project of whom the majority are women and children. Drinking water has received the highest priority under CDPs, which means a saving of anywhere between 1–5 hours of water collecting time for women. Other CDPs have included agricultural projects, construction of paths/bridges, health/nutrition projects and adult literacy classes. ●

Other examples of loan schemes include that in Pakistan, where rural women are benefiting from a scheme implemented by the Agricultural Development Bank of

---

* IFAD

Pakistan. The women are using the money to buy buffaloes and to develop cottage industries such as making carpets, blankets and knitted goods. Côte d'Ivoire, with support from the World Bank, is launching a project to increase women's access to agricultural extension, job training, literacy programmes, and initial funds.[31]

Projects combining credit, training and food aid are enabling women to improve their farming and to set up income-generating enterprises. In Bangladesh, the Vulnerable Groups Development programme, a joint venture by the government of Bangladesh, the World Food Programme and various NGOs, is helping the 42,000 women enrolled in the programme. Some are raising poultry and earning an income from the sale of chickens and eggs, others are taking part in a sericulture programme.

GAMBIAN WOMEN IMPROVE THEIR RICE FIELDS

Women are the main rice cultivators in The Gambia, but men are responsible for clearing the land and for building bridges and causeways in the paddies. Women were eager to learn more efficient farming methods, but the men often neglected maintenance once the food and cash benefits were withdrawn.

In 1987, WFP joined forces with the NGOs, and together they presented the villagers with an attractive package, supplementing the cash with food in an inventive way. In Jataba, for example, when the village chief signed the contract, he promised that the first 10 per cent of the work would be performed without immediate cash or in-kind compensation. This is called *tesito* or self-help work. The money – and the value of the food – owed to the villagers for this labour will be deposited in a bank account and used to cover maintenance work.

Through this scheme, the women are assured that the necessary servicing will take place. No money can be withdrawn from the account without the consent of the local village women's committee.

By the end of 1988, 20 of the 103 participating villages had become self-sufficient in rice. Over a period of 10 years, 6,000 hectares of swamp have been rehabilitated or developed. Bunds protect the paddies against saline filtration and help retain fresh water. Sluices and canals improve drainage and the leaching of salts and acid sulphate. Bridges and causeways ease access to the paddies. Before, children strapped to their backs, the women would waddle through the mud in the mosquito-ridden swamps to reach their fields.

The low-tech, low-cost approach encourages finding local solutions. For example, to avoid importing costly shovels, picks and axes, the NGOs trained and equipped local blacksmiths who now make all of the project's tools.

The women's training programme includes credit, mechanization and seed multiplication. Each village chooses a maintenance committee of three members – one must be a woman – selected for their farming skills. Newly developed land is distributed among villagers, particularly to landless families.

The women of Jataba and other villages can now manage their paddies in a more productive and efficient way. They have increased household food security, eased their work burden, and become more self-sufficient, while at the same time protecting the swamp-lands that are the basis of their own livelihood.

World Food Programme (WFP)

These examples show the many ways in which women from different cultures are using their knowledge and skills in working to improve the environment and in doing so are improving their living conditions and raising their status within the family and community. Many women are restricted by constraints, and the biggest constraint of all is the lack of information. In many countries, legislation exists giving women rights to education and land, but life for women in the rural areas is still governed by local tradition and customs, and the women themselves are not aware of their rights. These women need to be given the necessary information and education, and to be aware of the avenues open to them, as their voices need to be heard. Those with power should be listening to what women have to say. Statements by government ministers and international agencies recognizing the importance of women and advocating women's participation can have considerable influence. Furthermore, educated women, who have overcome the constraints, should do what they can to influence those in power. Women have much to contribute, but they need the empowerment to enable them to do so.

1 Dehlot, Colette (1990) unpublished PhD thesis, Penn State University, USA.
2 Mumtaz, Khawar (1989) 'Women, Development and Environment: Issues, Constraints and Potential', paper to National Conservation Strategy of Pakistan.
3 *Women's World*, December 1989, Rome, ISIS.
4 Savane, Marie Angelique (1990) United Nations High Commission for Refugees, personal communication.
5 UNFPA (1990) *State of the World Population*, New York, United Nations Population Fund.
6 Ibid.
7 Ivan-Smith, Edda, Nidhi Tandon, and Jane Connors (1988) *Women in Sub-Saharan Africa*, report No. 77, London, Minority Rights Group.
8 ILO (1988) *Women and Land*, Geneva, International Labour Office.
9 HABITAT (1989) *Women, Human Settlements, Development and Management*, Nairobi, United Nations Centre for Human Settlements.
10 *Appropriate Technology*, vol. 16, no. 3, 1989, UK, IT Publications, quoted in Sims, Jacqueline (1990) 'Effects of Environmental Factors on Women's Health', unpublished paper.
11 *The Tribune*, 3rd quarter 1986, New York, Women's Tribune Centre.
12 ICFTU (1985) *World Economic Review*, Brussels, International Confederation of Free Trade Unions.
13 UNFPA (1990) *State of the World Population*, op. cit.
14 FAO (1985) *Ideas and Action: Rural Women*, Rome, Food and Agriculture Organization of the United Nations.
15 FAO (1987) *Restoring the Balance: Women and Forest Resources*, Rome, Food and Agriculture Organization of the United Nations.
16 *Intermission*, September 1988, newsletter, Friends of Right Livelihood, UK.
17 Chipo-Cushnie Mayanga, Jamila 'Women Coping With Soil Erosion', *Tanzania Women's Magazine*, September 1989, Tanzania Media Women's Association.
18 Monimart, Marie (1989) *Women in the Fight Against Desertification*, Paris, Organization for Economic Cooperation and Development (OECD).
19 WFP, *WFP Journal*, January–March 1990, Rome, World Food Programme.
20 WHO (1990) 'Achievement of the International Drinking Water Supply and Sanitation Decade', unpublished WHO report.
21 ACWW (1990) *Countrywoman*, July/September, London, Associated Country Women of the World.
22 UNEP (1988) *The Global 500*, Nairobi, United Nations Environment Programme.
23 Yeboah-Afari, Ajoa (1989) 'Village Projects Conserve and Teach' in *Earthwatch*, no.37, London, International Planned Parenthood Federation.
24 d'Monte, Darryl (1989). Case Study: 'The Pavement Dwellers of Bombay' in *Against All Odds*, London, Panos Institute.
25 ACCION (1990) *International Bulletin*, Summer.
26 Madely, John (nd) 'The Success of Cameroon's Agricultural Policy', paper in *Food Policy* (UK).
27 Asia and Pacific Development Centre Workshop, October 1989.
28 Phillips-Howard, Kevin, D. (1987) 'Women's Cooperative in Kenya Fights Drought', *Ecoforum*, February, Nairobi, Environment Liaison Centre International.
29 Njan, Rebeka 'Learning to Grow', *New Internationalist*, June 1990, Oxford, New Internationalist Publications.
30 Kendall, Serita (1989) 'Growing Without Soil in Bogotá', *Earthwatch*, no. 37, London, International Planned Parenthood Federation.
31 World Bank (1990) *World Bank News*, August, New York, the World Bank.

6 CASE STUDIES AND PROJECT IMPLEMENTATION

The modernization of agriculture, with mechanization, extensive irrigation and the introduction of hybrid crop species has marginalized women's traditional knowledge of and experience in the use and management of natural resources. Development efforts rarely take people's knowledge into account, and certainly not women's expertise in such areas as soil conditions, seeds, crop varieties, and appropriate agricultural methods. Equally overlooked is women's expertise in water and fuel supplies.

ELIZABETH CECELSKI, 1987, ILO

THIS CHAPTER CONTAINS detailed case studies which illustrate the varied ways in which women are involved in the environment. The studies are the work of experts who have presented their assessments, analyses and conclusions, and can serve as models for use in similar environments and situations. In addition, the final section of the chapter presents an overview of women's participation in projects and programmes concerned with the environment. Particular reference is made to the strategies for planning and to the more important issues for research. The studies cover a range of topics in different areas. Each study has a particular focus; in some cases it is the improvement of the environment, in others the social aspect is more obvious.

The first two studies are concerned with women's use of the environment for their basic needs. Melissa Leach looks at women and forest resources in a village in Sierra Leone, and shows the importance of the forest to the women as well as the difficulties they face as a result of recent changes. The PROWWESS/UNDP case study describes a highly successful water-supply project in the Kwale district of Kenya. Important features of the project are the participation of women from the early stages, and the close co-operation between the government, donor agencies and a national NGO.

An example of an urban environmental project is provided by the Guarari Community Development Project in Costa Rica, which is aimed at providing low-cost housing for low-income families, while at the same time allowing conservation and protection of the natural environment. Women play a leading role in its planning and practical implementation.

The Samitis of Bankuru is a study based on an ILO project which had the prime aim of providing employment for landless and peasant women. In addition, however, the project has involved women in the rehabilitation of the environment by reclaiming wasteland; and the development of the women's groups has enabled them to acquire skills and to gain confidence.

The last two studies focus on the gender aspect of the particular projects concerned. Corinne Wacker shows the importance of working through women's groups in a programme to ensure a secure village water supply. Mary Hobley considers the relevance of gender and class with regard to the control of forest resources in a village in Nepal.

WOMEN'S USE OF FOREST RESOURCES FOR FOOD SECURITY AND INCOME GENERATION: SIERRA LEONE
Melissa Leach, IDS, Sussex

Close to the boundary of Gola North forest

reserve, in the Sierra Leonean part of the West African forest zone, lies a rainforest edge community, Madina. The hilly landscape is a rich mosaic of forest, rice farm, tree crop 'garden', and regrowing bush. The Mende people here cultivate rice and intercrops on annually-cleared land whose fertility is restored by forest fallow, and earn money from the sale of export tree crops, such as cocoa and coffee. However, they have long collected 'wild' plant and animal (bushmeat, fish) resources from the forest and fallow land. In varied ways, these are important for ensuring flows of food and money throughout the year.

Women use and rely on plant resources more heavily than do men. Women's food provisioning responsibilities are more immediate and varied. Men provide the main rice staple, but women are expected to help out with staple food provision during the 'hunger' season (July– September) before the rice harvest, and are keen to ensure that their own children eat well even when overall household supplies are low. Women are also responsible for providing the sauce (made with oil, vegetables, salt and, ideally, meat or fish) eaten with the carbohydrate staple.

Furthermore, women have fewer cash-earning sources than men, so forest products are more important to their incomes. Most village men have cocoa and coffee farms, and earn annual revenues from them. Some supplement their incomes with forest products, by selling bushmeat or palm wine, or making tools or baskets for sale, but only a few young and poor men rely more heavily on these income sources. Nearly all women treat forest product sales as a regular part of the repertoire of small scattered sources (including vegetable sales and trade) which make up their incomes. As women often spend their money on food, clothing and medicines for their children, rather than rely on unreliable contributions from their husbands, these earnings

contribute to household welfare.

FOREST FOODS

Mende use wild foods in a number of ways. Firstly, women collect and process them to make sauce ingredients. Some of these are so central to the diet that, ideally, they are eaten every day. Palm oil, which women extract from the fruit of the oil palm *tokpo (Elaeis quineensis)* by a painstaking process of pounding, washing and boiling, is a clear example. The oil palm grows wild on farms and fallow land, and has myriad economic, social and ritual uses which give it a central place in Mende life. Women use other wild plants occasionally, according to their seasonal availability and how much time they have to gather them, to add taste and variety to the diet. The seeds of *kpei (Coelocaryon sp.)*, a forest tree, are pounded to make a thick-textured soup during the dry season (December–March), for example. A variety of edible herbaceous plants spring up on newly burned farms between April and June, and women collect their leaves as alternatives to cultivated sauce vegetables. In the rainy season, they collect wild mushrooms *(fali)*, which are locally valued as a meat substitute.

Secondly, women use forest foods as snacks, especially for children whom they recognise to need small, regular quantities of food throughout the day. Fruit, such as the plum-like *ndawa (Parinari excelsa)*, is often so used.

Thirdly, wild foods can buffer food shortages. Most people use some to alleviate seasonal hunger and substitute for scarce ingredients every year. Certain foods appear at 'strategic' times of the year, or can be stored until these times. For example, people who have run short of rice before harvest and cannot afford to buy it can dig for bush yams *(ngawu)*. Palm oil is also scarce and expensive during the hunger season. Most women therefore try to collect the seeds of *fawei (Pentaclethra macrophylla)*

in December–February. They store these in their kitchens, and process them into a dark brown oil substitute when their palm oil supplies run short. Forest foods can also tide people over more severe periods of food shortage. People in Madina recall several of the famines of the last century by the name of the product most important for survival, such as *kpatoi*, when people survived by eating the seeds of the tree (*Pterocarpus santalinoides*).

INCOME

Forest resources also contribute to household food security indirectly, through the contribution they make to women's incomes. Women dominate the trade and marketing of forest products in many parts of the West African forest zone. In some areas there are well-developed markets for fruits and seeds. This is not the case in Sierra Leone, but women occasionally sell these products within their villages, especially at times of year when other income sources are scarce. For example, women sell the spherical fruit of *gboji* (*Spondias mombin*) in August.

The most important marketed bush items in Sierra Leone are firewood and palm oil. Firewood is a plentiful by-product of the bush fallow rice production system. Most of the preferred firewoods are common fallow species, and when a new farm is cleared, many dry, semi-burned branches are left on the land. Collecting, chopping and bundling firewood on the roadside to sell to passers-by or urban traders is a lucrative source of income. Farm firewood becomes available from April onwards, and provides income during the period of the year when food and money are in shortest supply.

The sale of locally processed palm oil in local markets is an important source of off-farm income. The palm fruit yields two kinds of oil. Women who have a surplus of the preferred red palm fruit oil usually process and sell it during the palm fruit cutting season (December–May). The palm kernels which are left no longer fetch the high export price they once earned during the colonial period. Nevertheless they can still be processed into kernel oil and sold locally. Most women store them in their kitchens and process them in the hunger season, in order to sell the oil when they need money most badly.

CHANGES IN
FOREST RESOURCE AVAILABILITY AND VALUE

Commercialization and forest degradation are affecting the use of forest resources throughout most parts of the West African forest zone. On the one hand, the increasing scarcity of forest products with no (or only prohibitively expensive) substitutes is increasing their market value in urban and forest-scarce rural areas, and stimulating sales from areas which still have supplies. On the other hand, as forest areas are replaced by more permanent forms of cultivation, farmers more often preserve and plant the most useful species on farmland; a form of indigenous agro-forestry they have long undertaken. As the local systems of 'tree tenure' assign rights of use of trees on farmland to the farmer, as opposed to the family or wider community which holds rights over trees on uncultivated land, farmland trees are well suited to systematic exploitation for commercial sale.

These two linked trends would appear to represent opportunities for women who live in degrading forest areas to increase their incomes. In practice, however, the prevailing relations of access to land, labour and produce restrict women's gains from forest product commercialization. In Madina, men are considered to have rightful claims over the palm fruit oil their wives process if, as is usual, they have negotiated access to palms and cut the fruit. In the past, husbands were rarely interested in the revenues from palm oil sales which were small compared with their coffee and cocoa earnings. But as the relative price of palm oil has increased, men have become keener to stake their claims over the oil and sell it for themselves. Many now leave only a few pints for cooking, and the lower-value kernels, to their wives. Similarly in the rural hinterlands of urban centres, where firewood marketing is highly profitable, Kamara (1986) found that men were increasingly involved, selling over 20 per cent of the wood. Men's superior rights to lineage land helps them claim the firewood resources on newly cultivated farms, to which the farm household has exclusive rights. Paradoxically, as the potential contribution of forest products to women's incomes increases, women can find it harder to hold on to the benefits.

Women in Madina also find it difficult to protect and preserve the trees which they want to use on farmland. Many plant small groups of fruit trees behind their kitchens, but the space is limited there. Men plant and preserve trees in their cocoa and coffee farms, but most women, without access to sufficient male labour to establish coffee farms and rarely able to inherit them, lack access to this permanently cultivated land, and grow only seasonal food crops. Thus the farmland trees to which most women have access are those their husbands preserve for their own use, as timber and to shade young tree crop seedlings. Although women can use the food and firewood products of these trees, their rights are not secure. One farmer felled a *fawei* tree from which three women in a nearby compound had regularly gathered seeds. It was overshading his coffee.

CONCLUSION

Mende women are the principal users of forest plant resources to satisfy household food and income needs. This gives them interest and knowledge which should make them key managers and key beneficiaries of efforts to conserve and enhance the

resource base, such as through social forestry, agro-forestry or 'innovative' forms of forest management.

However, just as women's weaker claims to labour, land, trees and produce often mean they lose out when ongoing changes render resource access more competitive, they may work against them in project situations. Interventions must therefore build in enough incentives for both men and women, or enhance and support women's rights and control, if women are genuinely to get the benefit.[1] ●

PEOPLE, PUMPS AND AGENCIES: THE SOUTH COAST HANDPUMP PROJECT
PROWWESS/UNDP

This is the story of one programme in the coastal province of Kenya, widely acclaimed to be a success. It began as the small South Coast Handpump testing project in 1983. Over a period of time the project changed, evolved and grew into the district-wide Kwale Water Supply and Sanitation Project covering an area 27 times the scope of the original project.

THE CONTEXT

In Kenya, economic and population pressures coupled with the fact that 90 per cent of the rural people (85 per cent of the total population of 19 million) did not have access to safe water in 1980, led to government interest in low-cost technologies including hand-pumps.

At the beginning of the UN Water Supply and Sanitation Decade there was no hand-pump in Kenya that was sturdy and did not break down frequently; that could be easily repaired by village people using simple tools; that was inexpensive and was being manufactured in the country. The concept of VLOM (Village Level Operation and Management of Maintenance) did not exist, nor did a VLOM hand-pump. The South Coast project aimed to develop a VLOM hand-pump for Kenya. Two locations, Diani and Masambweni, along 300 square kilometres of the coastal belt in Kwale district, were selected for the testing programme. The work was executed by the Ministry of Water Development (MOWD) with management support from the World Bank. It was financed by the government of Kenya (GOK) and the Swedish International Development Authority (SIDA) through UNDP/OPS.

Positive as well as negative factors had impact on the project from the beginning. The coastal belt had a clean, shallow aquifer, ten to twenty metres below the ground surface. There was a long tradition of using hand-dug shallow wells. The need was recognized as a result of severe water-related health problems including diarrhoea, and a cholera outbreak in 1979. The timing of the project was right; the government's current strategies were also appropriate. The 'district focus' policy emphasized 'full participation of the local community in the planning and implementation of development activities'. This provided the project with a legal administrative framework to implement community participation.

The concept of community participation is not new in Kenya. The Harambee (self-help) movement that has existed since independence has greatly contributed to development activities and has become the cornerstone of the Primary Health Care strategies in Kenya. There were, however, some misgivings, even predictions of failure. Two previous hand-pump projects in the area had failed. Both had completely covered people's wells and installed hand-pumps that could not be repaired when they broke down and people eventually had to dig new wells.

Naturally people were not enthusiastic about the arrival of yet another well-covering project. In addition, the population in the coastal belt was primarily Muslim which to many signified a potential disadvantage in stimulating women's participation.

DEVELOPMENT AND EXPANSION

Since the hand-pump project focused primarily on technology installation and development, not surprisingly the preparatory work and the first year of the project was led by three MOWD technicians who concentrated on addressing essential technical issues. The water levels of the underground water aquifer were monitored and the aquifer mapped; water quality was tested for bacteriological and chemical adequacy; seasonal fluctuations in water levels were noted; the presence of existing boreholes and wells was marked.

This early technical work laid the groundwork for the later high success rate in finding water. The project systematically improved drilling techniques, introduced coarse sand gravel packs to prevent sand caving into boreholes, improved well design and worked with manufacturers experimenting with different designs and materials for hand-pump components.

Within the first year, it was recognized that to develop pump maintenance systems in partnership with local communities, especially their women, would require specialized technical expertise of a different type than was available within the MOWD. This led to the inclusion of KWAHO (Kenya Water and Health Organization), a young Kenyan NGO, within the project. UNIFEM funds allowed KWAHO to post two sociologists to the project who trained five local women as extension workers. The KWAHO staff led the community organization work and trained 29 local women as pump caretakers. PROWWESS funds provided KWAHO with management support and training in participatory methodologies.

The community liaison team (one

woman, one man) hired and trained five local village women as extension workers. Together, the seven team members trained other village women in community organization, and development, maintenance and use of simple water supply systems. The UNIFEM project document 'Training of Women in the Development, Maintenance and Use of Simple Water Supply Systems' was structured in such a way that it allowed KWAHO to be truly responsive to community needs and also adjust its work to the pace and temperament of its technical partners who were testing 12 different types of pumps.

The main collaborators were in place. There were three more distant partners that were crucial for the continued existence of a financially fragile KWAHO. They were UNICEF, Private Agencies Collaborating Together (PACT), an American NGO, and WaterAid, London, a British NGO. Each agency involved in the project, irrespective of the size or duration of its contribution, played critical roles without which the project would have foundered in its early stages. Every agency involved was characterized by strong leadership willing to take risks, make long-term commitment and practise partnership.

The work of the KWAHO team motivated village women and men to organize themselves into water committees, raise money for maintenance of pumps and become trained in pump repairs. It proved that community involvement was not only possible but also worthwhile.

The project emerged out of the two years of transition (1985–86) with an even deeper understanding of the centrality of community involvement in the success of their endeavours. By 1987, a hand-pump suitable for village level operation and maintenance had been developed, the AFRIDEV. Only then could local people be trained in pump maintenance and repairs and pumps then handed over to local communities.

Pilot South Coast Project 1983–85

Area: 300 square kilometres

Population served: 21,000

Technical staff: 17

Social staff: 7

Village pump caretakers trained: 29

New installations

Hand-dug wells with hand-pumps: 10

Boreholes with hand-pumps: 89

Kwale Expanded Programme 1985–87

Area: 8,250 square kilometres

Population served: 46,750

Technical staff: 74

Social staff: 16

Health staff: 5

Village pump caretakers trained: 109

New installations

Boreholes with hand-pumps: 146

Spring captures: 23

Rainwater tanks: 17

Dams: 1

Demonstration latrines: 96

Currently, tasks are being increasingly routinized and institutionalized. Simultaneously, strategies are being developed and will be further refined for the adaptation of community involvement strategies to different technologies (rainwater tanks, spring captures and dams) and to different ecological and cultural zones.

ACHIEVEMENTS AND IMPACT

Besides building water systems and demonstration latrines, the project has had a profound impact at the village, government, NGO and donor levels:

1. *Effective and Sustainable Utilization:*
At the village level, the economic and social impact of effective and sustainable utilization is easy to discern. In areas where pumps have been installed and are being utilized, women consistently express relief and gratitude at not having to walk long distances to fetch water of questionable quality to the home.

Encouraged and supported by the approach of KWAHO extension workers, women have utilized increased availability of time and water for horticulture. Water groups have increasingly branched off into a variety of production activities including poultry keeping, processing of *bixa* (red oxide) and production of *khanga* (cloth). This has in turn increased cash contributions towards pump maintenance and the probability of its long-term survival.

Health statistics for Kwale district, based on out-patient clinic visits, show a clear and consistent decline in diarrhoeal diseases 'from 34,042 out-patient visits in 1984 to 19,420 in 1986'. Statistics from Muhaka Health Centre in the project area indicate a 50 per cent decline in diarrhoea and 71 per cent decline in skin diseases between 1985 and 1987.

2. *Dynamic Problem-solving Capacity (sustainability):* At the village level this has been instituted through the 125 user-created and user-supported water committees. These committees have become increasingly autonomous in functioning. They have elected leaders, collected local materials for construction, helped in pump installation, collected money for pump maintenance and have undertaken pump repairs.

- 135 village water committees
- all collect cash
- all have women treasurers
- families pay Ksh 1–10 per month
- totals range from Ksh 200–13,000
- 70 per cent have opened bank accounts
- all pumps are functioning
- committees have repaired pumps

Both women and men have gained confidence in themselves and in each other. This is evidenced by increased respect for women and their acceptance in public decision making. Young, female, extension workers are accepted and listened to with respect even by older men and women in a predominantly Muslim society. The importance of women as pump caretakers and on decision making committees is appreciated and supported by communities.

Groups have evolved their own rules and regulations to guide problem solving and conflict resolution. Decisions made by committees have been followed up by action. This includes the locking up of pumps, allowing members to pay in kind, dropping ineffective committee members, denying access to non-paying members and penalizing households that do not carry out mutually agreed duties such as cleaning pump surroundings on an assigned day.

As groups have gained confidence and a sense of efficiency they have increasingly used extension workers as resources. This has included asking for additional information, training or guidance in solving particularly persistent problems. The interface between the water committees and project staff is the source of a two-way information flow between project staff and people in communities.

At the agency level, working groups

Community Organization Process for Boreholes with AFRIDEV Hand Pumps

STAGE 1   Meetings with leaders and village members, information about the project, discuss roles and responsibilities of the project and the community.

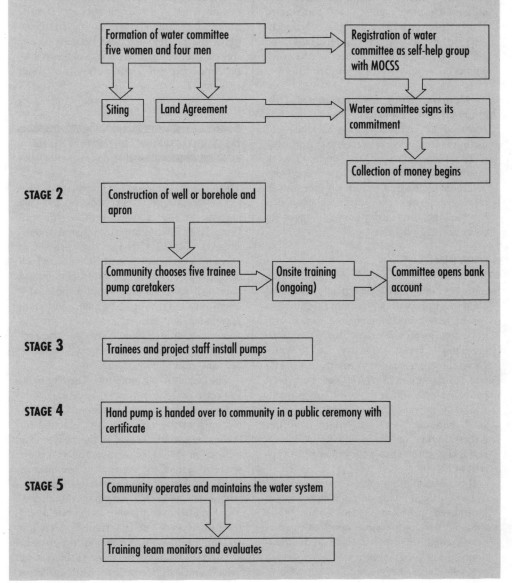

Formation of water committee five women and four men

Registration of water committee as self-help group with MOCSS

Siting

Land Agreement

Water committee signs its commitment

Collection of money begins

STAGE 2   Construction of well or borehole and apron

Community chooses five trainee pump caretakers

Onsite training (ongoing)

Committee opens bank account

STAGE 3   Trainees and project staff install pumps

STAGE 4   Hand pump is handed over to community in a public ceremony with certificate

STAGE 5   Community operates and maintains the water system

Training team monitors and evaluates

within each section meet regularly to monitor, evaluate and adjust strategies to ensure effectiveness. The highest committees – the project steering committee, which includes MOWD, KWAHO and donor representatives from Nairobi; and the project management committee – now include the KWAHO senior staff member. These committees also meet regularly and function to support project staff in problem solving. In order to ensure long term sustainability, the project needs to move closer to and work within the regular MOWD mechanisms.

3. *National Staff and Expanded Programmes (replicability):* The project is managed by competent Kenyan staff, and includes local people recruited from the Kwale region. Two SIDA personnel work in advisory capacities while one Peace Corp volunteer assists as a technician specialist in rainwater tanks. The project has expanded beyond the first experimental stages to cover an entire district.

OTHER IMPACTS
KWAHO's crucial role in operationalizing the community involvement approach and ability to work with government technicians has increased government and donor support for its involvement in water programmes. The Ministry of Water Development strongly supports KWAHO and has nominated KWAHO as the principal NGO with which it works. Government and donor experience in working with a small national NGO has led to a greater understanding of the problems of NGOs and a commitment to policy change in support of NGOs.

It is because of its achievements and continued struggle with some identified, yet unresolved problems, that Kwale offers valuable lessons for those involved in integrated community-based water and sanitation projects/programmes.

Kwale succeeded because it was able to develop mutually supportive relationships between community groups, government ministries, an NGO and several external donors who were willing to make long-term commitments, take risks and work together. This working together was made possible by a shared vision and growing conviction of the centrality of women and communities in achieving success. Despite different disciplinary and political philosophies the partnership held because of one shared overriding goal: achieving sustainable functioning of community-owned water systems. ●

THE GUARARI COMMUNITY DEVELOPMENT PROJECT
■■■■■■■■■■■■ World Conservation Union

The Guarari Community Development Project is a unique experiment in low-cost housing in the crowded central valley of Costa Rica. Two non-governmental organizations, CEFEMINA, a prominent women's organization, and COPAN, which campaigns for and helps build community housing, have stimulated and supported a grass-roots movement which addresses population and natural resources within a wide range of integrated activities. The project illustrates the roles of women, as planners and resource managers.

The Guarari Community Development Project is located in the fertile central plain of Costa Rica which, until recently, supported most of the agricultural production for the entire country. Most of the people (1.6 million in 1987) are concentrated in the western part of the plain, which embraces San José, Heredia and several other cities, with a density of 825 per square kilometre. The population is growing at the rate of 2.9 per cent a year. The government so far has no land-use plan for this region, nor is there an overall strategy to manage increasing urbanization in accordance with the principles of conservation of natural resources.

Guarari offers a model for housing low-income families in ways compatible with raising the standard of living of local people, encouraging the acceptance of smaller families and protecting and restoring the natural environment. Pioneered by women, this type of community development offers possibilities for peri-urban expansion which nevertheless provides a 'lung' or 'green belt' around large cities, reducing atmospheric pollution. Rural agricultural skills can be preserved and the productivity of the land renewed.

EVOLUTION OF THE PROJECT

Successive governments have made attempts, sometimes politically motivated, to cope with the increasing pressure of migrating peasants who had lost their rural lands and were attracted to jobs and the cultural life in the capital city of San José and other main cities, including Heredia, Cartago and Alajuelo. In the 1970s the Institute of Housing (Instituto Nacional de Vivienda y Urbanismo) (INVU) began buying up farms on the periphery of the city for slum clearance housing. Installation of urban services and the actions of squatters on these lands were very destructive of the natural environment, as the land was cleared of trees and other natural vegetation, producing, as well, conditions for many social problems. In many cases squatters moved on to the land before the promised housing, water, sanitation and electricity services were installed and without any advance planning for schools, health centres and other social amenities.

The government action, or lack of it, therefore gave land indiscriminately to those who were ready to grab it, without consideration for families waiting to move out of the older, squalid living conditions of the original slums.

CEFEMINA, which was established in 1981 as an independent, non-political organization dedicated to improving the lives of women, launched its own campaign against the lethargic government machinery, opposing the policy of allowing squatter communities, demanding the installation of urban services before housing construction took place and asking for virgin land on which to pioneer self-help community development which would preserve the natural environment and improve the quality of human life. CEFEMINA's interest from the start was to build a sense of community self-help, particularly among women, as well as group responsibility for house construction, management of shared facilities and group activities to meet other social needs of the residents.

Women emerged as the main protagonists for community-serving housing arrangements which would stimulate, rather than stifle, group responses to social needs. Thanks to the support and intervention of the Minister of Housing, Dr Fernando Zumbado, CEFEMINA and its partner COPAN were allocated a former coffee plantation near the provincial capital of Heredia, some 20 kilometres to the north-west of San José. Guarari was born.

GUARARI

Guarari is made up of 118 hectares of land, nine of which form a watershed area of steep banks of natural vegetation through which a small watercourse traverses the area from east to west. The site has a pleasant exposure toward the surrounding countryside and distant mountains. The land is part of the central plain which previously provided most of the agricultural productivity of Costa Rica. The plan includes conservation and rehabilitation of the watershed area. It is planned to accommodate 3,000 houses which will be part of a new urban metropolitan area. The programme of 'auto-construction' has been developed for impoverished families, many of them headed by women with young children. The houses are planned in '*conjunto residencial integrado*', that is, with small groups of houses clustered around a recreational area. Several examples were described:

This is the second project for 250 houses for poor people but also for some public workers like engineers and secretaries so that we can have an integrated neighbourhood.

In this other part the women wanted the houses to be close to each other in two irregular rows and to have a long park extending between the rows for recreation and a playground for the children.

Women are the principal activists in Guarari. As Dr Norma Kaminsky, who is in charge of CEFEMINA's health programme, explained:

The women are the leaders in this project. They are more organized than the men and participate in group activities as well as in house construction.

Another CEFEMINA member added:

Women are the main builders of the project in every sense – physical, social and psychological. They are the main builders of a collective identity. The main resource of the project is the involvement of the people in all the activities. Without the people there is nothing you can do. The people have taught us about community involvement.

Each group of houses will have the social and physical facilities necessary for a productive community life. The arrangement of houses into small groups enables them to adapt to the natural topography and preserves the natural habitat as far as possible. The houses are arranged around a pleasant recreational area with special amenities for the children.

The Guarari project is being developed on the principle that present and future

residents build the houses themselves – 'auto-construcción'. A project co-ordinator, who lives in Guarari, said: 'All the members of the community are involved in house-building and they all take part in the Assembly where all the decisions are taken.'

The government facilitates land acquisition and material; the beneficiaries provide the labour and final finishing of the units. Financial support is provided by the Banco Hipotecario de la Vivienda (BANHVI), which is a government credit bank. BANHVI provides the funds for land acquisition by INVU (the Housing Institute) which, in turn, accepted a project proposal from COPAN. COPAN has the capacity to hire technicians, buy materials, work with other organizations involved in social issues and generally administrate the housing developments. CEFEMINA has the philosophical and social structure for group work, especially with women.

The work at Guarari has only just begun. So far, 295 houses have been erected and another 200 are being built. Small-scale industries, such as rabbit breeding, production of medicinal plants and a nursery for the propagation of tree seedlings, are either at an experimental stage or still to be negotiated. The rehabilitation of the watershed is still on the drawing board. Water is so far only available for household use. Final success and sustainability cannot yet be measured. Nevertheless, many positive aspects emerged from direct observations and interviews on the project site.

There is a clear definition of the problem that the project seeks to solve, that is, the shortage of decent and appropriate housing for low-income families and women heads of household. All participants agree that the goal is to obtain appropriate living quarters in a healthy environment where other facilities also exist to foster a better way of life and there is a long-term commitment to achieving the goal.

Women have taken the lead in overturning the conventional housing designs of government and have negotiated with engineers and financing agencies for units which are better adapted to their needs, allowing proper supervision of children at play, more ventilation in kitchens and other work places and communal recreation facilities. They have learned to question any proposals put forward by government, to assess them against their own needs and to put forward their own counter-proposals with conviction.

There is strong evidence of close rapport between the participants and the lead organizations, CEFEMINA and COPAN. An effective working structure has evolved and all affiliated members are required to participate in one or more committees.

Increasing numbers of people are being trained in house building and in leadership and management skills. Construction techniques have been developed on the site as more and more local people have gained technical skills. Many of the women and men interviewed expressed satisfaction with the skills they had acquired through participation in the training programmes. The health/family planning committee members also showed their enthusiasm for both the methodology and content of the training they received.

There is a conscious effort on the part of the project's directors to use and generate local resources for the activities. Most of the building material is produced locally and on-site production of doors, window frames, wall planks and other prefabricated house parts has been successful. All the educational materials have been produced in the office of CEFEMINA by volunteer groups.

The population is aware of the need to preserve the existing flora and fauna and rehabilitate the watershed area that crosses the site. All those interviewed cited the positive learning aspects of the project. Without exception, they affirmed that their lives are better since they have been involved with the project. The experiences gained in community involvement, skills acquired through specific activities and the acquisition of a place to live were the most sustainable aspects of the project.

Based on the Guarari experiences, similar projects have been initiated at San Ramón, Alajuela (244 houses), and at Alajualita San José (104 houses), and there is no reason why these projects should not be repeated elsewhere. They would appear to be eminently replicable. Experience at Guarari is showing that this type of community planning is cost-effective and brings many additional benefits to both the inhabitants and the land they occupy. Guarari provides a model for peri-urban housing around large cities which can help ameliorate atmospheric pollution and provide a 'lung' or 'green belt' for the city. Government officials expressed themselves satisfied with this model and indicated that, in general, they would be happy to see it followed elsewhere. ●

THE SAMITIS OF BANKURA
International Labour Office

In a small village in West Bengal, a women's Samity (society) obtained a land donation in 1980 from private landowners who lacked the resources to develop the degraded land. With unwavering focus, and collective will, the Samity reclaimed the wasteland, and in 3 years the land was thick with trees on which tasar silk worms are reared. As news spread, other Samities were formed by women in surrounding villages, each with land donation from villagers and today, 1,500 women in 36 villages are members of such Samities. The groups have also organised supplementary income-generating activities, on an individual or group basis.

Samity members can now survive without 4

yearly migrations to distant districts in search of work because they have created employment for themselves by expanding the productive base of the local economy. Women's bargaining power as workers has increased because of their link with an asset-owning Samity. There is a new confidence amongst the members that they can influence the course of their own lives through the Samities, where 'all are responsible for all'.

The Samities have been supported by the Centre for Women's Development Studies (CWDS, New Delhi), and ILO's Programme for Rural Women (New Delhi). These organisations have provided technical guidance and counsel, and catalytic funding. Government schemes have emerged as the major source of funding.

Bankura is one of the 16 districts of the state of West Bengal. With a total geographical area of 6,881 square kilometres, it is the fourth largest in the state. It is one of the two districts in the state declared as a backward district.

Of the total geographical area, in 1987–88, 55.8 per cent was net area under cultivation, 14.5 per cent was area under forests, 13.1 per cent was area under non-agricultural use. As high as 6 per cent of the total land area has been specified as barren and uncultivated land, 3 to 6 per cent as cultivable wasteland and 6.7 per cent as fallow land. The remaining land area is under the permanent pasture of the grazing ground and area under miscellaneous tree crops.

The economic conditions of the population are fairly depressed. Sixty per cent of the cultivators are marginal farmers and 25 per cent are small farmers owning less than 2 hectares of land. Per capita income per year for a landless family or the family of small and marginal farmers has been calculated to be only about Rs 500, which is only about 50 per cent of the poverty level income at current prices. Consequently, some 40 per cent of the scheduled caste and

tribal populations (in particular Santhals) migrate temporarily each year from the western parts of the district to the adjoining districts of Burdwan, Hoogly and Howrah.

INITIATION OF THE PROJECT

The objectives of the Bankura project and its basic model were drawn from SEWA (Self-employed Women's Association) and WWF (Working Women's Forum). The organizations and the employment to be generated through them were not to be ends in themselves. They were to be the instruments of mobilization of poor rural women, to enable them to participate more effectively in the wider process of socio-political development through collective action, and to increase their voice in development decisions that affected their lives.

Even before site selection could take place or the research begin, the government of West Bengal invited the director of CWDS and one of its founder members to attend a Reorientation Camp for Migrant Women Agricultural Labourers, in May 1980, at Jhilimili, a village in Ranibandh Block of Bankura District.

Ranibandh is part of the least developed region of Bankura with a large concentration of tribal population. Originally a part of the vast area known as Jungle Mahal (Forest Estate), it used to be inhabited mainly by Santhals, a forest-dwelling tribe. During the last three centuries, other people increasingly penetrated and settled. Forests disappeared even more rapidly in the twentieth century, and soil erosion increased on the hilly slopes. Even cultivable land became increasingly less productive and droughts were frequent. Over the last few decades, therefore, thousands of men, women and children had taken to seasonal migration to the green revolution districts of Hoogly and Burdwan for employment in agriculture. Going on Namal (migration to the lowlands) to the women was the last resort for survival. To quote from the most authentic report on this camp:

Their main grievance was against the forest policy of the Government. For the tribal women, forest provided the basic means of livelihood. They used to collect, free of cost, fruits, flowers or leaves of Mahua, Peasal, Kendu and other trees. They used to gather leaves and brushwood and other minor forest produce without paying any charge. But during the last three decades gradually their customary rights had been abrogated. They were harassed, prosecuted, insulted – and above all were deprived of their supplemental income from forests.

BANDYOPADHYA, 1980

They were all from landless or marginal peasant households. Locally they could get casual work, in agriculture or otherwise for a maximum of 6–8 weeks. Deforestation had left them no option but to go on Namal. Daily wages were prescribed at Rs. 8 per day for migrant labourers, paid partly in kind. The travelling was arduous and dangerous. At the place of work, accommodation would be in stables or self-constructed shelters. Children had to come along with the mothers, and could therefore not attend school regularly. Infant mortality, abortions and a gradual loss of health were common phenomena, as well as sexual molestation by the employer or his recruiting agent.

The women formulated four demands in the camp: 1) restoration of their right of access to forest produce; 2) employment in their own area; 3) land and homesteads in their own right; and 4) protective measures for maternity and child care as provided to factory workers. Because the disorganization of their lives had also precipitated the destruction of other social norms, eviction and desertion of wives and families by hus-

bands had become widespread, wife-beating had increased, and women felt they could not get justice from the traditional caste and tribal councils.

A number of decisions were taken by the government to accommodate the women's needs, such as the restoration of their rights of free access to forests for collection of minor forest produce, and directions to local authorities to employ only local labour in all types of work generated by the government. The district administration was also instructed to allocate homestead land to the women who were found to be homeless, and to identify possible ways of generating new employment for women within the region in order to reduce their dependence on seasonal migration. All these decisions emanated from West Bengal's Minister for Land Revenue and Land Reform, and his chief officer, the Land Reforms Commissioner, both of whom were present at the camp. The Minister, however, decided also to call in the CWDS to initiate directly some experiments through the women's groups.

PRODUCTION AND MARKETING

The first samiti (organization) with a membership of 30 women from eight villages, was formed by the women who had joined the 1980 Jhilimili camp. Within nine months, three samitis were formed, with a membership running into hundreds; work had to be found immediately. With the help of state officials and the chairman of the local Panchayat Samiti (the block level council), three different types of activities were initiated. Women from the Jhilimili group received an agency from the local Forest Cooperative (Large Size Multipurpose Society, or LAMPS) to organize the collection of kendu leaves (used for making indigenous cigarettes), and sal seeds, activities that generated employment for over 200 women for three months. The organization at Chendapathar started producing sal leaf plates and cups with the help of small machines. The third group, at Bhurkura, received a gift of seven acres of wasteland from local peasants which they decided to convert into a plantation of Asan and Arjun trees on which tussar silk worms could be reared once the trees had matured.

The plantation at Bhurkura offered assured employment to a small group of women and provided an extraordinary demonstration effect. Between 1981 and 1988, 250 acres of wasteland were given to 12 women's organizations drawn from 35 villages in three blocks of Bankura district and one block from the neighbouring district of Purulia. Of this, 150 acres had been planted in 1988. In 1987, ten women's organizations generated about 36,000 workdays of direct employment, mainly through development of these plantations. This included land preparation, nursery seedling raising, planting and rearing the trees, including watering through dry seasons, and silkworm rearing in the older plantations. The women's care in rearing the plants ensured a survival rate of 98 per cent in contrast to 50 per cent in plantations developed by the Forest and Sericulture Departments. It also reduced the maturing period of the plants to two years; the experts had predicted four years as a minimum. So far the tussar-silk cocoons produced by the three organizations whose plantations began between 1981 and 1985 have all been bought by the Department of Sericulture.

TRAINING

Training in relevant skills has been a regular activity since 1982. The women have been trained in mechanized sal leaf plate making, silk-worm cocoon rearing, wasteland development, mechanized rope-making and improved goat and poultry management. The trainers are from government departments of Sericulture, Forestry, Livestock, the Khadi and Village Industries Commission, as well as voluntary bodies such as the Society for Promotion of Wasteland Development (SPWD) and the Action for Food Production (AFPRO). Continuous training has also been provided by the project staff of the CWDS in sericulture, accounts keeping and maintenance of records.

ORGANIZATIONAL DEVELOPMENT

The size of membership of the 12 samitis and the number of villages from which they are drawn vary. The first three organizations formed in 1981 are all multi-village groups. Their membership expanded from 400 in 1981 to 950 in 1988. Most of the later organizations, formed since 1985, are single village groups, formed around a plot of wasteland that had been given to them by local households. Membership of these groups is necessarily much smaller and ranges between 30 and 70 women. But the demonstration effect produced by the success of the plantations suggests that in the coming years these organizations may well expand their acreage as well as membership.

Literacy classes, adult education and child care services have been initiated in some villages. Several of the leaders have now become literate and are able to operate their own bank accounts and record their organizational activities. Two leaders from the oldest organization at Jhilimili have served for a full term of five years (1983–88) as members of their local Panchayat where they have emerged as genuine representatives of poor women's problems and interests.

Over seven years, the Bankura project has evolved from spontaneous group activity to a widespread movement of wasteland reclamation and income generating activities, directly covering 36 villages in two districts.

What is the samities' future?

Samities have received more offers of land, and are now exploring the feasibility of other land-based activities. Perhaps they will use the new patches to create village woodlots or raise mixed plantations with fodder, fuel, fruit, or house-building materials. Enterprises for individual women will certainly increase as their collective resources grow and enhance their revolving funds.

As a natural sequel to the momentum generated by the existing samities, new ones are being formed and others are under discussion in two adjacent districts, Purulia and Medinipur. They might evolve new land-use patterns, and a new set of activities, both for women's groups and for individual members.

We have learnt that actually it is the land that owns the people. We have worked hard to give the land a green cover, and in return it has clothed us with authority. We are advancing together. The journey has begun.

Bankura women are in control of their future. And they are not daunted by the fact that finally they will be wholly responsible for themselves. ●

PARTICIPATORY DEVELOPMENT PLANNING FOR SUSTAINABLE DEVELOPMENT WITH WOMEN'S GROUPS IN KENYA
Corinne Wacker, Zurich University

This study is an example of participatory development planning for sustainable development. It involved women's groups in the Laikipia District, Kenya, in the construction of water tanks to provide a secure water supply. A crucial factor was to achieve this by working with the women to generate knowledge, by adapting assistance to their needs, and by making the ways of collaboration clear to them. The study summarizes the outcome of this method and emphasizes the cultural and gender specific aspects. The participatory method was developed during my study of women's groups in Laikipia from 1986–89, which assisted a Swiss development programme in its co-operation with women's groups.

Historically, Laikipia (a Masai Clan name) was seasonal grazing ground for Masai pastoralists and a natural border to the neighbouring agriculturalists, the Kikuyu. During colonial times, the district belonged to the scheduled areas for British settlers. Since independence (1963) a number of farms were bought, mainly by Kikuyu farmers, and subdivided into small holdings. As it was formerly part of the colonial 'White Highlands',[2] Laikipia's infrastructure has been developed for large-scale farmers' needs. Today the immigrating population faces insecure ecological conditions and the necessity to build schools, roads, water projects, cattle dips, market centres and other infrastructure in collaboration with government in harambee self-help projects.

Many men work in towns outside the district, leaving the main part of farming on their smallholdings to the women. In various areas in Laikipia, more than 50 per cent of the peasant holdings are women-headed households. Besides involving themselves in self-help projects,[3] women also form their own groups of 20–50 neighbours, where they seek common solutions for the many problems they face with farming and household maintenance in a newly settled, ecologically and socially insecure context.

CONSTRUCTING WATER
TANKS WITH WOMEN'S GROUPS
Within a multisectoral programme of the Swiss Development Cooperation for sustainable development in Laikipia, a small side-line activity with women's groups, the construction of roof-catchment ferrocement water tanks to collect the rains developed into a very successful programme. The

examination of the features of the water tank programme leads to generalizations about planning sustainable development with women's groups which exceeded the scope of that specific programme and area. Within four years, 25 groups have built more than 600 ferrocement water tanks to meet domestic needs for water. These tanks each contain 500 gallons, enough water for cleaning, cooking and drinking for two months for a family of six. After some successful results with the first women's groups, the question of how this project would be standardized arose. What were the conditions for a sustainable development? Answers to these and other questions related to the organizational and social conditions of sustainable development were found through a process of participatory research and development planning with women's groups.

WOMEN'S CULTURE:
THE ROOT FOR SUSTAINABLE DEVELOPMENT

To plan sustainable development with women's groups in a participatory way became possible after evaluating the culture of the women and their groups. By the term 'culture', I mean the economic base, organization, knowledge and norms, regulations and authorities within groups.[4] Women have an important role in the informal management of resources,[5] and their main organizations to promote development are the women's groups. It took some time to understand that women's groups in Laikipia have roots in five different traditions, which are interacting today.

The majority of the 316 women's groups in Laikipia are formed by the rural farming population, mostly Kikuyu. Traditionally, both sexes were involved in subsistence production, their work was complementary and largely autonomous. Kikuyu men cleared the virgin forests and prepared the soils and women planted, harvested and prepared the crops.[6] Both women and men

were part of social organizations, based on lineages, clans and age-class sets, in which they co-operated for common concerns. In Laikipia, the eldest women's groups still existing today started some 30 years ago in the swamps which they reclaimed for cultivation. Their basis for co-operation is two Kikuyu traditions: *ngwathio* (a system of collaboration for cultivating and weeding the gardens between neighbouring women, in which once a week each woman receives the help of the others and reciprocates the assistance on equal terms). *Matega* is the tradition of bringing firewood and water to neighbouring women after they have given birth, and receiving the same service in return when in the same situation (systems of reciprocity). These two traditions of co-operation were extended by the women during the colonial period: in demarcated Native Highlands, by agricultural and trading activities, in addition to childcare and household tasks. But women were not involved directly in the modern economy.[7] In 1954 land adjudication (the Swynnerton Plan) in the Native Reserves introduced private ownership of land.[8] Women lost their traditional rights to the land and thereby the security to make a living by subsistence farming for themselves and their children.[9] The loss of security was not compensated by new income-earning possibilities, and poverty became widespread. Overloaded with work, with husbands absent for long periods, and struggling with poverty, women intensified their networks of co-operation. *Ngwathio* and *matega* systems were extended to various situations of need. In Laikipia women's groups formed by very poor people – jobless squatters, who live illegally in the forest or on land belonging to other people – act as crisis networks based on traditional subsistence co-operation; peasant women developed a variety of common projects around the same traditional bonds. The normative basis remained similar: each woman gives

assistance to a distinct group of other women who reciprocate in kind. Group leaders are respected elder women (moral authorities).

The self-organization tradition of women was reshuffled through Community Development policy into authoritarian structures in the 1950s, when, due to widespread poverty, native welfare policy was introduced in Kenya. Women joined *Maendeleo Ya Wanawake Clubs* for handicraft, housewifery and welfare activities.[10] A number of women's groups of Laikipia's large-scale farms still have Maendeleo Club activities today, often under the leadership of women who were trained during the late colonial time. Their rules consist in pooling funds to buy handicraft materials; a skilled, modern leader teaches a new technique to the members, who then produce items. Each member receives individual benefits related to her productivity and bears the financial risk if no customer can be found.

After independence Jomo Kenyatta, first president of Kenya, encouraged women to organize themselves into new women's groups, or *mabati*, to perform traditional dances and develop the country. A number of Maendeleo Clubs in Laikipia changed their names and started new activities. The women pooled funds in their circles mainly to buy land, aiming to become farmers, as their mothers had been before the squatter system and land-adjudication had altered the conditions.[11] During the Women's Decade, women's groups were encouraged to start income-generating projects with credits provided through Special Rural Development Funds and through the Women's Bureau.[12] Although peasant women in Laikipia need an income because job opportunities are scarce and farming is risky due to frequent drought, these income-generating projects failed when the risks were beyond women's control.

Today women's groups have different traditions and different rules, often within the same group. Rules of direct reciprocity and crisis assistance among members are rooted in traditional subsistence farming. Activities for improvement of the infrastructure or for buying land consist in pooling efforts and funds together and creating links towards broader formalized institutions through 'brokers' by providing self-help contributions. Income-generating activities are often built on systems of individual benefits related to the individual productivity. A majority of the groups is involved in several activities simultaneously ranging from an income-generating or household-oriented activity to a credit circle, and from a government-sponsored project to an autonomous self-help enterprise. This allows the women to find means of security in their groups. Peasant women's households face many risks, within an ecological context (rains, soil fertility and erosion), the market and from politics outside women's control. The groups help women to bear risks connected with the insecurities of the modern economy and the ecological risks of a semi-arid area. Apart from their involvement in women's groups, women are under-represented in the institutions at district and national levels that deal with issues that touch women's lives directly.[13]

REASONS FOR
SUCCESS OF THE WATER TANK PROGRAMME

The water tank project was successful because the proposal made was well-suited to the women's groups' control capacities and needs. The water tank programme brought only limited intervention by outsiders, and, once built, the water tanks are under the control of each individual woman. Therefore, group-internal regulations were only adapted to the rules connected with development assistance for a short time (three weeks of collaboration with the technician) and the groups could largely maintain their flexibility in relation to their various traditions and activities in Laikipia. The rule of the donor, that each group-member should receive one water tank, has parallels in the tradition linked to subsistence farming (direct reciprocity), the mode of financing is equal to the tradition of credit circles; problems arising from the fact that 'brokers'[14] create a dependency on outsiders were limited due to the short-term character of the intervention. Some groups manage larger, long-term projects in common, a shop, for example, but in general, as for credit circles, their rules are limited to pooling funds and redistributing them for individual use. In order to acquire some security, women have developed a range of strategies on the economic and political level. The key word is flexibility. The actual water tank construction time was two to three years, until all 20–30 members had their tanks built, but time is linked with poverty – the time cost of one tank is approximately equivalent to eight months of casual labour. Groups also need time to organize themselves, to make rules and control assets within the membership as well as within their local context. Sustainable development is built on the culture of the people. In areas like Laikipia, where men are migrant labourers and women sedentary peasants, and where the administration is not fully organized, sustainable development assistance was successful when built on the basis of the peasant women's work and organizations, when it was integrated in the existing production systems.

Standardization of the water tank programme became possible after a participatory evaluation process, during which all women's groups in a specific area were involved in planning and evaluating the project. The participatory planning started with solving problems in a group. Information was given to the women's groups, and they were helped in solving their problems with their own means.[15] Compared to classical evaluations, which bring knowledge from the people to the donor or government, participatory procedure seeks a dialogue with the women, in which their own capacity to solve problems and find solutions is strengthened. Through participatory evaluation we learned that networking processes of the project are limited. Women are overloaded with work[16] and have neither the means nor the time to travel far to teach water tank construction to other groups. As soon as a project brings influence and income it is likely to escape women's areas of control. The water tank programme was standardized by informing all groups in one area of the aim, scope and conditionalities of the tank construction. The groups could then decide if and when they would like to learn the new technique. Two trained masons travel to their area and teach one group after the other by constructing three tanks with them, afterwards the groups continue to construct tanks themselves and the masons come for periodic visits. Water projects based on the scarce river waters require various ministries to be involved in planning and monitoring on a national scale; they do not include women's participation in decision-making. History shows that women usually lost out when they had to compete for scarce resources and so they could develop only on land not colonized or used by others. In colonial Laikipia, such areas were the swamps, and then in the 1960s the land of former white ranchers became available. Today, natural resources which are not used (yet) by others include the falling rains before they join the rivers, the swamps, trees for bee-keeping, market shops in new centres and so on. Only peasant women, those who were once able to buy land, could construct water tanks on their farms. Squatter women without their own land lack the means to control long-term water projects to meet their needs. In large water projects, for example, dams or river catchments, although women contribute the main self-help labour for their construction, these projects frequently entail technological, financial and political risks, which are beyond women's control. Water is an available resource only when it is culturally accessible to the people: knowledge, means of control and organization, as well as the material requests (money, technology) have to be able to be managed by users in order to provide them with safe water.

SUSTAINABLE DEVELOPMENT AIMS TO REDUCE RISKS AND ENHANCE SECURITY

Although water projects may provide more security against ecological risks, for example, lack of rain, they can introduce new socio-cultural risks, when their planning does not conform to the culture of the people, in a learning process that enables the water-users to effectively manage the project once it is constructed and in use. Participatory development planning starts before the project is worked out. It considers the four elements of culture: the economic basis of the users (the peasant households, for example), their organizations (women's groups, for example), their norms, authorities and means of control as well as their knowledge of the use and maintenance of natural resources. A successful way to plan water projects with women's groups consists in having group discussions with them and by evaluating the water project from the point of view of its use (costs of maintenance, control of technology and decision-making) once it has been built. Only when the means of control for sustainable use are clear and the group decides to realize the project, does the actual planning of the construction start.

Nevertheless, unforeseen risks can arise at any time: ecological risk and socio-cultural risks, which have not been anticipated by the group before starting the construction. Sustainable development can be promoted only through strength in problem-solving. Participatory methods of

planning include the promotion of knowledge and control (decision-making) by the users before the project is technically built. To plan sustainable development, safety is a crucial factor. Women do need the normative, political and participative social control over the technical improvements a programme can provide. ●

GENDER, CLASS AND THE USE OF FOREST RESOURCES: THE CASE OF NEPAL
■■■■ Mary Hobley, Overseas Development Institute

This study is concerned with the human inter-relationship which determine how natural resources are controlled, and the ways in which these relationships are constructed through gender and class. Women as social beings are divided by their class, which determines their control over and access to both natural and social resources. Within classes they are divided by ideological and cultural barriers, by generational differences, and in their relationships to men.[17] Women are oppressed by men through their relationships at the level of households and in the wider economy, as subsistence producers and as part of the Third World rural production system.[18]

FOREST USERS – FOREST DECISION-MAKERS

The study of the interaction between women as forest resource users but not resource decision-makers shows how policies to promote participation of women in forest management must take account of the inter-relationships between women and men, poor and rich. Policies that focus on one group to the exclusion of others cannot promote effective change in access to resources, as appropriate action cannot be taken without understanding the relationships that constrain an individual's access to resources. This case study of forest use and decision-making in a village in the Middle

Hills of Nepal demonstrates how some women are systematically excluded from the decision-making process, but more importantly, how both poor women and poor men are prevented from participating.

Before examining the processes of women's participation in forest decision-making, it is necessary to understand the different relationships which women enter into with other women and men. The position of a woman within a household depends on whether it is her natal or marital home, a joint or nuclear household. This position permeates all her relationships within the household and also determines the way in which her labour is carried out. There is a hierarchy within households, dependent on the age and gender of the individual, which maintains the division between women and men and also the division between women. Women have many roles and relationships within a household that change over time: from woman as daughter, to head of household and wife.

Although there are differences in the division of labour between women within households and between women of different classes, the most striking are those between women and men. For example, planting of permanent resources such as trees on private land is considered to be a man's job; women say that they are unable to plant trees. The daily maintenance of all livestock through the provision of fodder and leaf litter for bedding is the work of younger women and children. Collection of forest products, firewood, grass and leaf litter is considered to be women's work, but cutting firewood with an axe for seasonal use (e.g. the monsoon) is considered to be men's work.

Men are fully dependent on women for collecting grass and dry leaves. Women have more knowledge about forests than men.

(GROUP DISCUSSION WITH WOMEN IN BANGAUN)

The labour involved in collecting forest products is mainly that of women. But not all women are equally dependent on forest resources for the provision of their needs: some wealthier women are able to use the resources from their private trees to supply household needs.

It became apparent in the course of fieldwork that the separation of women from men through the division of labour in forests and agriculture is reflected in the construction of two knowledge systems formed by gender and class. Men dominate the processes of exchange and sale, while women are involved almost exclusively in production for household use. Decision-making and knowledge of decisions within each of these areas are also concentrated in each gender.

This division meant that women were unable to answer questions that required knowledge outside their area of production: they were ignorant of decisions made about rights over resource use, payment of loans or similar matters.

Men were equally ignorant of decisions made by women about production for household use. Generally, the decisions made by women were unlikely to affect their legal/political access to resources. Decisions made by men did, however, directly affect women's physical access to resources.

Men often withheld information from women, whether deliberately or not, so that women were less able than men to control or influence decisions. Women had little understanding of their rights of access to local forests, whereas men generally understood their access rights and were aware of the legal status of the forest; a case of women's labour and men's control.

WOMEN'S LABOUR
VERSUS MEN'S DECISION-MAKING
The conflict between women's use of the forest and men's decision-making function became apparent when women were

brought into the male domain in the interaction of women with men in public meetings initiated by the project. Relations of
dominance between women and men
gained their full expression at these forest
meetings.

A clear description is given by one
woman of the problems that women face
when forced into a situation where they
must interact on an equal level with men:

**The foreigners told the villagers that because
women are the forest users they must also be
members of the forest committee. According to the
foreigners it should be compulsory for women to
attend the meetings. The men agreed to this and
women were allowed to become committee
members. However, women were informed of a
meeting only when a male committee member
chanced to meet them. Even if women attend
meetings they cannot voice their opinions: they
cannot speak against the opinions of their seniors.
When the men have finished speaking that is the
end of the meeting. . . . Men do not tell women
that they cannot speak at the meetings, but the
men do not want to be opposed by women.**

**Also, the women are reluctant to speak out because
they are afraid of making mistakes; they think that
people will laugh at them. . . . The important thing
is that men should realize the importance of
women's views regarding forest management. The
problem cannot be solved by outsiders imposing
such ideas on the men. If the men wish to dominate
women then that is what will happen.**

SAMA CHETRI, 1987; HIGH CASTE WOMAN

Women's lack of knowledge and involvement in the local level decison-making processes led to their intimidation at meetings.
One woman said that if women speak out at
meetings the 'men will say that the hen has
started crowing' (Kaki Ghimire, 1987, high
caste woman). One man commented on the
role of women in forest meetings and
indicated how he perceived the relationships between women and men with refer-

ence to decision-making:

**There are women on the committee:
there is one woman from every
household. Whether women are called
to meetings or not depends on the
amount of work at home. They are
called to the meeting if their
participation in the meetings is
urgent. . . . Calling all the women to
the meeting just hampers the work of
the agenda because discussion is not
substantial. . . . It is true that women
are the real users of the forest but our
women have not yet participated in the
meetings. They don't know much, they
can't give solid opinions. Let me tell you
one thing, I am a man. I attend the
meeting. If I am prepared to make the
female members of my family act
according to what I say, why should they
attend the meeting?**

BAHADUR CHETRI, 1987, HIGH CASTE MAN

Women's lack of access to knowledge about
decisions taken concerning the resources
they use transcends class divisions, and the
following sentiment was expressed by both
wealthy and poor women: 'There should be
a separate women's meeting because men
don't tell us anything' (Sobha Chetri, 1987,
high caste woman).

The relationships which construct
women's reality also dictate their exclusion
from decisions which control their access to
forest resources:

**Women do not know about forest
committees. Since women don't
understand about meetings they cannot
participate. . . . I don't know how to
speak at meetings. I want nothing to do
with forest committees – only men go to
meetings.**

KANCHI CHETRI, 1987, HIGH CASTE WOMAN

But women as a group are not homogeneous, some women were able to participate more actively in forestry meetings. Young unmarried women from wealthy households spoke out at forest meetings, whereas young married women from the same households did not. Similarly, women who have attained the highest status within their households, as wives to the household head, or are free of familial restraints, for example widows, are also more assertive amongst a mixed group of women and men. Daughters-in-law did not participate in forest meetings and when I asked them why they were silent, they said they were embarrassed to speak in front of their husbands. A woman's role within a Hindu household is defined by the need to maintain and enhance ritual purity. Woman as wife is ritually inferior to her husband. The deference which a wife must present to her husband continues through all aspects of her life and is expressed explicitly in the public arena through the women's embarrassed silence in meetings and non-participation in village decision-making.

Despite the fact that some women did speak out at forest meetings, women considered that their participation with men on forest committees was problematic because, previously, such committees were organized by male village leaders and not open to women:

It hadn't been decided by the village to put women on the committee. It was decided later when people from above came to the village. . . . The village leaders and male members of the village used to get together and hold meetings. Women were not involved.
SAMA AND SHYANGARI CHETRI, 1987,
HIGH CASTE WOMEN

Even though some men consider the participation of women as unnecessary, and some women as impossible, women accept that collection of forest products, and there-fore the need for forests, is mainly their responsibility:

Men don't care about the forest. They go to the teashop drink tea and talk, that's all they do. Women cook food and feed them. . . . Men don't have to cook so they don't have any concern about the forest. . . . It is women who need the forest. They need firewood to cook. Women can't advise men, even if they do the men don't listen to women. . . . Men preach to women about not cutting trees, but what can women do? they cannot cook food without firewood and they cannot collect firewood from other places.
GROUP DISCUSSION WITH WOMEN IN PALCHAGAUN, 1986

THE PRACTICE OF CLASS RELATIONS

As has been shown, gender relationships which determine the labour expended in the collection of forest products and access to forests also determine access to decision-making about forest use. Class relationships have similar determining effects. Men from wealthy households dominated forest meetings held in the villages. A man from a poor household describes how he perceives the relations between rich and poor in these forest meetings:

At meetings, the big [wealthy] people speak. How can they allow the poor people to speak? If they [the rich people] see that they can make money they come forward. They don't listen to the poor . . . The poor can never be happy. If they stand and speak the wind blows their sound away. If they sit and speak no one can hear them. The situation is never favourable.
THULO KAMI, LOW CASTE MAN

CONCLUSIONS

Although women's labour transfers forest products to the household, men's control over decision-making determines the future use of forest resources by women. Underlying this difference lies that between wealthy women and poor women and men. In the case of poor women and men, who have insufficient land available to release for tree-planting, local forests are the only source of forest products. In this case decisions made by wealthy men restricting access to local forests militated against those households with no private trees.

Given the constraints under which women and poor people operate in the public arena, to hold mixed meetings to discuss the use and control of local forests could not produce a representative view of forest-user needs. The conflict between women's needs to maintain the daily reproduction of the household and men's longer-term use of forest products could not be reconciled without extended periods of sensitive negotiation.

The challenge for forestry lies in the provision of skilled facilitators able to bring together divergent forest-user groups who are often divided on class and gender lines. Thus, training and reorientation of forestry departments and forestry training institutions and universities lies at the core of this process.

This study of forest use and forest decision-making demonstrates how class and patriarchal structures limit individuals' access to and control over forests. I therefore endorse Westoby's exhortation[19] as the way ahead for a social forestry where people are seen as individuals whose relationships with natural and social environments are constructed by the universal categories of class and gender:

Forestry is not about trees, it is about women and men, poor and rich. And it is about trees only in so far as trees can serve the needs of women and men, poor and rich.[20]

Certainly, progress will be made only when the people are able to speak of their needs and action can be facilitated to ensure the security of meeting these needs. ●

STRATEGIES FOR PLANNING AND SOME RESEARCH ISSUES*

■ Mary Boesveld, Leiden University, The Netherlands

Previous chapters have made abundantly clear that women are key actors in the struggle against environmental degradation and related issues. There is therefore an obvious need to address women directly in projects and programmes concerning this struggle.

However, the way to do this is not always apparent. What, in any given situation, are the crucial factors which determine the possibilities for women to participate in the struggle in a meaningful way? What are their needs, motivations and constraints? How can their knowledge and experience be taken into account, and how can they be involved in planning and decision-making?

The following overview considers the strategies concerning planning with women for sustainable development and wise use of natural resources. It also outlines some important research issues relevant to women's participation.

STRATEGIES
Participatory approaches
Although most development policy and planning still relies on solutions devised in Western centres of knowledge and expertise, over the past few years there has been an increasing emphasis on the importance of participatory approaches. This entails the direct involvement of the communities concerned in all aspects of development activities. Sustainable development requires participation of the people in the following three areas: 1) in diagnosing the problem; 2) in designing and planning improvements and solutions; and 3) in using and evaluating them.[21] The long-term success of many projects may be much more dependent on this type of direct participation than had previously been realized.

In particular, with regard to combating environmental degradation and establishing sustainable and wise use of natural resources, it is crucial to ensure that women, as key actors, can support the activities and will be motivated for implementation and long-term sustainability.

There are some handbooks and guidelines available on participatory approaches for various development activities.[22] These methods need to be assessed carefully, and then adapted to specific situations and problems.

The following paragraphs set out some of the main issues. Unlike the typical scenario where a development agency introduces solutions and then tries to persuade the target group to participate, participatory methods assume the concept of an aid–recipient relationship.[23] In this way, both the expert and the women concerned are seen as active agents of change, working together to solve environmental problems on the basis of a mutual sharing and exchange of knowledge, information, expertise and experiences as partners in a continuous dialogue.

Carrying out a base-line study at the beginning of a project or programme offers the first opportunity to start the dialogue. In the course of the project, some degree of regular self-evaluation helps in sorting out problems and seeking improvements. There are several guidelines on partnership in evaluation which could easily be adapted to other kinds of research in support of development activities.[24]

In training activities, a partnership approach can be used to build upon women's indigenous knowledge and revive and strengthen traditional skills. Local experts and extension workers can be trained in participatory approaches.

Development activities with a partnership approach need more time and effort than traditional approaches and consequently cost more money. This should be taken into account in proposals and budgeting for projects and programmes.

Gender Policy

All development activities, particularly those aimed at introducing sustainable use of natural resources and finding solutions for environmental problems, should be gender aware.

This means awareness of gender differences in interest, motivation, and perception of benefits, based on different tasks, responsibilities and access to resources. Furthermore, women and men have distinct domains of knowledge.

Throughout this book, it has been shown that survival tasks, providing the basic needs of the family, are largely women's responsibility. Environmental degradation makes it increasingly difficult to cope, and because they are hit first and hardest, women may also be the most highly motivated group to mobilize for the promotion of sustainable use of natural resources. It is, however, important for them to be helped gain some control of the resources they are using, and for their knowledge and expertise to be taken seriously.

Currently, gender awareness in development policy is often translated into separate projects for women, or into a special 'women's component' added to a larger project or programme. Some of these women's projects are quite well-organized and successful,[25] many suffer from limited financial and technical resources, isolation, and generally problems with continuation after external (donor) funding and support is stopped.[26]

For gender-aware development activities aimed at promoting sustainable use of natural resources, a careful assessment is needed of the local gender structure and ideology, in order to define the most appropriate policy. In some situations a separate project for women may be the best solution, but in those cases special efforts are necessary to prevent isolation and marginalization, and to provide sufficient funding and technical support as a means towards achieving long-term sustainability. Where possible, however, an approach that promotes the participation of women and men alike might have advantages. In those cases, special care should be taken to acknowledge women's expertise and their key role in the management of natural resources. It might also be necessary to help women in taking up leadership roles and support their empowerment. Such a project may not be easy to support, but a partnership approach treating both women and men equally, and with whom different options and solutions can openly be discussed, might help to solve problems.

As for development policy, women's organizations are generally considered to have an important role in supporting women's participation, strengthening decision-making, and ensuring long-term sustainability of development activities. For any project or programme it is important to ascertain the existence of a national or local organization, or movement, for promoting women's empowerment or their involvement in development efforts. Such an organization may also be mobilized generally to promote sustainable development and wise use of natural resources, and it could continue to support these efforts after the project has terminated.

Another aspect of gender policy is the engagement of local women experts and staff in the team of project workers on an equal basis with men. This will not only facilitate working with women on the project, but also underline the fact that women are taken seriously and generally promote their participation.

RESEARCH ISSUES

An understanding of problems of environmental degradation requires a complex combination of research into ecosystems and natural processes on the one hand and social structures and processes on the other. It is not possible to examine all the complexities of the interdisciplinary approach, but emphasis is given to those aspects which are particularly relevant to the issues raised in this book.

Rural women

The importance of women's contribution to the production of food and the provision of other basic needs is now routinely mentioned in development policy and planning, but often without a realistic assessment of women's work, their needs, motivations and constraints. Also, very little systematic information is available about differences in women's and men's access to resources and their different use of natural resources in various ecosystems. An exception is the study by Elizabeth Cecelski for the ILO.[27]

The relationship between environmental degradation, hunger and poverty, and women's tasks and access to natural resources, should be systematically investigated for different ecosystems. Questions relating to land rights and land use may be very important for projects and programmes aimed at sustainable use of natural resources in, for example, agro-forestry.

Urban women

There is relatively little research data available on women living in cities. Information is urgently needed on how women cope with waste disposal; water and air pollution; food, fuel and water shortages; general environmental health problems; and health problems related to working conditions.

Attention should also be paid to the informal networks and mutual support systems, as well as formal organizations, which women in poor neighbourhoods set up among themselves for mutual support and to improve their living conditions.[28] These networks and organizations may provide an excellent base for the introduction of improvements in the environment.

Population

Population policy and population control have always involved much debate, particularly with the increasing environmental degradation and decline of natural resources.[29] The possibility to plan wanted children should be considered as a basic human right, especially for women. In this regard, issues of birth control and family planning should be investigated in relation to women's other tasks and responsibilities. Research should focus initially on possibilities for women to increase their freedom of movement and range of choices through family planning.

Migration

In many cases migration might be directly or indirectly related to environmental degradation. More systematic investigation into this issue is needed, taking into account gender differences in migration patterns.

A special case is the increasing number of refugee camps, which generally have a disastrous effect on the environment. The demands for fuel and the attempts to grow subsistence crops can lead to large-scale environmental degradation in the area around the camps.[30] In such a situation of desperation research may be difficult; if possible, it should focus on alternative means of survival, in relation to a more sustainable use and management of natural resources.

Knowledge

The modernization of agriculture, with mechanization, extensive irrigation and the introduction of hybrid crop species has marginalized women's traditional knowledge of and experience in the use and management of natural resources. Development efforts rarely take people's knowledge into account, and certainly not women's expertise in such areas as soil conditions, seeds, crop varieties, and appropriate agricultural methods. Equally overlooked is women's expertise in water and fuel supplies.[31]

Related to knowledge are people's ideas about 'the nature of nature'. Cultural ideas and values determine the perceptions and attitudes of women and men towards the natural environment. Investigation into people's, and particularly women's, knowledge, expertise and cultural values, should be a common feature of any project or programme aimed at sustainable development.

EVALUATION OF DEVELOPMENT POLICY AND APPROACHES

In order to increase our knowledge of the appropriateness of development efforts in general, and specific approaches towards sustainable development and women's participation as outlined here, there should also be a continuous analysis of the policy and the methods adopted. Systematic investigations into the use of different participatory approaches, in varying circumstances, and into the successes and failures of different types of projects with women will certainly provide a means for avoiding inappropriate development policy and improving approaches. ●

1 Kamara, J.N. (1986) *Firewood Energy in Sierre Leone: Production, Marketing and Household Use Patterns*, Hamburg, Verlag Weltarchiv.

2 van Zwanenberg, R.M.A. and King, A. (1975) *An Economic History of Kenya and Uganda 1800–1970*, London, Macmillan.

3 Thomas, Barbara (1988) 'State Formation, Development, and the Politics of Self-help in Kenya', in *Studies in Comparative International Development*, vol. XXIII, no. 3, Eastern Michigan University.

4 Wacker, Corinne (1990) 'Sozio-kulturelle Nachhaltigkeit von Wasserprojekten, Nachhaltige soziale Prozesse und

die Nachhaltigkeit von Selbsthilfeprojecten', *Aquasan*, SKAT St Gallen, Switzerland.

5 Mackenzie, Fiona (1986) 'Local Initiatives and National Policy: Gender and Agricultural Changes in Muranga District, Kenya', *Canadian Journal of African Studies*.

6 Kenyatta, Jomo (1956) *Facing Mount Kenya. The Tribal Life of the Kikuyu*, London; Routledge, W. and K. Scoresby (1968) *With the Prehistoric People; the Akikuyu of British East Africa*, London.

7 Stichter, Sharon (1982) *Migrant Labour in Kenya. Capitalism and African Response 1895–1975*, London, Longman.

8 Sorrenson, M.P.K. (1967) *Land Reform in the Kikuyu Country: A Study of Government Policy*, Nairobi.

9 Byamukama, James (1985) *Land Law Reform and Women's Property Rights in Land in Kenya*, African Rights Research Association, Toronto; Davidson, Jean (1987). 'Without Land we are Nothing: the Effect of Land Tenure Policies and Practices upon Rural Women in Kenya', *Rural Africa 27*, Winter, Michigan State University.

10 Wipper, Audrey, 'The Maendeleo Ya Wanawake Movement in the Colonial Period: the Canadian Connection, Mau Mau, Embroidery and Agriculture', *Rural Africana*, 29 Winter 1975–76.

11 Maas, Maria (1986) *Women's Groups in Kiambu, Kenya*, research report no. 26, African Studies Centre, Leiden, The Netherlands; Wachtel, Eleanor, 'A Farm on One's Own: the Rural Orientation of Women's Groups Enterprises in Nakuru, Kenya', *Rural Africana* 29, Winter 1975–76.

12 ILO (1986) *Women's Employment Patterns, Discrimination and Promotion of Equality in Africa*, Geneva, International Labour Office.

13 Central Bureau of Statistics (1978) *Women in Kenya*, Nairobi; Staudt, Kathleen (1985) *Agricultural Policy Implementation: a Case Study from Western Kenya*, Kumarian Press.

14 Maas, Maria, op. cit.

15 Wacker, C., B. Meier (1990) 'Partizipative Methoden in der Entwicklungszusammenarbeit', *Wo sind die Fraun? Frauenforschung und Frauenforderung in der Entwicklungszusammenarbeit*, Ethnologische Arbeitsgruppe Fraun und Entwicklung Zurich (ed.), Zurich.

16 Abbott, S. (1974) 'Full-time Farmers and Week-End Wives: Change and Stress among Rural Kikuyu Women, PhD thesis, University of North Carolina, USA; Smock, Audrey Chapman (1987) 'Women's Economic Roles', in Killik, T. *Papers on the Kenyan Economy*, Nairobi.

17 Caplan, A.P. and J. Bura (eds) (1978) *Women United. Women Divided*, London, Tavistock Publications.

18 Vuorela, U. (1987) *The Women's Question and the Modes of Human Reproduction; an analysis of a Tanzanian Village*, Helsinki: Monographs of the Finnish Society for Development Studies No. 1.

19 Westoby, J.C. (1987) *The Purpose of Forests: Follies of Development*, Oxford, Basil Blackwell.

20 Hobley, M.E. (1990) 'Social Reality, Social Forestry: the case of two Nepalese panchayats', unpublished PhD thesis, Australian National University, Canberra.

21 Matlon, P. (1984) *Coming Full Circle: Farmers' Participation in the Development of Technology*, Ottawa, International Development Research Centre.

22 UNICEF/UNFPA (1985) *Manual for Fieldworkers*, New York, United Nations Childrens Fund; *A Resource Book on Community Development* (1985) Oslo, Redd Barna.

23 Stamp, Patricia (1989) *Technology, Gender and Power in Africa*, Ottawa, International Development Research Centre.

24 Fuerstein, Marie-Therese (1980) *Partners in Evaluation, Evaluating Development and Community Programme with Participants*, London, Macmillan; Naranan-Parker, Deepa (1990) *Participatory Evaluation: Tools for Managing Change in Water and Sanitation*, New York, PROWWESS/UNDP.

25 Mantemba, Shimwaayi (ed.) (1985) *Rural Development and Women: Lessons from the Field*, vols. 1 & 2, Geneva, International Labour Office.

26 Buvinic, Mayra (1984) *Project for Women in the Third World: Explaining their Misbehaviour*, Washington, International Center for Research on Women.

27 Cecelski, Elizabeth (1985) *The Rural Energy Crisis: Women's Work and Basic Needs*: Perspectives and Approaches for Action, Geneva. International Labour Office; ILO (1987) *Linking Energy with Survival*, Geneva, International Labour Office.

28 Muller, M.S. and D. Plantenga (1990) *Women and Habitat. Urban Management, Empowerment and Women's Strategies*, Amsterdam, Royal Tropical Institute.

29 World Commission on Environment and Development (1963) *Our Common Future*, Oxford, New York, Oxford University Press; Schrader-Frechette, K.S. (1981) *Environmental Ethics*, Pacific Grove CA, Boxwood Press.

30 Cecelski (1985) and ILO (1987) op.cit.

31 Shiva, Vandana (1989) *Staying Alive: Women, Ecology and Development*, London, Zed Books Ltd, and Delhi, Kali for Women.

ANNEX I
DEFINITIONS
OF KEY TERMS*

acid rain. Term used to describe fall-out of industrial pollutants, sometimes literally as acidified rainfall and sometimes as dry deposition. Most of these pollutants come from burning fossil fuels or from vehicle exhausts. Acid rain damages trees, crops and plants; acidifies lakes, rivers and groundwater; and corrodes buildings.

biogas. A methane-rich gas produced by the fermentation of animal dung and human dung, or crop residues, and used as fuel or as fertilizer in many developing countries.

biomass. Scientific term used to describe the dry animal and plant matter found on the face of the planet.

biotechnology. A generic term for those technologies that seek to use living organisms (or parts of) to modify existing forms of life or to generate new life; the application of biological organisms, systems or processes to industry.

chlorofluorocarbons (CFCs). Chlorine-based compounds used as aerosol propellants, refrigerants, coolants, sterilents, solvents and in the production of foam packaging used by the fast-food industry. CFCs are environmentally dangerous on two accounts: they are greenhouse gases, trapping the earth's radiation before it can escape into space, and thus heating the planet through the 'greenhouse effect'; they also release chlorine as they break down, which reacts with ozone and destroys the ozone layer above the earth.

desertification. The term used to describe the increase of desert land as a result of human activity.

ecosystem. A community of organisms and their inter-related physical and chemical environment. It can apply equally to a geographical area of land or ocean, or to the entire planet.

genetic engineering. The transfer of genes between organisms of different species.

greenhouse effect. Growing levels of carbon dioxide and other gases in the atmosphere which form a blanket around the earth, holding in much of the solar radiation which would otherwise escape into space.

over-grazing. The overstocking of land with grazing stock can all but eliminate plant cover, particularly when the animals are clustered in small areas, such as a waterhole, or kept on the same land for a long period. Eventually the land is laid bare. The soil is then vulnerable to erosion and ultimately desertification.

ozone layer. A layer of pale blue gas in the earth's stratosphere, which protects us from the ultraviolet radiation from the sun.

salinization. When land is too salty to support plant life it is said to be salinized. Salinization occurs when the delicate salt balance of the soil is upset, thus allowing salts to build up in the root zone of crops or, worse still, to form a saline crust on the surface.

soil erosion. Dispersal of soil due to the action of wind and rain.

sustainable development. As outlined by the Brundtland Commission, sustainable development is: 'development that meets the needs of the present without compromising the ability of future generations to meet their own needs'.

---

* Adapted from: *Renewing the Earth*, Seamus Cleary, CAFOD.

ANNEX II
A GUIDE TO EDUCATION AND ACTION

THIS BOOK PROVIDES a basis for study and further activities. The main text provides information on a range of issues and topics related to women, environment and development, which can be studied in greater depth by following up the specific references at the end of each chapter. Further information can be obtained from the sources listed in the Bibliography and the organizations detailed in Annex III. The book can also be used as a guide at the practical level. The case studies provided in Chapter 6 are examples of what can be done in particular circumstances, and could serve as models for future projects, especially with regard to people participation. The section on strategies for planning (Chapter 6) is also of use to those involved in the more practical aspects of development policy.

Another important area of study/activity is participation in discussions and meetings. This Annex contains some guidelines on organizing such meetings and gives examples of how the material available in the book can be utilized.

The gathering together of a group of people, some experts, others seeking knowledge, in either a formal or informal structure, with an exchange of ideas and information, and discussions leading to conclusions and action can be a valuable exercise. There are three main types of gathering: a one-day (or half-day) meeting; the more ambitious seminar; and the workshop, which is usually of a more specific and practical nature. In all cases thorough advanced planning is essential, taking into account the target audience, the venue, facilities available, and so on. There should be a well-defined purpose, an agenda and timetable and a competent person in charge who can lead and guide discussions.

The Guidelines for Planning and Conducting a Seminar provide a useful checklist and can be adapted to smaller, less formal meetings.

GUIDELINES FOR PLANNING AND CONDUCTING A SEMINAR

1. Be sure about the purpose of the seminar.

2. Organize speakers/experts well in advance to give them time to prepare for the seminar and their papers on particular topics.

3. Arrange advance media coverage if you wish to have the purpose of the seminar made known publicly. Invite the media to cover the seminar if you want the message and outcome made known to a wider audience.

4. Select a skilled chairperson who can gauge when to adjourn or to break up into group discussions.

5. Identify resource people who can act as group discussion leaders and rapporteurs who will write down the main ideas. In the absence of skilled rapporteurs some advance training is recommended to ensure that group discussions are adequately reflected in the plenary session or in the final report.

6. Select participants according to the objectives of the seminar. Ask them to bring their experiences in written form, pictures or on tapes, for use in the workshop sessions.

7. Choose an environment appropriate to the seminar topic, for example, at the vil-

lage level if related to the rural poor.

8. Provide basic facilities and ensure adequate working space as well as secretarial and clerical support for participants.

9. Consider the use of audio-visual material – tapes, slides, charts – as tools to provide the focus for discussion.

10. Have a definite schedule prepared to present to participants and stress that the goals be achieved within that time-scale.

11. As an introduction, arrange an informal session to allow participants to become acquainted. This will encourage a relaxed atmosphere and free exchange of views.

12. At the commencement of the seminar, make the purpose clear to the participants.

13. The organizer should have some idea of the anticipated outcome and be prepared to intervene and state this.

14. Do not overtax participants, particularly on the first day. Allow adequate time for private study and social activities.

15. To maintain interest and alertness, plan a range of approaches – practical exercises, simulated games, 'brainstorming', breaking into small groups, etc.

16. Ensure ongoing evaluation and feedback to participants.

17. Allow flexibility according to what evolves in the course of the seminar and do not rule out any alternatives.

18. Try to overcome cultural barriers through observation and sensitivity.

19. Follow up the seminar with analysis and evaluation.
Source: Asian and Pacific Centre for Women and Development

The environment is a subject area which embraces many topics, and a meeting on an environmental topic lends itself to active participation.

Everyone is affected by the environment, and has some experience of environmental problems, for example: the local water supply; health in the home and working environment; changes affecting the surroundings, involving issues such as loss of trees, or disposal of garbage.

THE ONE-DAY MEETING

This type of gathering should be centred on a presentation delivered by an expert speaker or speakers, and should follow a set format.

For the time available, it is better to select one particular topic or issue relating to women and the environment. The programme can be adapted to suit the type and number of participants, whether it is for members of a group or organization, or for a wider audience. The total number of participants should ideally be in the region of 20 to 50.

General plan for a one-day meeting

Examples of suitable subjects: Women and Water; Women as Consumers; Women and Natural Resources; the Local Environment.

1. **Welcome**: Participants should be informed of the details of the programme, including timing of sessions and breaks.

2. **Environmental awareness exercise**: This is optional, but it is a useful way of involving the participants from the beginning, and it enables them to focus on the subject of the meeting. It can be in the form of a simple questionnaire, either on the environment in general or on the specific subject for the meeting. For example, participants can be asked to list (or think of) three negative aspects of their local environment (environmental problems), and three

positive aspects. Another idea, using this book, is to ask participants to list the global environmental issues (Chapter 2) in the order of importance from their individual point of view.

3. **Introduction to the subject**: Fact sheets can be prepared in advance using extracts from the book. Other information could include copies of recent newspaper articles highlighting relevant local or national issues. A short video could also be shown.

4. **Speaker(s) on the subject**: Speakers should be experts on the subject, preferably with practical experience and/or personal involvement.

5. **Discussion**.

6. **Recommendations and ideas for action**.

Using this basic plan, the following is an example of a meeting on a specific topic, Women and Water, giving reference to use of the book and other suggestions.

One-day meeting on women and the environment: women and water

The meeting room/entrance hall should have visual displays of photographs, posters, and so on, showing women carrying water, using water, health and hygiene, pictures of water, and lack of water – rivers, rain, drought and so on.

1. **Welcome**.

2. **Environmental Awareness**: Participants could list the different ways they use water during one day.

3. **Introduction to subject**: Fact sheets: extracts from the following chapters could be used: Chapter 2 – section on water; Chapter 3 – Women as Water Collectors, include A Day in the Life of Aling Maring; Chapter 4 – Basic needs – reference to water; Chapter 5 – from section Women

Working to Improve the Environment – The SWACH Project.

If relevant to the meeting, one of the case studies (Chapter 6) involving women and water supply could be included.

4. **Speaker(s)**: For example, representative from local or national government water service; health official; expert involved in water projects.

5. **Discussion**: Encourage participants to contribute by explaining their local problems.

6. **Recommendations and ideas for action**:
- Prepare guidelines for safe water use;
- Prepare guidelines for conserving water;
- Carry out an investigation into sources of pollution of local water supply;
- Organize campaign against water pollution.

THE SEMINAR

Seminars consist of several sessions over several days. They usually have a more formal structure and aim to produce a document with specific recommendations. A seminar is best suited for between 30 and 50 participants and is usually divided into plenary sessions, attended by everyone, and smaller working groups. A panel of invited experts is a good way of stimulating discussion. At the end of the seminar, definite conclusions should be framed, including a written report and recommendations for action.

THE WORKSHOP

A workshop differs from the previous gatherings in that it is more practical and action oriented. It is designed for a small number of participants (no more than 15), each making their own contribution to the discussions and action. The emphasis

PLAN FOR A SEMINAR

	First day	Second day	Third day	Fourth day	Fifth day
09.00–10.30	—	Introductory lecture on the Environment as a Global Issue	Speakers (experts) on three topics relating to Women and the Environment (possible topics: water, energy, farmers, urban environment)	Presentation of reports from the three Working Groups, followed by discussion	Presentation of Plans for Action. Discussion
10.30–11.00 (*coffee/tea*)	—				
11.00–12.30	—	Women, Environment and Development Lecture and discussion	Working Groups on each of the three topics	Continued	Conclusions: Adoption of Recommendations
12.30 (*lunch*)	—				
14.30	**Arrival of participants, registration**	Women and Environmental Problems (range of topics) Panel and discussion	Women as Agents of Change Panel and discussion	Working Groups on action: Policy Responses Grass-roots	Continue if necessary Closure of seminar
16.30–17.00 (*coffee/tea*)	—				
17.00	**Welcoming addresses, introduction of participants**	Reception	Working Groups complete reports	Working Groups complete reports	
18.30	**Introduction to the seminar (film/s)**				
19.30 (*dinner*)	—				

should be on an exchange of ideas and experiences directed towards achieving a specific goal. This type of activity could be particularly useful in providing an opportunity for those with practical experience of working with women in the environment to meet and discuss the issues involved and to recommend possible solutions.

Plan for a workshop (of one to three days)

A workshop should be informal, but there should still be a timetable and it is very important to have a skilled, experienced moderator in control of the proceedings, and to allow sufficient time for the conclusions of the workshop.

1. **Welcome**: Introduction to the subject. Purpose of workshop, setting out targets to be achieved.

2. **Presentations by participants to be followed by discussions**.

3. **Conclusions**: report, recommendations, agreement on code of practice.

IDEAS FOR ACTION

There are many ways in which an individual or a group can be actively involved in making a positive contribution to the environment. This can be achieved in the home, by wise use of resources such as fuel, whether it is firewood or electricity. In the community, action can be taken on unsightly litter or garbage dumps, and recycling campaigns can be organized (see Box below).

It is useful to investigate the planning mechanisms, local and national, so that individuals and groups know the ways in which possible action can be taken. Another means of involvement is through national and international environmental organizations and movements.

It is also very important to make contact with those who have influence and power, in international organizations and in national governments, so that they are aware of the relevance of women in relation to environment and development, and of the issues concerning the environment presented in this book.

SCRAP NEWSPAPER COLLECTION CAMPAIGN IN HONG KONG

Foreword

The overuse of paper is a serious problem in Hong Kong. According to 1988 statistics from Environmental Protection Department, waste paper is the second largest sector of household waste out of 4,600 tons of solid waste generated per day. Hence, the promotion of paper recycling is necessary.

In response to this phenomenon, the Hong Kong Earth Day Organizing Committee organized the Scrap Newspaper Collection Campaign on 8 April 1990. The campaign was co-ordinated by the Conservancy Association – Hong Kong Environment Centre, a member of the organizing committee. In the campaign; 48 community organizations and 70 primary and secondary schools have collected 159 tons of scrap newspaper in two weeks' time. Hence 600 tons of pulp was saved in the process of paper-making.

Aims

(1) To encourage citizens to participate in scrap newspaper collection and recycling.

(2) To illustrate the delicate inter-relationship between paper recycling and environmental protection, and

(3) To provide possible channels for scrap newspaper collection and recycling.

Programme Schedule

26 February
Sending of invitation letters to community organizations and children and youth centres.
7 March
Deadline of application for community organizations.
17 March
Two working committees for the 48 participating community organizations. Publicize in the Professional Teachers' Union's Newspaper to invite schools to participate.
24 March
Deadline of application for schools.
26–31 March
Scrap Newspaper Collection in schools.
2–8 April
Scrap Newspaper Collection in community organizations.

2–10 April
Transportation of newspaper from schools and community organizations for recycling.

22 April
Presentation of souvenir to community organization and school collecting most paper on the Earth Day Carnival.

A gift counter was set up during the Earth Day Carnival to distribute gifts to citizens who had donated 10kg of newspaper to collection centres.

18–25 April
Evaluation in community organizations.

23–28 April
Evaluation in schools.

12–16 May
Packing and transportation of souvenir to 70 schools.

21 May–15 June
Information gathering for the report.

1–31 July
Printing and distribution of report.

Programme Detail

Date:
8 April 1990 (Sunday)

Participating Organizations:
Social services organizations and local organizations are invited to join the programme.

Participating Details:
(1) Organizations are required to publicize the programme in their locality.
All promotional items will be supplied by the Earth Day Organizing Committee.

(2) Organizations should decide their collection time and venue.

(3) Organizations should assign staff or volunteers to collect, record and deliver coupon to citizens who donate newspaper to the organization.

(4) The Earth Day Organizing Committee will make transport arrangements for delivery of newspaper within one to four days after the campaign.

Programme Details:
(1) Only scrap newspaper will be collected

(2) The collected newspaper should be clean and tied with ropes.

Gifts and Souvenirs:
(1) For every 10kg of newspaper, donated by citizens, a gift coupon will be given. With this coupon, citizens may obtain a souvenir in Earth Day 1990 Carnival.

(2) Souvenir packs will be delivered to each participating organizations

(3) Winners in the campaign will be awarded souvenirs at the Earth Day 1990 Carnival.

Application:
Please complete the application form and send to the Earth Day Organizing Committee on or before 7 March 1990 (GPO Box 167, HK). For further enquiries, please contact Miss Echo LAI at 8155805.

Promotion Material
Scrap newspaper
can be used to wrap our
rubbish, to start fire in BBQ.
Do you know that, a pile of waste
paper can be transformed into a pile
of money $$$$?

The total amount of solid waste ▶

generated by domestic households per day is 4,600 tons, in which waste paper is the second largest sector among all wastes. The waste paper is either dumped in landfill sites or burned in incinerators, or exported to South-East Asian countries at a relatively low price. Meanwhile, a local waste paper manufacturer has to import shipments of waste paper with high transportation costs from foreign countries.

Do you think that this phenomenon is rather ridiculous? The fact is that Hong Kong citizens do not have a clear concept of waste classification. In many other foreign countries like Japan, Canada and America, their citizens are used to separating wastes into different categories: waste paper, plastic bags, bottles, etc. Through simple classification, these countries have surplus waste returnables for export, but in Hong Kong, we are still dumping these resources into our landfill sites and incinerators.

Who can modify this situation? You, as an ordinary citizen, can help very much.

Please put your scrap newspaper on your shelves and donate them to a nearby collection centre on 8 April 1990 – Scrap Newspaper Collection Campaign, your waste paper can be channelled for recycling and become recycled paper. A gift coupon will be given to you for every 10kg of newspaper sent.

Please take note of the collection time in your district; please join the Scrap Newspaper Collection Campaign. We are in urgent need of your participation.

Report on Scrap Newspaper Collection Campaign
Earth Day (Hong Kong)

ANNEX III
LIST OF
ORGANIZATIONS

UNITED NATIONS SYSTEM

Food and Agriculture Organization (FAO), Via delle Terme di Caracalla, I-00100 Rome, Italy.

International Fund for Agricultural Development (IFAD), Via del Serafico 107, I-00142 Rome, Italy.

International Labour Organization (ILO), 4 chemin des Morillons, CH-1211 Geneva 22, Switzerland.

United Nations Children's Fund (UNICEF), 3 United Nations Plaza, New York, NY 10017, USA; *also* Palais des Nations, CH-1211 Geneva 10, Switzerland.

United Nations Centre for Human Settlements (HABITAT), UN Office at Nairobi, PO Box 30030, Nairobi, Kenya; *also* DC-2 Room 946, United Nations, New York, NY 10017; *also* Palais des Nations, CH-1211 Geneva 10, Switzerland.

United Nations Development Fund for Women (UNIFEM), 304 E 45th St, 6th floor, New York, NY 10017, USA.

United Nations Development Programme (UNDP), 1 United Nations Plaza, New York, NY 10017, USA; *also* UNDP European Office, Palais des Nations, CH-1211 Geneva 10, Switzerland.

United Nations Educational, Scientific and Cultural Organization (UNESCO), 7 place de Fontenoy, F-75700 Paris, France.

United Nations Environment Programme (UNEP), PO Box 30552, Nairobi, Kenya; *also* (Liaison and Regional Office), Palace des Nations, CH-1211 Geneva 10.

United Nations Population Fund (UNFPA), 220 E. 42nd Street, New York, NY 10017, USA; *also* UNFPA Liaison Office, Palais des Nations, CH-1211 Geneva 10, Switzerland.

United Nations Research Institute for Social Development (UNRISD), Palais des Nations, CH-1211 Geneva 10, Switzerland.

International Research and Training Institute for the Advancement of Women (Instraw), PO Box 21747, Santo Domingo DN, Dominican Republic.

World Bank, 1818 H Street NW, Washington, DC 20433, USA; *also* 66 Avenue d'Iena, F75116, Paris, France.

World Food Programme (WFP), Via Cristoforo Colombo 426, I-00145, Rome, Italy.

World Health Organization (WHO), Avenue Appia, CH-1211 Geneva 27, Switzerland.

Information on the activities of these organizations in the field of women and the environment can be obtained from the above addresses.

NON-GOVERNMENTAL ORGANIZATIONS

African NGOs Environment Network, PO Box 53844, Nairobi, Kenya.

Asian and Pacific Development Centre, Periavan Duta, PO Box 12224, 50770 Kuala Lumpur, Malaysia.

Associated Country Women of the World (ACWW), Vincent House, Vincent Square, London SW1P 2NB, United Kingdom.

Baha'i International Community, Office of the Environment, 866 United Nations Plaza (Suite 120), New York, NY 10017, United States of America.

Both ENDS (Netherlands IUCN Committee), Damrak 28–30, 1012 LJ Amsterdam, Netherlands.

Caritas Internationalis, Piazza San Calisto 16, I–00153 Rome, Italy.

CEFEMINA, PO Box 5355, San José, Costa Rica.

Centre for Our Common Future, Palais Wilson, 52 rue des Paquis, 1201 Geneva, Switzerland.

Centre for Science and Environment, 807 Vishal Bhavan, 95 Nehru Place, New Delhi, India.

Commonwealth Secretariat, Marlborough House, Pall Mall, London SW1Y 5HX, United Kingdom.

Development Alternatives with Women for a New Era (DAWN), c/o IUPERJ, Rua Paulino Fernandes, Botafogo 22270, Rio de Janeiro, Brazil.

Earthscan Publications, 3 Endsleigh Street, London WC1H 0DD, United Kingdom.

Environment Liaison Centre, PO Box 72461, Nairobi, Kenya.

European Development Education Network, c/o Breedstraat 16a, 1811 HG Alkmaar, Netherlands.

European Environment Bureau, 20 rue du Luxembourg, B–1040 Brussels, Belgium.

Friends of the Earth (International), c/o Peter Lammers, PO Box 17170, 100 JD Amsterdam, Netherlands.

Friends of the Earth (UK), 26–28 Underwood Street, London N1 7JQ, United Kingdom.

Greenpeace (International), Keizersgracht 176, NL 1016 DW Amsterdam, Netherlands.

Greenpeace (UK), Canonbury Villas, London N1 2PN, United Kingdom.

Habitat International Coalition (HIC), 313 Frankenslag, 2582 HM The Hague, Netherlands.

Institute of Development Studies, University of Sussex, Brighton BN1 9RE, United Kingdom.

International Alliance of Women, PO Box 355, Valetta, Malta.

International Confederation of Free Trade Unions (ICFTU), 37–41 rue Montagne-aux-herbes-potagères, B–1000 Brussels, Belgium.

International Council of Jewish Women, 6 avenue de Budé, 1202 Geneva, Switzerland.

International Council of Women, 13 rue Caumartin, 75009 Paris, France.

International Council on Social Welfare, Koestlergasse 1/29, A–1060 Vienna, Austria.

International Development Research Centre (IDRC), 250 Albert Street, Box 8500, Ottawa, Canada.

International Documentation and Communication Centre (IDOC), via S. Maria dell'Anima, 30, 00186 Rome, Italy.

International Federation of Business and Professional Women, Cloisters Business Centre, 8 Battersea Park Road, London SW8 4BG, United Kingdom.

International Federation of University Women, 37 Quai Wilson, CH–1201 Geneva, Switzerland.

International Institute for Environment & Development (IIED), 3 Endsleigh Street, London WC1H 0DD, United Kingdom.

International Organization of Consumers Unions (IOCU), 9 Emmastraat, 2595 EG The Hague, Netherlands.

International Organization of Consumers Unions (IOCU), PO Box 1045, 10830 Penang, Malaysia.

International Planned Parenthood Federation (IPPF), Regent's College, Inner Circle, Regent's Park, London NW1 4NS, United Kingdom.

International Reference Centre for Community Water Supply and Sanitation, PO Box 93190, 2509 AD The Hague, Netherlands.

Isis – Women's International Cross-Cultural Exchange, 3A chemin des Campanules, CH–1219 Aire – Geneva, Switzerland.

League of Red Cross and Red Crescent Societies, Case postale 372, 17 chemin des Crets, CH–1211 Geneva 19, Switzerland.

Lutheran World Federation, PO Box 2100, 150, route de Ferney, CH–1211 Geneva 2, Switzerland.

MATCH, 200 Elgin Street, Suite 1102, Ottawa, Canada.

Medical Women's International Association, Herbert Lewin St. 5, D–5000 Cologne 41, Germany.

Overseas Development Institute, Regent's College, Inner Circle, Regent's Park, London NW1 4NG, United Kingdom.

Oxfam, 274 Banbury Road, Oxford OX2 7DZ, United Kingdom.

The Panos Institute, 9 White Lion Street, London N1 9PD, United Kingdom.

Sierra Club, 408 C Street NE, Washington DC 20002, United States of America.

Society for International Development (SID), Palazzo della Civiltà del Lavoro, I–00144 Rome-EUR, Italy.

Soroptimist International, Royal Mile Mansions, 50–40 North Bridge, Edinburgh EH1 1QN, United Kingdom.

Transnational Network for Appropriate/Alternative Technologies (TRANET), PO Box 567, Rangely, ME 04970, United States of America.

Womankind, 122 Whitechapel High St., London E1 7PT, United Kingdom.

The Women's Environmental Network, 287 City Road, London EC1V 1LA, United Kingdom.

World Association of Girl Guides & Girl Scouts (WAGGGS), Olave Centre, 12c Lyndhurst Road, London NW3 5PQ, United Kingdom.

World Conservation Union (IUCN), World Conservation Centre, CH–1196 Gland, Switzerland.

World Council of Churches (WCC/CCPD), PO Box 2100, CH–1211 Geneva 2, Switzerland.

World Federation of Methodist Women, 103 bis route de Thonon, CH–1222 Vesenaz-Geneva, Switzerland.

World Information Service on Energy (WISE), Postbus 5627, 1007 AP Amsterdam, Netherlands.

Women's International League for Peace and Freedom, 1, rue de Varembé, Case postale 28, 1211 Geneva 20, Switzerland.

World Press Centre, Southgate Office Village, 284A Chase Road, London N14 6HF, United Kingdom.

World Resources Institute, 1709 New York Avenue NW, Washington DC 20006, United States of America.

World University Service, 5, chemin des Iris, CH–1216 Geneva, Switzerland.

World Young Women's Christian Association (YWCA), 37 quai Wilson, 1202 Geneva, Switzerland.

Worldwide Fund for Nature (WWF), World Conservation Centre, CH–1196 Gland, Switzerland.

Worldwide Fund for Nature (WWF), Panda House, Godalming, Surrey GU7 1XR, United Kingdom.

SELECTIVE BIBLIOGRAPHY

Agarwal, Bina (1986) *Cold Hearths and Barren Slopes. The Woodfuel Crisis in the Third World*, London, Zed Books.

Bertell, Rosalie (1985) *No Immediate Danger: Prognosis for a Radioactive Earth*, London. The Women's Press.

Boserup, Esther (1989) *Woman's Role in Economic Development*, London, Earthscan Publications Ltd.

Buvinic, M., M.A. Lycette and P. McGreevy (1983) *Women and Poverty in the Third World*, USA, Johns Hopkins University Press.

Centre for Science and Environment, *State of India's Environment 1984–85*, the Second Citizen's Report, New Delhi, India.

Cernia, M. (1985) *Putting People First: Sociological Variables in Rural Development*, New York, Oxford University Press.

Cleary, Seamus (1989) *Renewing the Earth*, London, CAFOD.

Commonwealth Expert Group (1989) *Climate Change: Meeting the Challenge*, London, Commonwealth Secretariat.

Commonwealth Expert Group (1989) *Engendering Adjustment for the 1990s*, London, Commonwealth Secretariat.

Dankelman, Irene and Joan Davidson (1988) *Women and Environment in the Third World: Alliance for the Future*, London, Earthscan Publications.

DAWN (1988) *Development, Crisis, and Alternative Visions; Third World Women's Perspectives*, London, Earthscan Publications Ltd.

Day, Jennie (1984) *Women in Food Production and Agriculture in Africa*, Rome, Food and Agriculture Organization of the United Nations.

Elkington, John and Julia Hailes (1989) *The Green Consumer Guide*, London, Victor Gollancz Ltd.

FAO (1990) *Sustainable Development and Natural Resource Management*, Rome, Food and Agriculture Organization of the United Nations.

FAO (1985) *Tropical Forest Action Plan*, Rome, Food and Agriculture Organization of the United Nations.

FAO (1990) *Women in Agricultural Development*, Rome, Food and Agriculture Organization of the United Nations.

FAO/SIDA (1987) *Restoring the Balance: Women and Forest Resources*, Rome, Food and Agriculture Organization of the United Nations, Stockholm, Swedish International Development Agency.

Hare, F. Kenneth (1985) *Climate Variations, Drought and Desertification*, Geneva, World Meteorological Organization.

HABITAT (nd) *Women, Human Settlements, Development and Management*, Nairobi, United Nations Centre for Human Settlements.

Hardoy, Jorge, and David Satterthwaite (1989) *Squatter Citizen: Life in the Urban Third World*, London, Earthscan Publications Ltd.

Henrichsen, Don (1987) *Our Common Future: A Readers Guide*, London, Earthscan Publications.

Heyzer, Noeleen (1987) *Women Farmers and Rural Change in Asia*, Kuala Lumpur, Malaysia, Asian and Pacific Development Centre.

Huston, P. (1979) *Third World Women Speak Out*, New York, Praeger Publishers.

ILO (1990) *Environment and the World of Work*, Director General's report to the 77th Session of the International Labour Conference, Geneva, International Labour Office.

ILO (1987) *Linking Energy with Survival*, Geneva, International Labour Office.

ILO (1988) *Women and Land*, Geneva, International Labour Office.

International Women's Tribune Centre (1987) *It's Our Move Now: a Community Action Guide* to the UN Nairobi Forward Looking Strategies for the Advancement of Women.

IPPF *People* (quarterly development magazine with supplement *Earthwatch*), London, International Planned Parenthood Federation.

IUCN, UNEP, WWF (1980) *World Conservation Strategy*, International Conservation Union, Gland, Switzerland (World Conservation Strategy II forthcoming).

Ivan-Smith, Edda, Nidhi Tandon, and Jane Connors (1988) *Women in Sub Saharan Africa*, Minority Rights Group Report no. 77, London.

Leghorn, K. and A. Parker (1981) *Women's Worth*, Boston, Routledge, & Kegan Paul.

May, John (1989) *The Greenpeace Book of the Nuclear Age*, Toronto, McClelland & Stewart.

Ministry of Foreign Affairs, The Netherlands (1989) *Women, Water and Sanitation*, The Hague, Ministry of Foreign Affairs.

Momson, Janet (1991) *Women and Development in the Third World*, London, Routledge.

Monimart, Marie (1989) *Women in the Fight Against Desertification*, Paris, Organization for Economic Cooperation and Development (OECD).

Munslow, B. with Y. Katere, A. Ferf and P. O'Keefe (1988) *The Fuelwood Trap: a Study of SADCC Region*, London, Earthscan Publications Ltd.

New Internationalist (monthly magazine), Oxford, New Internationalist Publications.

NGLS, *Voices from Africa* (publication series), Geneva, United Nations Non-governmental Liaison Service.

OECD (1989) *Focus on the Future: Women and Environment*, London, International Institute for Environment and Development.

Panos (1989) *Against All Odds*, London, Panos Publications.

Pearce, David, Anil Markandya and Edward B. Barbier (1989) *Blueprint for a Green Economy*, London, Earthscan Publications Ltd.

Pietila, Hilkka and Jeanne Vickers (1990) *Making Women Matter: The Role of the United Nations*, London, Zed Books Ltd.

Plant, Judith (1989) *Healing the Wounds: The Promise of Ecofeminism*, Philadelphia, PA, Santa Cruz, CA, New Society Publishers.

Seager, J. and A. Olson (1986) *Women in the World: an International Atlas*, London/Sydney, Pan Books.

Shiva, Vandana (1989) *Staying Alive, Women, Ecology and Development*, London, Zed Books.

Speth, James Gustave (1988) *Environmental Pollution: a Long-Term Perspective*, New York, World Resources Institute.

Starke, Linda (1990) *Signs of Hope; Working Towards Our Common Future*, Oxford and New York, Oxford University Press.

Srinivasan, Lyra (1990) *Tools for Community Participation: a Manual for Training Trainers in Participatory Techniques*, New York, PROWWESS/UNDP, distributed by PACT Media Services (accompanying video also available).

Timberlake, Lloyd (1988) *Africa in Crisis* (2nd ed.), London, Earthscan Publications Ltd.

Tolba, M.K. (1987) *Sustainable Development: Constraints and Opportunities*, London, Butterworth.

UNEP (1989) *Action on Ozone*, Nairobi, United Nations Environment Programme.

UNEP (1988) SWMTEP (United Nations

System Wide Medium Term Environment Programme 1990–95), Nairobi, United Nations Environment Programme.

UNEP/GEMS (1987) Environment Library no. 1, *The Greenhouse Gases*, Nairobi, United Nations Environment Programme.

UNEP/GEMS (1989) Environment Library no. 2, *The Ozone Layer*, Nairobi, United Nations Environment Programme.

UNEP/WHO (1988) Global Environment Monitoring System, *Assessment of Freshwater Quality*, Nairobi, United Nations Environment Programme, Geneva, World Health Organization.

UNESCO (1988) Man and the Biosphere Programme, *Man Belongs to the Earth*, Paris, UNESCO.

UNFPA (1986) *The State of the World Population 1986*, New York, United Nations Population Fund.

UNFPA (1989) *The State of the World Population 1989*, New York, United Nations Population Fund.

UNFPA (1990) *The State of the World Population 1990*, New York, United Nations Population Fund.

United Nations (1989) *World Survey on the Role of Women in Development*, New York.

van Wijk–Sijbesma (1985) *Participation of Women in Water Supply and Sanitation*, The Hague, International Reference Centre for Community Water Supply and Sanitation.

Vickers, Jeanne (1991) *Women and the World Economic Crisis*, London, Zed Books Ltd.

Walgate, Robert (1990) *Miracle or Menace: Biotechnology and the Third World*, London, the Panos Institute.

Wallace, Tina with Candida March (1990) *Our Work is Just Beginning: A Reader on Gender and Development*, Oxford, OXFAM.

Ward, Barbara (1988) *Progress for a Small Planet*, London. Earthscan Publications.

Wells, Troth, and Foo Gaik Sim (1987) *Till They Have Faces – Women as Consumers*, Penang, Malaysia International Union of Consumer Unions, and Rome ISIS.

Whittow, John (1979) *Disasters*, Georgia, USA, University of Georgia Press.

WHO (1989) *Our Planet Our Health*, Geneva, World Health Organization.

WHO (nd) *Women, Water and Sanitation*, Geneva, World Health Organization.

WHO/UNEP (1986) *Pollution and Health*, Geneva, World Health Organization.

Wijkman, Anders and Lloyd Timberlake (1984) *Natural Disasters: Acts of God or Acts of Man*, London, Earthscan Publications.

WMO/ICSU (1989) *Global Climate Change*, Geneva, World Meteorological Organization.

WMO/UNEP (1990) *Scientific Assessment of Climate Change*, Policy Makers Summary of the Report of Working Group 1 to the Intergovernmental Panel on Climate Change, Geneva, World Meteorological Organization.

Women, Environment and Development (1989) seminar report, London, Women's Environmental Network.

World Commission on Environment and Development (1987) *Our Common Future*, Oxford/New York, Oxford University Press.

World Resources Institute (1989) *Participatory Rural Appraisal Handbook*, Washington.

World Resources Institute (1990) *World Resources 1990–91*, Oxford/New York, Oxford University Press.

WWF (nd) *The Importance of Biological Diversity*, Gland, Switzerland, World Wide Fund for Nature International.

Zivetz, Laurie (1990) *Project Identification, Design and Appraisal: a Manual for NGOs*, Canberra, Australian Council for Overseas Aid.

AUDIO-VISUAL

ODA Video *Planting a Future*, Environmental Aid in Action, available from ODA, London.

UN Centre for Human Settlement (HABITAT) audiovisual catalogue, available from HABITAT offices in Nairobi, Geneva, New York.

UNDP *Borrowed From Our Future* (a video on the environment), also videos on water and on health, available from UNDP, New York.

UNEP Film and video catalogue, available from UNEP, Nairobi.

UNFPA Audio-Visual guide, available from UNFPA, New York.

UNICEF Videofilms on the SWACH Project, available from UNICEF, New York.

TVE Bulletin (quarterly guide to films on development and the environment), London, Television Trust for the Environment.

INDEX